The College Writing Toolkit

Frameworks for Writing
Series Editor: Martha C. Pennington, Georgia Southern University

The *Frameworks for Writing* series offers books focused on writing and the teaching and learning of writing in educational and real-life contexts. The hallmark of the series is the application of approaches and techniques to writing and the teaching of writing that go beyond those of English literature to draw on and integrate writing with other disciplines, areas of knowledge, and contexts of everyday life. The series entertains proposals for textbooks as well as books for teachers, teacher educators, parents, and the general public. The list includes teacher reference books and student textbooks focused on innovative pedagogy aiming to prepare teachers and students for the challenges of the 21st century.

Forthcoming:

Writing Poetry through the Eyes of Science
A Teacher's Guide to Scientific Literacy and Poetic Response
Nancy Gorrell with Erin Colfax

The "Backwards" Research Guide for Writers
Using Your Life for Reflection, Connection, and Inspiration
Sonya Huber

Exploring College Writing
Reading, Writing, and Researching across the Curriculum
Dan Melzer

Tend Your Garden
Nurturing Motivation in Young Adolescent Writers
Mary Anna Kruch

Becoming a Teacher Who Writes
Let Teaching be Your Writing Muse
Nancy Gorrell

Writing from the Inside
The Power of Reflective Writing in the Classroom
Olivia Archibald and Maureen Hall

Arting, Writing, and Culture
Teaching to the 4th Power
Anna Sumida, Meleanna Meyer, and Miki Maeshiro

Seriously Creative Writing
Stylistic Strategies in Non-Fictional Writing
Sky Marsen

Reflective Writing for English Language Teachers
Thomas S. C. Farrell

The College Writing Toolkit

Tried and Tested Ideas for
Teaching College Writing

Edited by
Martha C. Pennington and Pauline Burton

equinox

LONDON   OAKVILLE

Published by Equinox Publishing Ltd.

UK: 1 Chelsea Manor Studios, Flood Street, London SW3 5SR
USA: DBBC, 28 Main Street, Oakville, CT 06779

www.equinoxpub.com

First published 2011

British Library Cataloguing-in-Publication Data

A catalogue record for this book is available from the British Library.

ISBN   978 1 84553 452 3   (hardback)
        978 1 84553 453 0   (paperback)

Library of Congress Cataloging-in-Publication Data

The college writing toolkit: tried and tested ideas for teaching college writing/ edited by Martha C. Pennington and Pauline Burton.
    p. cm. – (Frameworks for writing)
  Include bibliographical references and index.
   ISBN 978-1-84553-452-3 – ISBN 978-1-84553-453-0 (pbk.) 1. English language—Rhetoric—Study and teaching (Higher) 2. Report writing—Study and teaching (Higher) 3. English language—Study and teaching (Higher)— Foreign speakers—Handbooks, manuals, etc. 4. College teaching—Handbooks, manurals, etc. I. Pennington, Martha Carswell. II. Burton, Pauline.
  PE1404.C614 2010
  808'.0420711-dc22
                        2009036174

Typeset by S.J.I. Services, New Delhi
Printed and bound in Great Britain by Lightning Source, Milton Keynes, UK

Contents

Editor's Preface

The need for English language skills is increasing worldwide, with ever larger numbers of students requiring academic and professional writing skills in English as their first or second language. Around the world, college or university level writing is currently taught in different ways: as part of a general English curriculum, as an autonomous subject, and, increasingly, as an aspect of undergraduate and graduate studies in specific fields. The great demand for English language writing skills has focused considerable attention on writing pedagogy, spurring a great deal of activity and innovation in the content, methods, and modes of delivery of writing instruction in the current day. And the demand for writing skills in other languages is also increasing.

The College Writing Toolkit: Tried and Tested Ideas for Teaching College Writing is intended as a resource book for any higher education teacher or program focused on writing skills and students' writing needs in general or in specific fields. With contributions from writing specialists around the United States as well as from several other countries, it addresses the writing needs of student writers in first-year composition, general English studies, and other fields who may be first-language or second-language speakers of English. This book is a resource for college/university teachers of writing and teachers in other fields looking for good ideas for integrating writing practice into classroom and out-of-class activities, for using writing as part of critical thinking and discussion, for innovating in giving feedback on and marking their students' written work, and for integrating writing with computer practices.

Within an overall goal of acquiring writing skills and learning the conventions of academic and professional discourse communities, the individual chapters cover a variety of functions and goals, including writing for effective communication based on rhetorical awareness of different purposes and contexts, writing for analysis and synthesis of different voices and sources of information, writing for exploration of inner and outer worlds, writing for learning and creating, writing for self-expression and construction of identity. The collection offers activities that can be used in autonomous writing classes and in fields such as business, technology, communication, sociology, history, literature, and language studies.

The activities are original, practical, and flexible. The originality of the chapters is captured in activities that involve integration of personal beliefs and experience into academic writing, analysis and argument using literary and non-literary texts, research based on print sources as well as ethnography and interviews, discipline-based writing and project work, self-guided assessment of writing, and computer-based activities to support writing processes. The authors present their lesson ideas in a pedagogic framework which offers a rationale, clear directions for practice, and suggestions as to how the activities can be adapted to different contexts. Activities designed for second-language writers are easily adaptable to first-language writers, and those that have been tried and tested with students in the U.S. are also adaptable to students in other countries.

The College Writing Toolkit, in its contributions from a diversity of contexts and in its variety of emphases and creative approaches, is a reflection of the collective creative energy of the present era in writing pedagogy at college/university level. Anyone concerned with writing instruction in higher education might therefore want to consider opening this toolkit and rummaging around in it to try to find some writing aids that could prove useful for their students and contribute to their own teaching toolkit.

– Martha C. Pennington
Series Editor, Frameworks for Writing

Contributors

Olivia Archibald (PhD, University of Iowa) is a Professor of English at Saint Martin's University in Lacey, Washington. Archibald is currently co-authoring with Maureen Hall *The Power of Reflective Writing in the Classroom* (Equinox, 2010) and recently carried out research on the stories of Holocaust survivors which was published in Narrative Inquiry. Alongside her teaching and research, Archibald chairs the English Department and facilitates activities for faculty development at her university.

Nahla Nola Bacha (PhD, University of Leicester) is an Associate Professor of Applied Linguistics/TESOL at the Lebanese American University (Lebanon), where she has administered and taught in the Academic English Program for over twenty years. She has published internationally in English for Academic and Professional Purposes, second language writing, and discourse analysis, and co-authored textbooks for the national Secondary English Curriculum. Currently, she is researching the role of ESL/EFL Programs in second/foreign language academic contexts.

Pauline Burton (PhD, University of Bedfordshire) is a Senior Lecturer at the Community College of City University, Hong Kong, teaching Academic and Professional English. She has also taught first-year composition in the US and English to international graduate students in the UK. She co-edited *Bilingual Women:*

Anthropological Approaches to Second Language Use (Berg). Her doctoral research focused on creativity in writing and teaching English as a second language in Hong Kong.

Sally Chandler (PhD, Wayne State University) teaches composition, digital rhetoric, and creative nonfiction at Kean University in Union, New Jersey. Her research interests include communication across difference, ethnographic and feminist methods for research and teaching, and digital literacies. Recent work has appeared in *Computers and Composition*, *Composition Studies*, *Oral History*, *Feminist Teacher*, and in *Digital Writing Research: Technologies, Methodologies, and Ethical Issues* (2007).

Michelle Cox (PhD, University of New Hampshire) is an Assistant Professor of English and Writing Across the Curriculum Program Director at Bridgewater State University in Massachusetts, where she teaches second language sections of composition and a range of undergraduate and graduate writing workshops and seminars. Cox, who specialized in Composition Studies, has co-edited two collections on second language writing and has published other works in that area and on workplace writing and composition pedagogies.

Andrew Delohery (MA, Western Connecticut State University) is the director of The Learning Center at Quinnipiac University, where he manages programs for academic support and retention. Delohery, who teaches in Quinnipiac's first-year composition program, co-authored *Using Technology in Teaching* (Yale University Press, 2005) and contributed to *Direct from the Disciplines* (Heinemann, Boynton-Cook, 2006). He also serves on the Editorial Board of The *Learning Assistance Review*, the journal of the National College Learning Center Association.

Gita DasBender (PhD, New York University) is a Senior Faculty Associate in the Department of English at Seton Hall University, where she is Coordinator for Second Language Writing. Her research interests include second language writing, generation 1.5 students, creative non-fiction, and the essay. She has published on collaborative practices in the preparation of college teachers of writing and on critical thinking in college writing. She is currently Secretary-Treasurer of the New Jersey College English Association.

Idoia Elola (PhD, University of Iowa) is an Assistant Professor of Spanish and Applied Linguistics & Second Language Studies at Texas Tech University. Her research focuses prominently on second language writing with emphasis on revision, collaborative writing through the use of social web technologies, and issues of writing fluency and grammar among Spanish heritage speakers. She has published articles on foreign language writing, collaborative writing, and the use of technology in the language classroom.

Sara Hillin (PhD, Texas Woman's University) is an Assistant Professor of Rhetoric and Composition at Lamar University in Beaumont, Texas. She teaches courses in first-year and advanced composition as well as pedagogy and American literature. Her research interests are classical rhetorical theory, composition pedagogy, feminist rhetorics and gender studies.

Suzanne Hudd (PhD, Yale University) is an Associate Professor of Sociology at Quinnipiac University, where she teaches courses in social stratification and research methods and co-chairs the Writing Across the Curriculum Program with Robert Smart. She is currently engaged in a year-long sabbatical project, with funding from the American Sociological Association, in which she is researching the pedagogical goals and praxis of writing in sociology.

Kate Kessler (PhD, Indiana University of Pennsylvania) is an Associate Professor in the School of Writing, Rhetoric, and Technical Communication at James Madison University. Before earning a PhD in Rhetoric and Linguistics, Kessler taught English at Chambersburg High School in Pennsylvania. Kessler has run the Marine Corps Marathon and has hiked the entire Appalachian Trail. In summer 2009 she taught her university's Appalachian Trail Seminar, leading students on hikes along central Virginia's Blue Ridge Mountains.

Robert T. Koch, Jr. (PhD, Indiana University of Pennsylvania) is an Assistant Professor of English and Director of the Center for Writing Excellence at the University of North Alabama. His doctoral work was in English Composition, and his scholarly interests include writing centers and reflective practice in the teaching of writing.

Sky Marsen (PhD, Monash University) is a Senior Lecturer in Linguistics and Communication at Victoria University of Wellington, New Zealand. Marsen, who has a background in linguistics, comparative literature, cognitive science, and information and communication studies, has published *Professional Writing: The Complete Guide for Business, Industry and IT* (Palgrave, 2nd edition, 2007); *Communication Studies* (Palgrave, 2006); and *Narrative Dimensions of Philosophy: A Semiotic Exploration in the Work of Merleau-Ponty, Kierkegaard and Austin* (Palgrave Macmillan, 2006).

Dan Melzer (PhD, Florida State University) is the University Reading and Writing Coordinator and an Associate Professor of Composition in the English Department at California State University, Sacramento. With a background in rhetoric and composition, he coordinates the University Writing Center and the Writing Across the Curriculum Program at CSUS. His work has appeared in *Language and Learning Across the Disciplines, The WAC Journal*, and *Kairos*.

Molly Hurley Moran (PhD, University of New Mexico) is a Professor of English in the Division of Academic Enhancement at the University of Georgia. Her publications include articles and chapters on writing, books on contemporary British novelists Margaret Drabble and Penelope Lively, and *Finding Susan* (Southern Illinois University Press, 2003), a memoir about the disappearance and murder of her sister, an experience which led to publications and workshops in the field of writing and healing.

Lisa Nazarenko (MA, Hunter College, City University of New York) is a Lecturer in the English Department of the University of Vienna and Lecturer and Didactic Advisor at the University of Applied Sciences Technikum Wien (Vienna). With academic background in TEFL, Nazarenko has taught EFL, ESP, and Academic English for over 20 years in the USA, the former USSR, Portugal, and Austria. Professional interests include writing, vocabulary, reading skills, and materials development in those areas.

Ana Oskoz (PhD, University of Iowa) is an Assistant Professor of Spanish in the Department of Modern Languages and Linguistics at the University of Maryland Baltimore County. She researches communications technologies in language learning, including online chat, discussion boards, blogs, and wikis for language development, to promote cultural discussions, and to enhance second language writing and intercultural competence. She has published on error correction, classroom-based assessment, and the use of technology in the language classroom.

Martha C. Pennington (PhD, University of Pennsylvania) is a Professor of Writing and Linguistics at Georgia Southern University, where she teaches linguistics courses in addition to first-year writing. Pennington is the editor-in-chief of *Writing & Pedagogy* and has published widely in applied linguistics, the teaching of writing, and computer-assisted language learning, including *The Computer and the Non-Native Writer: A Natural Partnership* (Hampton Press) and *Writing in an Electronic Medium: Research with Language Learners* (Athelstan).

Robert Smart (PhD, University of Utah) is a Professor of English and Department Chair of the English Department at Quinnipiac University, where he teaches advanced writing, Irish and Gothic Studies courses. Smart is the founding editor of *The Writing Teacher* (National Poetry Foundation), co-editor of *Direct From the Disciplines* (Heinemann, Boynton-Cook, 2006), and author of The *Nonfiction Novel* (UPA, 1984). He has published on Irish and Gothic Studies in several anthologies, and in *Postcolonial Text*.

Mark Sutton (PhD, University of South Carolina) is an Assistant Professor of Writing at Kean University in Union, New Jersey, where he coordinates the College Composition program. His doctoral emphasis in English was on Composition and Rhetoric, and his research interests focus on pedagogy, particularly collaborative writing, basic writers, and professional development. He has published articles in *Issues in Writing, LORE, Research and Practice in Developmental Education*, and *Composition Studies*.

Gillian Schwarz (MA, University of Leeds) is a Senior Lecturer in the English Department of the University of Vienna. With academic background in English Language Teaching and Linguistics, Schwarz has taught EFL, ESP, and Academic English for over 20 years in England, Kuwait, Argentina, and Austria. Her professional interests are in the areas of curriculum and materials development, focusing particularly on writing and reading skills.

Katherine E. Tirabassi (PhD, University of New Hampshire) is an Assistant Professor of English and Coordinator of the Thinking and Writing Program at Keene State College, where she teaches composition/literacy theory and writing. She has published articles on archival research, composition pedagogy, and writing center theory/practice. Her dissertation, "Revisiting the 'Current-Traditional Era': Innovations in Writing Instruction at the University of New Hampshire, 1940–1949" received the 2008

CCCC (College Composition and Communication Conference) James Berlin Memorial Outstanding Dissertation Award.

Zuzana Tomaš (PhD candidate, University of Utah) teaches pre-service teachers at the University of Utah and ESL at Westminster College, Salt Lake City. She conducts research in second language writing and teacher education and is a recipient of the Ruth Crymes Fellowship for Graduate Study and the Mary Finocchiaro Award for Excellence in Pedagogical Materials. Most notably, Tomaš is an Olympian who represented her native Slovakia in the marathon race at the 2008 Beijing Olympics.

Carter Winkle (MA, University of South Florida) is an English Language Instructor with a background in Applied Linguistics specializing in second-language composition at Miami Dade College. Additionally, Winkle is a guest lecturer of graduate and undergraduate ESOL endorsement courses for Barry University's Adrian Dominican School of Education, where he is also working toward a PhD in Curriculum and Instruction. His research interests include second-language writing, formative assessment, and generative curriculum.

1 Tools of the Trade: The College Writing Teacher in a New Age

Pauline Burton and Martha C. Pennington

I. A Toolkit for College Writing Teachers

The purpose of this book is to provide college teachers and university professors with "tried and tested" ideas for teaching writing or for incorporating writing into their classes. Our conception is a social constructivist one (Vygotsky, 1962, 1978) of college/university teaching as a distinctive community of practice (Lave and Wenger, 1991; Wenger, 1998) or as linked communities of practice, in which we create our own approaches suitable to our contexts, learning from each other and passing our best ideas to each other as colleagues.

The community of writing experts includes those with language and writing degrees, such as English, Rhetoric/Composition, Linguistics, and Applied Linguistics, as well as disciplinary specialists focused on writing in their own fields. Within that community of practice, distinctive types of approaches and expertise have been created for the teaching of writing in first-year composition and for teaching through writing in the disciplines. As indicated by the craft metaphor expressed in the title, the philosophy underlying this book is one of apprenticeship and mentoring in a teachers-teaching-teachers model of the development of expertise. Through such mentoring and participation, the community itself is continually extended and renewed.

This is a period in literacy development within colleges and universities in which approaches to improving the writing ability of students are being re-examined and created anew. The days of writing taught on a basis of literature are fading as writing teachers and other educators realize the need to teach writing related to other forms of information, genres, and purposes. The writing-across-the-curriculum movement is strong and growing, supplementing and even sometimes replacing the teaching of writing as an autonomous area. In this era of reconsideration of the foundation of university study, even as first-year writing courses are under scrutiny, writing is gaining more not less importance as those in the disciplines are coming to realize the extent to which writing differs from one context to another and how central writing is to their students' learning and expression of knowledge.

We have adopted the *College Writing Toolkit* metaphor to signify that the book offers something practical which college/university instructors can use to aid them in crafting lessons focused on writing. We mean *Toolkit* to imply "tools of the trade" more than finished recipes or steps to be applied exactly as described. Our sense of this *Toolkit* is of an idea-book that is both less than and more than a recipe book. While providing specific activities and plans for teaching, it is *less than* a book of recipes in that the ideas must still be adapted to specific circumstances. At the same time, it is *more than* a book of teaching plans in the sense of being grounded in theory as well as offering the specifics of implementation.

The *Toolkit* metaphor expresses our conviction that thinking is shaped not only through teaching and learning but through the process of writing (Sharples, 1999; Tynjälä, Mason, and Lonka, 2001). In his poem "Digging," Seamus Heaney presents the idea of writing as hard yet productive labor and his pen as the tool of his trade in the same way as the spade had been for his father and grandfather (Heaney, 1966). Even though the physical process of writing has been radically changed by new technologies (Yancey, 2009), the mental labor involved can still be arduous, especially when a new literacy, such as academic discourse, is being acquired.

The tools of our trade as college/university writing teachers are not just the pen or the computer but comprise in addition creative ideas for task-based pedagogy, a teaching approach that has evolved largely through theory and practice in second-language research and instruction (Crookes and Gass, 1993; Ellis, 2003; Long, 1985; Long and Crookes, 1992; Prabhu, 1987). As the following chapters show, it is the application of such ideas in the classroom, and their improvement through practice – hence "tried and tested" – that enables university students to write their own identities as fledgling scholars, researchers, language learners, aspiring professionals, and members of discourse communities: in Kathleen Blake Yancey's phrase, as "citizen composers" (Yancey, 2009: 8).

II.   The Teacher as "Bricoleur" in a New Age for College Writing

As the chapters in this book demonstrate, successful teaching depends not simply on the implementation of fixed steps in an assignment, but on a deep knowledge of the needs and interests of one's own students. Such knowledge underlies the art, as well as the craft, of teaching, and accounts for something of the "magic" of the individual teacher as well (Pennington, 1999). The college writing teacher, alongside the professor using writing in the disciplines, functions in the current day as both craftsperson and artist, working with known tools and approaches while developing a new frontier of teaching. This educational context requires the skills of a pedagogical "bricoleur" (Denzin and Lincoln, 2000; Lévi-Strauss, 1972) – that is, someone who creatively marries expertise to resources to fit the requirements of new teaching situations, students with new interests and needs, and the demands of a fast-changing world outside the university as well as within it. The writing teacher, while being more principled in applying theory to practice than the semi-skilled, rough-and-ready handyperson that is the original bricoleur of Claude Lévi-Strauss' conception (Lévi-Strauss, 1972), is no less ingenious a practitioner in using the means at hand.

III. Themes and Design of the Book

There is diversity in the teaching situations and also in the intellectual frameworks and backgrounds of the contributors to this book. This diversity is reflected in the various types of stimulus for writing activities, the "call to write" which Kessler refers to in her chapter. The stimuli to writing that are suggested by our contributors include not only reading literature or reflective and popular essays, but also carrying out ethnographic research and interviews, responding to writing prompts and authentic situations in the students' own lives, and sharing by students of each other's work in the classroom and through wikis and blogs. We see such diversity as a strength and source of richness: there is productive history and a depth of knowledge in these varied approaches to writing instruction.

We identify the following as common themes among the contributors to this volume:

Student-centered pedagogy;
Task-based methodology;
Writing and learning as a process, facilitated by new technologies;
Writing as a tool for thinking, learning, and constructing identity;
Writing as a means of introducing students to new discourse communities, both academic and professional;
The importance of specific feedback on writing from the instructor and peers;
The value of teaching rhetorical awareness for effective communication with specific audiences.

These common themes reflect the continued co-existence of stages in the historical development of college composition pedagogy – development that is outlined by Kathleen Blake Yancey in her report for the National Council of Teachers of English on writing in the 21st century (Yancey, 2009). As the chapters in this book demonstrate, new approaches to the teaching of writing adapt and enrich earlier professional paradigms, rather than replacing them entirely. College composition can draw upon a robust intellectual tradition – a tradition that can only gain strength by evolving through shared practice to meet the needs of new technologies, new audiences, and new literacies among college and university students.

The contributors to this book trace the origins and history of activities that have worked in specific settings with particular groups of college/university students yet are amenable to adaptation to other teaching contexts. The focus on activities facilitated a common design for all of the chapters, moving from the guiding theory and description of an activity through its implementation, critical reflection, and recommendations for future applications. This design is a model of reflective practice corresponding to the staged process of a creative task (Amabile, 1983, 1996; Cropley, 1997; Csikszentmihalyi, 1996). There was a sense of excitement we, as editors, had as contributions came in and we found yet another inspiring idea to try out in the writing classroom. We hope our readers will be similarly inspired to try out, adapt, and creatively remodel the activities of the chapters in this collection to suit their own classroom situations and teaching styles.

IV.   The Contributions

The contributions reflect the wide-ranging nature of college/university writing instruction: first-year composition, writing across the curriculum, English as a second/foreign language, writing in languages other than English, and electronically mediated communication. We have grouped the chapters into five sections, according to the major focus of the writing activities that each of them describes, as follows: Writing from Personal Experience, Argumentation and Writing from Sources, Writing for Specific Contexts, Interactive and Self Assessment, and Working with Technology in the Writing Classroom.

Writing from Personal Experience

The chapters in the first section deal with activities for novice writers – typically, first-year university students, including speakers of English as a second or foreign language. The contributors suggest various ways of teaching writing based on personal experience to help bridge the apparent gap between personal and academic discourse. They include personal essay (Archibald), literacy snapshots (Cox and Tirabassi), writing about students' strong beliefs (Moran) or about people they consider local heroes (Burton), and writing humorous stories from personal experience (Pennington).

In the first chapter, "The Personal Essay as a Tool to Teach Academic Writing," Olivia Archibald considers how best to introduce first-year students to new forms of discourse and techniques of revision. She advocates the use of the personal essay as a tool to teach academic writing, arguing that classic essays by authors such as George Orwell and Annie Dillard can fruitfully be used to make students aware of and to learn to balance within their papers two essential components of academic writing: the "inner story" of evaluation and reflection, supported by the "outer story" of description. With a wealth of practical detail, Archibald describes a workshop sequence through which students draft and revise their own essays about an experience of personal transformation. Through this process, novice writers develop the rhetorical skills they need to make the subsequent transition to writing thesis-based argumentative papers, using Archibald's "inner/outer" frame.

In "Snapshots of Our Literacies," Michelle Cox and Katherine E. Tirabassi present a creative non-fiction writing project based on personal narratives that has been used successfully in the first five weeks of university writing courses in a variety of pedagogical settings, including English as a Second Language (ESL) classes. The students craft "snapshot essays" as brief descriptive narratives responding to writing prompts that are focused on writing, reading, discourse communities, and literacy. Through the process of drafting and feedback from peers and instructors, students build up their essay with the support of detailed instructions. This workshop-based project, which was developed as a way to counteract students' resistance to revision, also serves to move students away from the five-paragraph essay still mandated in many high schools in the United States, and (in the case of ESL classes) to go beyond the sentence-level focus of much second-language writing instruction. The students are thus socialized into the discourse of university-level writing while drawing on their own varied literacies to assist in the transition.

Molly Hurley Moran, in "Empowering Basic Writers Through 'This I Believe' Essays," argues in favor of using personal writing as a pathway to academic writing, and discusses the difficulty of finding reading material that engages the interest of novice writers such as those in her first-year developmental classes yet which moves them beyond the narrow confines of five-paragraph essay models. Moran's solution is to structure her semester-long basic writing course around National Public Radio's "This I Believe" essays, which are inspirational short pieces written by anyone who wishes to speak about a deeply held belief. Moran recounts how she utilizes the print and audio-based versions of these essays to develop her students' writing through cycles of reading, journaling with writing prompts, discussion, paper drafting, and feedback from herself and their peers. She discusses improvements that she has made to the course in the light of experience and suggests further applications for student writers at every level of these inspired and inspiring stimuli to writing.

In her chapter, "Local Heroes, Local Voices", Pauline Burton presents a first-year composition activity in which students read a variety of texts (fiction and non-fiction) about courage and discuss the nature of heroism, and then identify and select their own choice of "heroes" on the university campus and in surrounding communities. Students contact their potential interviewees to secure an interview, formulate the questions they plan to ask, and carry out background research. They then conduct and record the interviews, working in pairs, and later craft magazine articles from the interviews with a student audience in mind, representing the "voice" of their interviewees as faithfully as they can. Burton's project is designed to engage first-year college/university students' interest through a theme rooted in personal experience and to facilitate discovery of new understandings that they can gain through the process of research and writing.

Martha C. Pennington, in "A Funny Thing Happened To Me: Introducing Oneself Through Humor," uses the personal funny story as a means of creating a classroom writing community while introducing novice writers in an enjoyable way to peer work, drafting, and the requirements of writing. In a series of writing workshops, Pennington's students read, critique, and write in response to a range of humorous texts, from the comic tales of classic writers such as Washington Irving to regional humor and different sub-genres of jokes. They describe and analyze their reactions to the humor in these texts and create funny stories of their own, drawing on personal experience. A particular aspect of the assignment is its requirement that students draw a moral or generalization from the story that they use to frame their story. In the humanistic tradition of writing pedagogy, the activity described in this chapter privileges personal experience and the development of an individual voice, while also requiring a focus on narrative and on detailed and creative uses of language.

Argumentation and Writing from Sources

The chapters in the second section relate to key skills in academic writing: building an argument and integrating source material. A "delayed thesis" essay (Hillin), combining literature with exposition (DasBender), a paraphrase integration task (Tomaš), and writing a critique (Bacha) are presented as approaches to teaching such skills. The latter three chapters appear to support the contention that the differences between writing instruction for first-language and second-language writers are differences in degree rather than kind, as the students are, in both cases, learning new modes of discourse.

Sara Hillin's chapter, "The 'Delayed Thesis' Essay: Enhancing Rhetorical Sensitivity by Exploring Doubts and Refutations," is based on teaching argumentation to advanced composition students, and, in particular, teaching rhetorical sensitivity and awareness of opposing points of view. The activity which Hillin uses to facilitate such awareness is a short "delayed thesis" essay, written as a preparatory exercise for a longer research-based paper. As Hillin points out, this is not simply a matter of changing the organization and moving the thesis to a later part of the essay. Her assignment requires the student writer to conceptualize opposing audiences and seriously discuss the claims such audiences might present before moving into counterclaims and refutation. The comments of Hillin's students on the value of this exercise are illuminating, and it is worth considering how the activity could be adapted to less advanced classes to encourage all writing students to use doubting as a tool of persuasion. The value of a developed ability to explore doubts and refutations as a way to enhance rhetorical sensitivity not only inside but also outside the academy – from disputes between family members to international negotiation – can hardly be overestimated.

In "Literature-with-Exposition: A Critical Thinking and Writing Assignment," Gita DasBender writes from a teaching context with which some readers will be familiar: teaching composition as part of a university program in which literature is the primary focus. She argues that no kind of text should be excluded from writing instruction; rather, the instructor's task is to "re-imagine" the use of literary texts in combination with texts of other kinds to teach the academic writing skills of summary, analysis, critical thinking, building an argument, and integrating references. The approach DasBender advocates is to group the chosen texts – short stories, expository essays, and poems – around a single theme and to guide student writers towards connecting the ideas expressed in each. She outlines a working method of thinking through writing in which a series of writing exercises are combined into a final coherent paper – an approach similar to the "snapshot essay" method outlined by Cox and Tirabassi. It is worth noting that DasBender discusses the teaching strategies she uses to adapt the activity from first-language to second-language writers – strategies that underline the possibilities for adaptation of all of the contributions in this volume.

Zuzana Tomaš, in "Paraphrase Integration Task: Increasing Authenticity of Practice in Using Academic Sources," raises a perennial problem in source-based writing by student writers, especially (she suggests) students writing in a second language: plagiarism. Tomaš draws together the work of theorists in the field to discuss the various reasons, cultural and pedagogical, that plagiarism arises, and she draws on her own teaching and research experience to offer a developmental activity for a specific skill in academic writing: integrating paraphrases of source material into an original argument. Tomaš notes that there is a dearth of teaching material enabling students to practice this skill within an authentic context and so to develop the complex abilities required to properly incorporate other people's work within one's own. Her paraphrase integration task, presented with a wealth of examples, seeks to bridge the gap between sentence-level exercises and the complex task of integrating multiple sources in a research paper. This is an activity that could be beneficial to first-language as well as second-language writers in the college/university classroom.

Working in an English composition classroom with Arabic-speaking students in a Lebanese university, Nahla Nola Bacha, in her contribution, "Teaching Critique Writing: A Scaffolded Approach," recounts how she teaches critique writing to develop first-year students' critical thinking and awareness of text types.

Bacha describes a staged teaching and learning process designed to provide scaffolding to help her students become independent learners. Their goal is to produce five-part essays based on contemporary critiques, working in small groups. In doing this, the students practice skills such as introducing a source, summarizing its main ideas, agreeing or disagreeing with those ideas, and using paraphrase and direct quotation to support their opinions. In an adaptive "bricoleur" use of technology, Bacha applies plagiarism-detecting software not to check up on her students, but for the students themselves to evaluate the originality of their work and revise accordingly.

Writing for Specific Contexts

The contributors in this section present ideas for writing instruction that is geared to specific contexts: a wider curriculum of writing studies and academic literacies (Melzer), writing across the disciplines (Smart, Hudd, and Delohery), professional discourse communities (Marsen), and authentic audiences outside of the academy (Kessler).

In his account, "Academic Discourse Mini-Ethnography," of the academic ethnography project he developed for first-year and second-year composition courses, Dan Melzer takes a social constructivist stance regarding students' negotiation of and admission to the discourse communities and disciplines represented in colleges and universities. He maintains that the main goals of composition courses are two-fold: (1) to introduce students to the academic discourse communities that they are about to join and (2) to help them consider how academic discourses connect and conflict with their personal discourse communities and "self-sponsored literacies." His solution is to ask the students to investigate as ethnographers the academic discourse communities that they aspire to join and to present their findings from texts, interviews, and surveys through class presentations and a final report. Melzer offers key pointers for success in a "complex and demanding" project: linking the assignment to a wider curriculum, giving it enough time, and providing a basis for deep understanding through reading and discussing model ethnographies. Melzer's comments serve as a useful reminder that although activities can be adapted to a variety of teaching situations, there are usually practical constraints on such adaptations; and a transplanted activity needs to be fully integrated with the intended outcomes of a wider program of study in order to thrive.

In the second chapter in this section, "Using Writing Across the Curriculum Exercises to Teach Critical Thinking and Writing," Robert Smart, Suzanne Hudd, and Andrew Delohery present a "concentric model" of critical thinking. This model postulates a hierarchy of linked cognitive tasks, moving from *prioritization* (deciding the order of importance of ideas), to *translation* (putting those ideas into one's own words), and then to *analogizing* (comparing ideas from one source with those from another, including one's own experience). This model is used as the basis for creating writing prompts for informal writing tasks, otherwise known as "writing-to-learn" (WTL) tasks. Such tasks are linked to the wider goals of a class, and can be used to provide a basis for working on longer formal papers within a specific discipline. In this chapter, Smart and colleagues show how this approach is applied in faculty workshops and in an upper-division class for sociology students. Their specific examples demonstrate how powerful the concentric thinking model can be as a basis for writing in the disciplines, and also how it can be adapted to different contexts in which critical thinking and mastery of academic discourse are required.

In the next chapter, "Writing the 'Professional': A Model for Teaching Project Management in a Writing Course," Sky Marsen presents an approach to instruction in professional writing derived from narrative theory. Marsen's approach to writing instruction for professional purposes was developed in the university classroom with undergraduate students and has also been applied with professional and business clients. Marsen argues that narrative theory can be used not only as a means of explicating professional texts, but as a source of valuable concepts and strategies for writers.

Countering the common and superficial view of writing instruction as a secondary and remedial activity in business and professions, Marsen positions writing as "part of a network of mutually reinforcing activities" in realizing any successful project. The author outlines a semester-long workshop course using narrative theory as a framework for discussing case studies such as the Challenger disaster and for teaching project management through text analysis and writing.

Kate Kessler's chapter, "Writing for an Authentic Audience," links the aims of first-year composition with the rhetorical demands of writing for an authentic audience. She refers to the shift in writing pedagogy towards "post-process" writing, which embodies concern for product and rhetorical sensitivity to an audience, as prompting her decision to use real issues and real audiences with her writing students. As Kessler points out, these students are learning how to participate in public and civic discourse while discovering that effective writing can produce real outcomes. She cites "the call to write" – having something to say and using writing to say it – as a powerful motivator, and the examples she gives of student work and their comments on the course support this claim. "Post-process" does not, however, mean that process is absent: Kessler outlines a workshop sequence in which students draft and redraft their writing and move from a relatively simple text (a letter) to a more complex one (a proposal). Like other contributors to this volume, Kessler is aware of the importance of providing scaffolding for writing activities, and of the art of knowing when and how to provide it.

Interactive and Self Assessment

Assessment is often a contentious issue in writing instruction, touching as it does on questions of power, trust, equity, and the near-universal shift in higher education towards regarding students as consumers. The chapters in this section show how structuring assignments and making clear the criteria on which they are evaluated can increase students' reflectivity and ability to assess their own work (Nazarenko and Schwarz), while also providing appropriate feedback together with fair and transparent evaluation of student writing (Koch).

Developing students' reflectivity through guided self-assessment in every stage of a writing activity is the theme of Lisa Nazarenko and Gillian Schwarz's chapter, "The Write Path: Guiding Writers to Self-Reliance." Nazarenko and Schwarz regard such reflectivity as a key aspect of improving student writing and comment that can take some time to achieve. They present a set of activities they have used with second-language students in the second semester of a first-year university writing course, structured around writing an opinion essay. Key features of their teaching approach are guidelines for the assignment, model texts, hands-on interaction in the classroom, controlled prewriting, peer consultation and feedback, focused feedback from the instructor that mirrors the assignment guidelines, revision and redrafting, workshops and conferencing, and the use of structured reflection and feedback sheets throughout the process. The authors point out that, since the activity is broken down into clear steps, it is flexible and easy to adapt to different teaching situations and ability levels. They also point out that it is easier to address problems with student work at the prewriting stage than to fix them later – a point with which many instructors will doubtless concur.

Robert T. Koch, Jr., in "Conference-based Writing Assessment and Grading," provides a detailed framework for an approach to assessment and grading that uses conferencing and marking sheets (rubrics) with first-year composition and basic writing students in the final week of a multi-week essay assignment. A student paper is compared to a clear set of grading criteria both by the instructor and the student in advance of a conference in which a grade is assigned on the basis of discussion. Students are expected to bring a copy of their essay, a reflective letter, and a one-page written grade justification to the conference. Koch argues that although the grade that is assigned is final for the paper, it is developmental for the student, based on the discussion in the conference of how the grading criteria were applied to the student's work. Through this activity, which is repeated through the semester, students deepen their understanding of the characteristics of good academic writing and their awareness of their own strengths and weaknesses as writers. Comments from Koch's students indicate that most appreciate their involvement in the grading process and the insights which it provides for reflection, revision, and further improvement.

Working with Technology in the Writing Classroom

All of the contributions to this book, to a greater or lesser extent, address the applications of a range of technologies to support teaching and learning activities. The three chapters in the final section foreground the uses of technology to develop digital literacy (Chandler and Sutton), give individual feedback on student work (Winkle), and develop academic writing skills through using wikis and chats (Oskoz and Elola).

Sally Chandler and Mark Sutton, in "Scavenger Hunt: A Model for Digital Composing Processes," present an online Scavenger Hunt as a way to help students learn to manage composing in digital environments. Working with first-year university students, they use the Hunt as an early assignment both to develop students' ability to utilize course management software and to socialize them into the skills and practices they will need in order to learn effectively in digital spaces. Chandler and Sutton describe a cluster of writing-related activities in the Scavenger Hunt, such as reading critically, gathering information, giving and receiving feedback, and responding to writing prompts. They stress collaborative learning as a key part of this activity, since one of its intended learning outcomes is to encourage "thinking about writing as intimately tied to social processes." This assignment continues to evolve as the authors respond to student behaviors and comments and to changes in the needs and abilities of students from year to year.

Feedback on student writing using embedded digital audio files is the subject of Carter Winkle's chapter, "Virtual Mediation: Audio-

Enhanced Feedback for Student Writing." Writing from a background of research and teaching among second-language students in the United States, Winkle argues that this form of feedback can be matched to students' specific level and needs, thus providing customized assistance for individual learners. Knowing the individual student, the instructor can provide appropriate feedback on writing, offering dynamic, interactive assessment through online, virtual mediation for the student's own revision. Winkle does not see this method as a substitute for conferencing but as a practical and effective solution for distance learning and teaching situations such as his own, in which face-to-face meetings are not always possible. Winkle gives clear instructions so that even the most non-technologically savvy of readers could implement the virtual mediation method with ease. He also notes that the approach can be effective with first-language as well as second-language writers.

One of the most valuable aspects of using new technology in teaching writing is the opportunity afforded for collaborative work, especially through the medium of social networking software. In the final chapter in the book, "Academic Writing in the Foreign Language Class: Wikis and Chats at Work," Ana Oskoz and Idoia Elola argue persuasively for the value of collaborative writing in developing reflective thinking, improved accuracy, and shared knowledge of language use, among both first-language and second-language writers. Describing the acquisition of academic writing skills solely through individual study as a "daunting and solitary task," they present their use of wikis and blogs as a tool to help students in an advanced university-level Spanish class write more effectively in an academic context using their second language. As Oskoz and Elola point out, however, collaborative writing does not supersede the value of individual writing in preparing for the world of work and developing independent thinking.

V.   Conclusion

We believe that this collection provides a vivid picture of the *Toolkit*, or the various *Toolkits*, representing the vast store of expertise for teaching writing as well as for teaching through writing at college/university level worldwide. We hope that it achieves our aim of providing useful material for the various academic communities whose practices involve writing and writing pedagogies and that it will contribute to the ongoing evolution of those communities, aiding them in the teaching of writing and the promotion of diverse applications of writing to develop and express disciplinary knowledge. To the extent that it succeeds, this work can, as we would like to imagine, play a role in inspiring excellence in teaching and so contribute to the making of literate citizens for the world of today and tomorrow.

References

Amabile, Teresa M. (1983) *The Social Psychology of Creativity*. New York: Springer-Verlag.

Amabile, Teresa M. (1996) *Creativity in Context: Update to The Social Psychology of Creativity*. Boulder, Colorado and Oxford: Westview Press.

Crookes, Graham and Gass, Susan M. (eds.) (1993) *Tasks and Language Learning: Integrating Theory and Practice*. Clevedon, Avon: Multilingual Matters.

Cropley, A. J. (1997) Fostering creativity in the classroom: General principles. In Mark A. Runco (ed.) *The Creativity Research Handbook*, *Volume 1*: 83–114. Cresskill, New Jersey: Hampton Press.

Csikszentmihalyi, Mihaly (1988) Society, culture and person: A systems view of creativity. In Robert J. Sternberg (ed.) *The Nature of Creativity* 297–312. New York: Cambridge University Press.

Denzin, Norman K. and Lincoln, Yvonna S. (eds.) (2000) *Handbook of Qualitative Research* (2nd edition). Thousand Oaks, California: Sage Publications Inc.

Ellis, Rod (2003) *Task-Based Language Learning and Teaching*. Oxford: Oxford University Press.

Heaney, Seamus (1966) *Death of a Naturalist.* Faber Pocket Poetry. London: Faber & Faber.

Lave, Jean and Wenger, Etienne (1991) *Situated Learning: Legitimate Peripheral Participation.* New York: Cambridge University Press.

Lévi-Strauss, Claude (1972) *The Savage Mind.* London: Weidenfeld and Nicolson. Translation of *La Pensée Sauvage* (1962). Paris: Librairie Plon.

Long, Michael H. (1985) A role for instruction in second language acquisition: Task-based language teaching. In Kenneth Hyltenstam and Manfred Pienemann (eds.) *Modeling and Assessing Second Language Development* 77–99. Clevedon, Avon: Multilingual Matters.

Long, Michael H. and Crookes, Graham (1992) Three approaches to task-based language teaching. *TESOL Quarterly* 26(1): 27–56. Reprinted in Kris Van den Branden, Martin Bygate and John M. Norris (eds.) (2009) *Task-Based Language Teaching: A Reader* 57–81. Amsterdam: John Benjamins.

Pennington, Martha C. (1999) Rules to break and rules to play by: Implications of different conceptions of teaching for language teacher development. In Hugh Trappes-Lomax and Ian McGrath (eds.) *Theory in Language Teacher Education* 99–108. London: Longman.

Prabhu, N. S. (1987) *Second Language Pedagogy.* Oxford: Oxford University Press.

Sharples, Mike (1999) *How We Write: Writing as Creative Design.* London and New York: Routledge.

Tynjälä, Päivi, Mason, Lucia and Lonka, Kirsti (2001) Writing as a learning tool: An introduction. In Päivi Tynjälä, Lucia Mason, and Kirsti Lonka (eds.) *Writing as a Learning Tool: Integrating Theory and Practice* 7–22. Dordrecht, Boston, and London: Kluwer Academic Publishers.

Wenger, Etienne (1998) *Communities of Practice: Learning, Meaning, and Identity.* New York: Cambridge University Press.

Yancey, Kathleen B. (February 2009) Writing in the 21st century: A report from the National Council of Teachers of English. Urbana, Illinois: National Council of Teachers of English. Retrieved on 3 July 2009 from http://www.ncte.org.

Vygotsky, Lev S. (1962) *Thought and Language.* Cambridge, Massachusetts: MIT Press.

Vygotsky, Lev S. (1978) *Mind in Society: The Development of Higher Psychological Processes* (eds. Michael Cole, Vera John-Steiner, Sylvia Scribner and Ellen Souberman). Cambridge, Massachusetts: Harvard University Press.

Part 1
Writing from Personal Experience

2 The Personal Essay as a Tool to Teach Academic Writing

Olivia Archibald

I.   Background

In this chapter, I focus on the technique of using the personal essay as an instructional tool to introduce students to academic writing. For the last decade, I have bypassed traditional approaches to teaching college composition and, during the first weeks of such courses, bypassed a focus on the thesis-supported academic essay. Instead, I assign a series of personal essays for students to read, followed by an assignment that asks them to write about an experience in their lives that transformed them in some way. My purpose is to use personal essays as models of how and when writers move into reflection and evaluation in writing forms based on personal experience. I also use these models to illustrate how writers balance their evaluative claims with specific details. The goal underpinning such an emphasis is that, upon completion of this section of the course, students will have developed writing strategies that they can then apply successfully to the remainder of the course's writing assignments, which focus on argumentative essays supported by textual evidence.

Why use the personal essay to illustrate and reinforce skills of reflection and evaluation? The personal essay, as essayist Scott Russell Sanders notes, is "the closest thing we have, on paper, to a record of the individual mind at work and at play" (Sanders, 1989: 33). Its claim to fame in the nonfiction world is its ability to render the writer's thoughts as s/he describes, narrates, or analyzes the subject. Its form is often associated with a "naturalness, openness, [and] looseness as opposed to the regularity, and strictly ordered quality of conventional prose discourse" (Klaus, 1989: 156). As essayist Edward Hoagland states, a personal essay is the "human voice talking, its order the mind's natural flow" (Hoagland, 1982: 25). This "voice talking" shares with the reader not only the specific details of the information; it simulates the mind's movement in a way that presents the essay's purpose through reflections and evaluations of experiences rather than through a directly stated thesis. Such a form offers for writers the freedom to explore ideas in unfettered ways, "like finding one's way through a forest without being quite sure what game you are chasing, what landmark you are seeking" (Sanders, 1989: 34). Such a form offers to readers of personal essays the gift of seeing how a mind other than their own evaluates the events described in a way that avoids "a fatal faithfulness to a fixed idea" (Woolf, 1925/1953: 220).

The personal essay's history can be traced back to the 16th century Frenchman Michel de Montaigne, who was the first author to call his writings "essays" (Montaigne, 1575/1965). Montaigne's essays are personal, tentative, and digressive, presenting to succeeding generations of essayists a form for writing about personal experience. [1] Since his writings could not be called letters or treatises, Montaigne termed his pieces *essais*, the French word for a trial, an attempt. To read an essay by Montaigne is to journey with him while he explores his experiences, puts "on trial" his subjects, and shows us how he reaches his conclusions. As he says in "Of Vanity": "My style and my mind alike go roaming" (Montaigne, 1575/1965:

761). His pieces give us the appearance of a mind "roaming" as he shares with the reader his process in arriving at his judgments. As with the seemingly stream-of-consciousness forms used by other personal essayists, his "lusty sallies" are artful rather than careless and accidental:

> I go out of my way, but rather by license than carelessness. My ideas follow one another, but sometimes it is from a distance, and look at each other, but with a sidelong glance. (Montaigne, 1575/1965: 761)

Montaigne's essays and essays by writers in Montaigne's tradition of the personal essay are the "show me how you got the answer" prose of the writing world. Just as a geometry problem requires math students to explain how they reached their conclusion, a personal essay fulfills this course of action when writers explain their development and progression of thoughts about the experiences they describe. Such essays typically reveal explanations of the process of the writer's thinking on the subject, on the experiences the essayist details. To render the process of their thinking in such a way is to challenge writers to reflect and evaluate the topic. For students given opportunities to read and write in this genre, the personal essay becomes an excellent form to encourage skill-building in the areas of specific detail and evaluating evidence, whether the evidence is personal experience or text-based.

It is the very nature of the personal essay's habit of sharing with readers the process of how the writer reaches a conclusion that has become my principal reason to use the form in the beginning weeks of a composition course.

II.   Description of Activity

This series of assignments is developed for first-year students enrolled in my College Writing I class, the initial course of a year-long writing program. The course meets for 50 minutes three times per week. The entire *personal essay* section, from the first assigned reading to the final draft of the assigned essay, takes three weeks of class time. Beginning the second week of the course, students are assigned 7–8 personal essays to read and a personal essay to write. This essay becomes the first project of four major writing assignments given in the course.

The readings and writing assignment for this portion of the course are designed to enable students:

1. To hone skills in balancing specific detail with critical evaluation, two essential components of academic writing.
2. To experience and practice thinking, reading, and writing as essentially related activities, with the assumption that, in order to write effectively, one must think clearly and read critically.
3. To understand writing as a creative and cyclical process of planning, drafting, and revising.
4. To transfer the abilities and skills learned in this activity to writing assignments that require an argumentative thesis, supported by textual evidence.

Step One: Introducing the Concepts of "Inner" and "Outer" (1 class)

Before assigning any personal essays to read, I introduce to students the concept of the essay's *inner and outer stories.*[2] I tell students that a good essay, regardless of whether it is a personal story or an argumentative essay, involves two distinct but deeply interconnected stories. In a personal essay, these realms are the story of one's experiences and the story of one's thoughts – that is, respectively, the "outer" story and the "inner" story.

As students begin to brainstorm what these categories might mean, I write on a white board student comments and definitions. At the end of such discussions, I will often see listed under the heading for *outer story* examples such as:

- what happened to the person
- what we see or hear or taste
- the coffee cup sitting on my desk
- Joe's tennis shoes
- the world outside our brains

For examples of the *inner story*, student comments typically revolve around such phrases or notions as "what is inside my mind" and "the story of my thinking." I add to their inner story examples the words *reflection*, *evaluation*, and *critical thinking*. We discuss what these terms have represented to them when they have heard them mentioned in the past and what the terms might now represent when considering the two components of the essay. This inner/outer story paradigm will become our analytical lenses for the next few weeks, our conceptual framework to examine professionally written essays and evaluate student-written pieces.

Step Two: Using Personal Essays as Models (6–8 classes)

When choosing personal essays for students to read in this early section of my course, I have discovered through trial and error that certain essays work better than others. Since I'm seeking essays that illustrate how and when writers evaluate within their essays, I'm interested in personal essays which do that in obvious ways. One such essay that I typically use in the first few days is George Orwell's "A Hanging" (Orwell, 1945). In this piece, Orwell powerfully narrates the story of a hanging in Burma that he witnessed as an officer of the British Government. In the course of most of the essay, Orwell presents only the outer story events. But when the prisoner avoids stepping in a puddle on the way to his execution, Orwell shares with us his thoughts as he moves into a reflection of what he sees and gives us the reason for his essay:

> It is curious, but till that moment I had never realized what it means to destroy a healthy, conscious man. When I saw the prisoner step aside to avoid the puddle I saw the mystery, the unspeakable

wrongness, of cutting a life short when it is in full tide. This man was not dying, he was alive just as we are alive. All the organs of his body were working – bowels digesting food, skin renewing itself, nails growing, tissues forming – all toiling away in solemn foolery. (Orwell, 1945: 15)

Reading these evaluative comments made by Orwell about his experience, the only time in the essay when Orwell moves into the inner world of his thoughts, we know that Orwell is writing an essay against capital punishment. When students discuss "A Hanging," I ask them to consider how their reading experience would have differed if Orwell had not included this paragraph. I want them to understand the significance of evaluation and reflection within the essays they read and write. I share with them times when I have received student-written papers without that *inner story*, such as the instance when a student wrote about making the winning basketball shot, but never evaluated the experience, so that we readers were left to guess how important the event was to her. We talk about how essays without rhetorical moves into the *inner story* lack good writer control of effect make us wonder what the reason for the essay is, and cheat us from seeing the workings of a mind different from ours.

A good essay requires not just "the mind at work" evaluating the evidence; it requires specific details to support the writer's claims. Another point of focus when discussing Orwell's (1945) piece is finding specific details from the outer world that pull us into the essay with him, so that he is not just telling us about the experience; he is showing us as well. In small groups, students create a list of outer world details that Orwell uses successfully within his essay. Their oral reports often include references to Orwell's ability to create a scene and his skill to surprise them with his use of descriptive language, citing such phrases as "sickly light like yellow tinfoil" (Orwell, 1945: 13). By this time students are writing their own personal essay about an experience that changed them. Based on the group reports, we create a checklist of outer story strategies that they will follow as they write their own essay.

Orwell's "A Hanging" is an essay by a professional writer whose skills and artistry allow him to give us minimal evaluation, but still produce a brilliant piece of nonfiction. Although I consistently use it for its ability to emphasize the power of the inner story, "A Hanging" is a problematic model to use when I want to emphasize the practice of regularly interweaving within the outer story the writer's evaluations and reflections, a rhetorical strategy I will return to later in the course when we begin to write thesis-supported argumentative essays. One of the best essays I have found to provide such a model is a chapter from Annie Dillard's *An American Childhood* titled "The Chase" (Dillard, 1987) in essay anthologies. Dillard's theme of always grasping tenaciously to one's goals in life recurs throughout the essay as she and a boy are chased through her neighborhood by a person whose car had been hit by one of their snowballs:

> He chased us silently, block after block. He chased us silently over picket fences, through thorny hedges, between houses, around garbage cans, and across streets. Every time I glanced back, choking for breath, I expected he would have quit. He must have been as breathless as we were. His jacket strained over his body. It was an immense discovery, pounding into my hot head with every sliding, joyous step, that this ordinary adult evidently knew what I thought only children who trained at football knew: that you have to fling yourself at what you're doing, you have to point yourself, forget yourself, aim, dive. (Dillard, 1987: 47)

Dillard's artful weaving of outer story and inner story here and throughout her essay consistently reminds us of her purpose for the piece, bombards us with specific sensory details so we can experience the chase with her, and offers ample examples of strategic how's and when's to add critical thinking within an essay. In the above example, Dillard lets us know in obvious ways when she shares the inner story, and we get to see a mind at work when we read the sentence that begins: "It was an immense discovery, pounding into my hot head…." Inner story examples such as this allow students to consider the possible places and purposes writers critically think within an essay, including the purpose of reinforcing the theme. As in Montaigne's essays and those by writers who follow in his tradition, the enactment of the inner story allows the reader to see how the writer processes his experiences.

Another personal essay that makes an obvious move into the story of thought is Alice Walker's "Am I Blue?" (Walker, 1981). This essay uses the narrative of a horse named Blue to reflect on the unjust treatment of animals and humans:

> My partner's small son had decided he wanted to learn how to piece a quilt; we worked in silence on our respective squares as I *thought*…[author's ellipsis; emphasis added]
> Well, about slavery: about white children who were raised by black people, who knew their first all-accepting love from black women, and then, when they were twelve or so, were told they must "forget".… (Walker, 1981: 5)

As Walker and the boy piece together the quilt, Walker "pieces together" a series of reflections on injustice in the world. Without these critical moves, the essay becomes a story arguing only for animal rights. With these reflections, the essay becomes an argument for just treatment of all, taking the remaining sections of the narrative to a different level of understanding.

During discussion of an essay like Dillard's (1987) or Walker's (1981), I use the occasion to emphasize the importance of balancing the inner/outer realms. If the writer presents little or no outer story within the essay, the paper floats futilely in the sky, bloated with generalizations and without the necessary weight from specific details to give it substance. If the writer presents little or no inner story, as with the basketball player who never critically discussed her experience, the outer world keeps us too earthbound to see the essay's purpose and to know how to interpret the narrative and evidence. Writing an essay is a balancing act, and, when the writer has been successful, we readers are gifted regularly with ideas from both realms.

Other essays I have assigned through the years as models of personal essays in this section of the course include Scott Russell Sanders' "Grub" (Sanders, 2003), Annie Dillard's "Living Like Weasels" (Dillard, 2003), Marilyn Schiel's "Levi's" (Schiel, 2003), George Orwell's "Shooting an Elephant" (Orwell, 1945), E. B. White's "Once More to the Lake" (White, 1977), Joan Didion's "On Going Home" (Didion, 1968), Sanders' "The Inheritance of Tools" (Sanders, 1987), and Didion's "On the Road" (Didion, 1979).

Step Three: Giving the Writing Assignment (1 class)

After students have read and discussed three of the seven or so essays assigned in this section of the course, I distribute a handout with specific information about the first paper they will write in the class: A personal essay about a transformative experience. In a recent course, students received an assignment sheet with the following directions and evaluation criteria:

> Alice Walker's essay "Am I Blue," as with other essays you have been reading, is about an event that has an extraordinary effect on her life. Write an essay, 4–5 pages, detailing an event that (or a person who) has transformed you, something that changed you in some significant way.
>
> Whatever event (or persons) you choose to write about, you will want to write about it with enough detail for readers to understand why it is important, and you will want to write about it with enough evaluation of detail for readers to understand why it is important.
>
> **Evaluation**
> Your paper's evaluation will be based on the following criteria:
>
> 1. How well have you followed the requirements of the assignment?
> 2. How well is the essay supported with detail?
> 3. How well does the essay provide depth of thinking and evaluation of detail?
> 4. How well does the paper reveal creativity?

5. How well does the paper provide an organizational structure and signals that assist the reader to "move" through the paper?
6. To what extent does the text reveal evidence of editing, crafting, and proofreading?
7. How well has the writer handled the "process" of writing this essay, including participation in writing/editing workshops and meeting all deadlines?
8. How well does the essay demonstrate a command of standard academic conventions?

Besides writing about a transformative experience, other subjects for personal essays that I have assigned through the years when teaching this section of the course include writing about an important object, a special place, an exceptional trip, or a significant person in their lives. As with the transformative experience assignment, directions emphasize presenting adequate detail and evaluation for readers to understand the importance of the writer's subject.

After the assignment is distributed and discussed, students are asked to consider possible topics for their essay and to be prepared for a Brainstorming Workshop at the next class meeting.

Step Four: Brainstorming Workshop (1 class)

Students spend the next class period working on prewriting activities created to generate topic ideas. Stages of this activity include the following:

1. *Clustering.*[3] Students cluster for 5 minutes on the topic "Transforming Events in My Life."
2. *Listing.* Students are asked to examine their circled words, find the one that "speaks to them the most," and write that word/phrase on the top of another sheet of paper. This word or phrase becomes the focus for the next step: Students are asked to list for five minutes any ideas or other specifics about this word/phrase.

3. *Freewriting.*[4] This particular activity takes 20–25 minutes. Once students are finished with listing, I ask them to choose the event that seems to hold the most potential for them to write about as a subject of their personal essay. I then give them a series of 5-minute freewriting exercises, using the following prompts:

   - Return in memory to a particular moment in time, an important time in this event that you will narrate. You can see in "your mind's eye" this particular day. Is it autumn? Summer? Are you inside a house? On a sidewalk in your neighborhood? In a classroom? Where do you see yourself in this moment? Write for 5 minutes about all that you see in this moment of time.
   - Staying with this moment in time, write for 5 minutes about all that you hear. Perhaps you hear conversation. Perhaps you hear a teakettle boiling on the stove. Perhaps you hear tree leaves rustling in the wind. Write for 5 minutes about what you hear.
   - Staying with this moment, write for 5 minutes on all that you smell in this moment. Perhaps you smell trees decaying because the season is autumn and you are outside. Perhaps you smell cabbage cooking or an old musty couch. Perhaps you are in a hospital and everything smells a bit "sterile." Write about this for 5 minutes.
   - Write for 5 minutes about what was going through your mind at that moment. What were you were thinking about? What was going on in your "inner world"? What were your thoughts at that time?
   - Write for 5 minutes about what you think about the experience now. Some time has passed since the event occurred. You perhaps did not understand the significance of what happened at that moment when it occurred. But today the moment holds significance for you. For some reason, you chose this moment in time as an important scene in your story. Why is it so important in your

transformative experience? What do you think about this moment now?

Once students have completed the prewriting activities, they share their experiences with the prewritings and often express preferences as to which activity worked best as an idea generator for them.

At some point during our discussion, I guide the discussion to experiences with their freewriting. My reasons to use these particular questions as freewriting prompts are twofold: I want students to anchor their writing in one or more scenes so readers can "enter" their essays and experience through sensory descriptions of what the writers have experienced; and I want to reinforce the importance of inner stories, so we readers of students' essays are gifted with observing a mind at work and witness through development of theme the advancement of the essay's purpose. I return to the concepts of inner and outer stories, drawing parallels to the questions students addressed in the freewriting exercise. The first three questions generate material that, if used in their essays, becomes part of their outer stories; the last two questions generate material that hold potential for inner stories. At the end of the workshop, I suggest that, if students decide to change their subject for the essay, these writers should return to the "moment in time" prompts for a freewriting activity about the new subject outside of class time. Before class is over, I caution students to choose a transformative event that they will be comfortable sharing as a written piece with other classmates.

Step Five: Peer Group Workshop and Conference with Faculty (2–3 classes)

Alongside detailing specific directions and grading criteria, the writing project handout includes due dates for the first paragraph, first complete draft, and final draft. Students' first complete drafts are due on the fifth class after their essays were assigned. Before these are turned in to me, students meet in writing groups to read and respond to their group members' essays. Each reader completes a Reader Response Form for each essay read (see Appendix). Questions on the response forms have been developed from evaluation criteria given on the assignment handout.

I collect the drafts at the conclusion of the workshop and, for the next two scheduled class meetings, meet individually with each student in 10-minute conferences. By the time students revise their essays, they have received ample feedback, both from peers and from me.

Step Six: Final Drafts Collected and Graded

Final drafts are typically due a week after student conferences. As with other major writing assignments, these papers are handed in within a folder, with all drafts and writing group reader response forms included. Essays are evaluated and returned one week later.

III. Implementation

I teach two introductory (College Writing 1) courses each fall semester and have used the personal essay as a way to introduce students to academic writing for the past decade. Students in this composition course are typically traditional-aged first-year college students who have graduated from high school the previous spring.

Other demographics of these classes generally reflect the overall composition of the school. Saint Martin's University has a diverse campus, with 30% of the student body coming from ethnic groups that are primarily Latinos/Hispanics, Asians, Pacific Islanders/Hawaiians, and African Americans. The average gender composition of the courses approximates equal numbers of males and females. The average number of students in each course is eighteen.

Beginning in 2002, I started teaching College Writing 1 classes in our library's computer-supported classroom, a move to enhance possibilities for active learning. Students are assigned at one point during most classes a brief in-class writing assignment, such as summaries/reflections of course readings, progress reports on major papers, prewriting activities related to major papers, and synthesis of course concepts. During the personal essay component of the course, I often have students use the computers during class time for prewriting activities, reports on progress with a paper, and discussion of assigned readings. Students then email me these in-class writings.

Whenever students are not using computers, I arrange the classroom so students can focus on the class activity without computer intrusion. For example, if I want to briefly introduce a concept or explain an assignment, students either turn off their computer screens, or I stand in the back of the classroom and students turn their chairs toward me and away from the computers. During class discussions of assigned readings and writing experiences, students move their chairs away from the computers and form a circle in the center of the room. Everyone in class is expected to speak at these seminars.

Peer review writing workshops are held in three or four library study rooms, which are small rooms adjacent to the classroom, each room perfect for a writing group composed of four-to-five students. Before the class begins, I decide the composition of these groups, based on such criteria as leadership skills, writing ability, and dependability. I visit each group briefly during the workshop, but most of the time students are on their own to read and respond to their group members' essays via the Reader Response Form sheets.

The brief 10-minute writing conferences with each student necessitate on my part a concise list of 3–4 priorities I will discuss, and allow a one-on-one teaching approach on matters particular to their papers that I might not cover in large-class instruction. My responses to drafts on any major writing project in these writing conferences during the semester typically focus on ideas, development, organization, and overall clarity (Bean, 1996: 226–227).[5]

A frequent discussion point in conferences about students' transformative stories centers on a pattern I often see in first drafts of a personal essay – and I'm convinced that they learned this from writing their elementary school book reports – the habit of "dumping" all reflections and evaluation at the end of the piece. I discourage this format, not only because I want students to write a more artful personal story. I am interested in having students hone their ability to effectively balance evaluative claim with specific detail, a skill I hope they will transfer and apply to thesis-supported argumentative essay assignments. In a good college paper, the thesis does not just appear in the introduction and conclusion; it is interwoven throughout the essay via such strategies as transitional moves and evaluation/reflection of evidence presented.

IV.   Reflections and Recommendations

The overall quality of the argumentative papers assigned after the transformative essay assignment has convinced me to continue using personal essays to introduce students to academic writing. Final drafts of argumentative essays often reflect, among other achievements, successful skills in determining where critical moves should be made to evaluate the evidence presented and in critically evaluating the evidence in light of the thesis – two writing skills emphasized earlier via studying and practicing the personal essay's narrative strategies and thematic development.

To make the transition from personal essays to thesis-supported argumentative papers, I initially return to the inner/outer paradigm for a discussion of where the interrelated "stories" of specific detail and evaluation often appear in argumentative essays. Rather than detailing the specifics of personal experiences, the outer stories within argumentative essays are generally specific details from such sources as course texts, interviews, and library research. The inner stories are the writer's evaluations, reflections, and critical thoughts on these details, along with strategies such as transitional tactics, as the writer presents and develops the thesis. Just as with personal essays, the act of balancing details with evaluative claims within an argumentative essay involves rhetorical skills, so the essay does not suffer from unsubstantiated claims and/or evidence presented with little or no connection made to the thesis.

As with the personal essays, the first drafts of students' argumentative essays are often deficient in balancing the inner and outer worlds, but show improvement and a much better understanding of these strategies after peer workshops, faculty conferences, and the opportunity to revise. Because of such experiences, I am convinced that, without an emphasis on techniques that support revision, students would be less successful in understanding and enacting the writing skills this teaching technique stresses. My experience through the years as a teacher of college writing has provided me concrete comparative evidence that students become better writers less from first drafts of the assignments we give them than from their work of deep revision on subsequent ones.

I plan to continue to use the personal essay as an introduction to academic writing and have made the following modifications to this technique as I approach a new academic year:

- After students have completed their first draft, I have added as a class activity a workshop that entails having students highlight with markers or with computer tools sentences in their papers that reflect where they have critically evaluated and/or reflected on the event they narrated, and places that give the reader specific sensory details of the event. Students will be able to more easily see writing strategies they employ to negotiate inner/outer realms and use these insights in revision and future essay writing.

- I am adding the activity of using a web-based course management system like MOODLE for posting first drafts online so that these can be read by group members prior to the scheduled in-class peer review writing workshop.
- I have added as readings more examples of model essays that reflect ethnic diversity.
- I will be "publishing" students' final drafts online through a web-based course management system that is available for class members.

In addition to my original goal of using the personal essay as an introduction to academic writing, I have also discovered further advantages of such an instructional emphasis. At the end of the semester, students often state that this paper is their favorite assignment because they have been given an opportunity to examine an important part of their life that they had not examined so thoroughly before. They appreciate that their introduction to college writing permits them to use their own experiences. For faculty whose background includes knowledge of great essays and literary works, another advantage of this approach is its ability to use faculty knowledge in teaching academic writing.

Before they move into more systematized forms of discourse, I have found that using the personal essay to teach composition can be liberating for students and can hone critical thinking skills, its unfettered form allowing their ideas to "follow one another" but connect with a "sidelong glance" (Montaigne, 1575/1965: 761). As Sanders (1989: 34) describes his experiences of writing in this form, the personal essay presents to students opportunities to play with concepts while they find their way through forests of ideas, "dodging and circling, lured on by the sounds of unfamiliar birds, puzzled by the tracks of strange beasts, leaping from stone to stone across rivers, barking up one tree after another." Opportunities abound for composition faculty to build on the basic techniques of using the personal essay as a springboard into academic writing and for the development of critical writing skills.

Notes

1. Essayists in the tradition of Montaigne include such writers as Virginia Woolf, E. B. White, Annie Dillard, Edward Hoagland, Max Beerbohm, Scott Russell Sanders, Joan Didion, Phillip Lopate, and Alice Walker.
2. The notion of "inner and outer stories" as a general principle of the essay form is a concept I learned from Carl Klaus, director of the University of Iowa Masters in Writing Nonfiction Program in the early 1990s.
3. Also called such terms as "webbing" or "treeing," clustering is a prewriting activity to help writers generate ideas at any stage of their writing process through visual mapping. In the middle of a sheet of paper (or on computer), students circle the concept they will explore. Around the circled word, they write the major parts of this concept, circle these words, and connect the circled words with lines to the main topic. Students then repeat this process with the new ring of circled words; they write ideas/details that come to mind, circle these words, and connect them with lines to the specific word from which the idea came. Each new circled word offers the possibility of new ideas. I've used clustering as an idea generator in writing workshops attended by all ages and levels of writers.
4. Freewriting explores a topic by writing about it for a period of time without stopping and with little regard to issues like grammar or spelling.
5. Practices that stress revision in writing, such as multiple drafts, writing groups, and faculty-student writing conferences, are familiar emphases in composition pedagogy and writing textbooks published during the last three decades, thanks to the influence of the Writing as Process movement in Composition Studies. As faculty development director at my university, I anchor many writing-across-the-curriculum workshops on the superbly helpful *Engaging Ideas* by Bean (1996). Bean's book integrates writing as process concepts with activities that encourage habits of inquiry via problem-based assignments.

References

Bean, John C. (1996) *Engaging Ideas: The Professor's Guide to Integrating Writing, Critical Thinking, and Active Learning in the Classroom.* San Francisco: Jossey-Bass.

Didion, Joan (1968) On going home. *Slouching Towards Bethlehem* 164–168. New York: Farrar, Straus and Giroux.

Didion, Joan (1979) On the road. *The White Album* 173–179. New York: Farrar, Straus and Giroux.

Dillard, Annie (1987) *An American Childhood* 45–49. New York: Harper & Row.

Dillard, Annie (2003) Living like weasels. In Robert Keith Miller (ed.) *Motives for Writing* (4th edition) 84–88. Boston: McGraw Hill.

Hoagland, Edward (1982) What I think, what I am. *The Tugman's Passage* 24–27. New York: Random House.

Klaus, Carl H. (1989) Essayists on the essay. In Chris Anderson (ed.) *Literary Nonfiction: Theory, Criticism, Pedagogy* 155–76. Carbondale: Southern Illinois University.

Montaigne, Michel de (1575/1965) *The Complete Essays of Montaigne* (trans. Donald M. Frame). Stanford: Stanford University Press.

Orwell, George (1945) A hanging. *Shooting an Elephant and Other Essays* 13–18. New York: Harcourt, Brace, & World.

Orwell, George (1945) Shooting an elephant. *Shooting an Elephant and Other Essays* 4–12. New York: Harcourt, Brace, & World.

Sanders, Scott R. (2003) Grub. In Robert Keith Miller (ed.) *Motives for Writing* (4th edition) 62–67. Boston: McGraw Hill.

Sanders, Scott R. (1987) The inheritance of tools. *The Paradise of Bombs* 102–110. Athens: University of Georgia Press.

Sanders, Scott R. (1989) The singular first person. In A. Butrym (ed.) *Essays on the Essay: Redefining the Genre* 31–42. Athens: University of Georgia Press.

Schiel, Marilyn (2003) Levi's. In Robert Keith Miller (ed.) *Motives for Writing* (4th edition) 57–61. Boston: McGraw Hill.

Walker, Alice (1981) Am I blue? *Living By the Word* 3–8. New York: Harcourt Brace Jovanovich.

White, E. B. (1977) Once more to the lake. *Essays of E. B. White* 197–201. New York: HarperPerennial.

Woolf, Virginia (1925/1953) First Series. *The Common Reader.* New York: Harcourt Brace Jovanovich.

Appendix

Your Name_____

Name of Writer_____

Answer these questions after carefully reading the draft.
1. Write below what you think the purpose – the main point – of this essay is.
2. What suggestions can you give this writer to make his/her purpose clearer to the reader?
3. List places in the essay where you find the specific sensory descriptions (sights, sounds, smells, tastes, touch) especially strong
4. List places in the essay where you think additional specific sensory would improve the essay.
5. What suggestions can you give the writer:
    • to improve the opening of the essay?
    • to improve the way the essay is organized?
    • to improve the conclusion?
6. List places in the essay where you find the writer has been successful in giving us a reason why certain information is being shared.
7. Other comments?

3   Snapshots of Our Literacies

Michelle Cox and Katherine E. Tirabassi

> You need to get some writing down on paper and to keep it there long enough so that you can give yourself the treat of rewriting. What you need is a ballpoint pen so that you can't erase and some cheap paper so you can deliberately use a lot of it…. Where are your notes to yourself? Where are your lists?... Where are your quoted passages? Where is your chaos? Nothing comes of nothing!
> – Ann Berthoff, "Recognition, Representation and Revision" (Berthoff, 1981: 19)

Background

"Snapshots of Our Literacies" is a creative non-fiction writing project that asks students to develop brief descriptive narratives in response to writing prompts focused on writing, reading, discourse communities, and literacy. Students then select from these short narratives to craft a snapshot essay – an essay composed of these "snapshots" of experiences, linked together by a common thread or theme.

The two of us began to develop this writing assignment when we were both graduate instructors in master's programs at the University of New Hampshire. The assignment continued to evolve as we both worked on our doctoral degrees in Composition Studies at that same university, and as we each became assistant professors, one at Keene State College in New Hampshire and one at Bridgewater State University in Massachusetts. Over these past ten years, we have used this project in mainstream, honors, and ESL sections of first-year composition, in classes ranging from 18 to 24 students.

This assignment began as a response to student resistance to revision. Influenced by the works of Ann Berthoff (e.g., Berthoff, 1981), Peter Elbow (e.g. Elbow and Belanoff, 1999), and Donald Murray (e.g. Murray, 1996), we believed that writers learn the most about writing while revising, but that writers need to gain experience with invention and revision strategies to see the potential for discovery and learning while drafting. Though we would discuss revision during class, students would often labor extensively over that first draft, and wouldn't want to budge when it came to revising for a second draft. So we decided to create an assignment with an explicit focus on revision, placing this project at the very start of the semester, to introduce students to the social writing process approaches we would use all semester. A segmented or, as Toby Fulwiler calls it, a "snapshot" essay (Fulwiler, 1999) seemed perfect for this type of project, since it allows students to write multiple short pieces, which are more easily revised as discrete pieces before creating a more cohesive essay. Here's how we address this process in the assignment description:

> Generating short writings will give us multiple chances to experiment with stylistic choices, narrative strategies, and revision techniques. Sometimes, when we write a longer essay, we feel "locked into" that first draft, perhaps since it represents such an investment of time and effort. Long first drafts can feel as if they've been etched in concrete – unmovable, intractable, set. But short pieces of writing can be endlessly played with, transformed, explored. I

didn't discover the "treat of rewriting" until my second semester of graduate school. Hopefully, you will discover this much earlier than I did. Revision is the time when you are free to play with language, experiment with form and voice, and explore your ideas and memories more deeply.

This assignment also began as a response to students' misconceptions about writing, reading, and literacy. They often entered our first-year writing courses thinking that writing and reading took place only in English classes and that "literacy" referred to only the basic ability to read and write. We believed that enriching their perspectives on writing, reading, and literacy would be empowering for students, as they would come to recognize and write about their own multiple literacies, as well as develop a broader view of the many writing and reading activities they would be doing across the curriculum. To introduce these ideas of writing, reading, and literacy, we include the following definitions in the assignment description:

> **Discourse community:** A group of people who are connected by a common discourse. Composition scholar Lynn Z. Bloom defines discourse community in this way: "When several (or more) readers share a background, common values, and a common language, they may be considered a discourse community…. [A]ll the words, all the languages we understand (including the nonverbal communication of body language and social conventions), invariably influence how we write" (*The Essay Connection*; Bloom, 2006: 5). Discourse communities tend to use a specialized discourse and prefer certain genres for communicating with each other. Some examples of discourse communities: fans of the Boston Red Sox, knitters, biochemists.
>
> **Literacy:** You may be familiar with the definition of literacy as the ability to read and write. We are using a more current definition of literacy here. Composition scholars talk about people as having multiple literacies at multiple levels. If you can read and write within a particular discourse community, then you are *literate* in that discourse community. For example, I am literate in the world

of knitting, becoming literate as a Boston Red Sox fan, but not at all literate in the world of biochemistry.

Literacy sponsor: Literacy studies scholar Deborah Brandt defines a literacy sponsor as an agent that brings someone into a particular literacy (Brandt, 1998). For example, I am a sponsor to my sister's developing knitting literacy, because I often help her learn how to interpret knitting instructions and give her knitting books that I've found helpful. Those knitting books were my literacy sponsors because they helped me become literate in the world of knitting.

As we became more aware of the second language writers in our classrooms and more knowledgeable about the field of second language writing, we began to see the merits of this project for drawing on the multiple resources these students bring to their writing. In *Critical Academic Literacies*, A. Suresh Canagarajah introduced the framework of "resource-as-deficit" and "difference-as-resource" (Canagarajah, 2002: 218) to describe two possible stances in relation to second language writers – the former seeing second language writers as limited, as less-than native English speaking students, and the latter recognizing the additional resources these students bring to their writing in English. To help second language students view their first language literacies as resources, we added the following invitation to the assignment description:

> If you use English as a second (or third, etc.) language, feel free to write about literacy experiences you had while writing or reading in your first language. Second language literacy builds on first language literacy, so it's valuable to reflect on all of your literacy experiences, across languages, educational systems, and cultures. You may also choose to focus on writing experiences you had while writing and reading in English. It's up to you.

Second language students often feel that they are starting from scratch when developing literacy in an additional language, but first-language literacy creates a foundation for second-language literacy (Bauer, 2009; Cummins, 1991; Roberts, 1994), and awareness of these connections is empowering for multilingual students.

For all students, writing about their own literate backgrounds allows them to see what literacies they bring to the college classroom, literacies that they can draw from and build upon. As Anne Ruggles Gere points out in "Kitchen Tables and Rented Rooms: The Extracurriculum of Composition," many rich literate practices occur beyond the classroom walls and these experiences can also shape students' attitudes and beliefs about writing and their "motivation to revise and improve composition skills" (Gere, 1994: 78). The prompts allow students to explore both curricular and extracurricular experiences that have shaped their beliefs and attitudes toward writing and revision and to articulate to themselves and to their readers who they are as writers.

In addition, this project has the benefit of being a great icebreaker in the first-year writing classroom. Students learn a great deal about each other's experiences from reading each other's drafts during workshops, and the instructor gains a rich understanding of the students' past experiences with writing, reading, and language, as well as how the students' identify and describe themselves as writers and readers – important information for developing a challenging yet encouraging space for writing over the course of the semester.

II.   Description of Activity

Writing is an experimental act. In the search for meaning, the writer – and the artist, the actor, and the scientist – proceeds by trial and error. I hook one word to another, reach up above the workbench and grab a different word; plug a clause into a sentence, turn it around and try it again; shape a paragraph, taking a little off the end, building up the middle, sharpening the leading edge.
– Donald Murray, *Crafting a Life in Essay, Story, Poem* (Murray, 1996: 136)

We dedicate the first five weeks of the semester to this project. The description of our process follows.

First Week

Students discuss "Writing as Inquiry" by Bruce Ballenger (Chapter 1 of Ballenger, 2007) and readings about discovery and invention strategies by Donald Murray (Murray, 1996), read over the Snapshots of Our Literacies assignment description and writing prompts, and choose a "Writing about Writing" prompt. Here are a few of the prompts from this section:

1. **Favorite Writing Experience:** Think about a piece you wrote that is important to you. What makes this piece special to you? What did you write about? How did you go about writing this piece? Did you write it inside or outside of school? How has this writing experience continued to influence you? If you shared what you wrote, what kind of feedback did you receive? Rather than think about a piece, you could also think about writing in a certain genre, such as poetry, letters, arguments, or writing in a journal. Develop a brief narrative that highlights an aspect of your favorite writing experience.

2. **Worst Writing Experience:** Think about a writing experience that had a negative effect on you. Did this experience take place in school or outside of school? How was the experience negative? Was it stressful? Did you feel embarrassed? Were you unfamiliar with the discourse or genre you were expected to write in? If you shared what you wrote, what kind of feedback did you receive? How has this experience continued to influence you as a writer? Develop a brief narrative that highlights an aspect of your worst writing experience.

3. **Picturing a Writer:** What do you envision when you picture a writer? What does this writer write? Where does this

writer write? What does this writer look like? What kinds of tools does this writer use to write with? Compare yourself to this writer that you envision. How do you compare? Where do your ideas about writers come from? Write a brief narrative that explores what you envision when you picture a writer in comparison with who you are as a writer.

4. **Feelings about Writing:** What are your first thoughts when you think about writing? What are your first feelings when you are given a writing assignment in school? Where do these thoughts and feelings come from? Do you remember the first time you felt this way about writing? Do you remember a time when you felt differently about writing? If so, what changed your feelings? Write a brief narrative that depicts your feelings about writing.

5. **Writing Inventory:** As a form of prewriting, make a list of the kinds of writing have you done. What genres have you written in (i.e. journal entry, email, lab report, proposal, essay, research paper)? What places have you written for (i.e. a workplace, school, an organization)? What audiences have you written for? What purposes have you used writing for? After making this list, write a snapshot on what you discovered about who you are as a writer.

6. **Your Writing Process:** How would you describe your writing process? Do you use a dictionary or a thesaurus? Do you have people read your writing and give you feedback as you write? What are the steps you take when you write? Do you brainstorm, make an outline, write multiple drafts? How do you feel when you write? Does your writing process differ if you are writing for school versus writing outside of school? How do you find topics to write about? Do you have different writing processes for different genres of writing (i.e. email, journal entry, lab report)? Do you have different writing processes depending on which language you write in? Write a brief narrative that depicts your writing process.

While the above prompts could elicit short responses to each question, we instead ask students, at the beginning of the writing prompt section, to develop narrative stories, phrasing our instructions as follows:

> In most of the prompts, I list a number of questions, but you don't need to worry about answering every question. In fact, it would be better if you didn't. Read the prompts until you come across a question that sparks a particular memory, something worth exploring through writing, and then write. In each piece, I would like you to use personal writing (writing from your experiences, using the word "I"), and a narrative (story-telling) voice.

Students are randomly divided into writing groups of 3–4 students, remaining in these groups during this project. During this early stage in the project, we simply ask students to share their drafts with their writing groups and to have conversations about the content of the pieces, asking each other questions about the literacy experiences. Our aim is to create an encouraging and comfortable space for writing at this point. For homework, students select another "Writing about Writing" prompt.

Second Week

Students read "Reading as Inquiry" by Bruce Ballenger (Chapter 2 of Ballenger, 2007) and select writing prompts from "Writing about Reading" prompts, which mirror the ones about writing, entitled *Favorite Reading Experience, Worst Reading Experience, Reading Inventory, Picturing a Reader, Feelings about Reading,* and *Your Reading Process*. In class, we also spend some time writing to these prompts, and students begin to revise the snapshots they've been developing, drawing from a series of revision prompts we developed (which are published under the title "Playing with Revision;" Cox and Tirabassi, 2008). Here are a few revision prompts that students have found particularly useful with this project:

1. **Do You Really Mean It?** Revision gives the opportunity to reflect on and further develop your ideas. Read over your draft, and ask yourself if you still believe or agree with everything you wrote. Write reflective notes in the margins as you read, and then revise, while referring to these notes.

2. **Looping:** Look through your draft and identify a line that calls out to you, one that seems to hold meaning. Take out a new piece of paper, copy this line at the top, and freewrite from it, pushing to further develop meaning as you go. Look over this new writing, identify another line that calls out to you, and repeat the process.

3. **Unbury a Story:** Find a line in your essay that seems to hide a story, and unbury that story. You might find a line that "tells" but doesn't "show." Open up that story. Belief statements, such as "I can't write," often hold one or more stories within them. Choose one of these stories to tell.

4. **Add, Add, Add:** Comb through your essay and add details that help your audience better understand what you see and mean when you use certain words. Change vague nouns (*car*) to specific nouns (*Nissan Quest*), general adjectives (*red*) to specific ones (*metallic cherry*), direct statements (*my minivan handles well*) to metaphors (*When shifting across three lanes to get to my exit, my minivan handles like what I imagine a racecar to feel like, hugging the road while cleanly gliding to the next lane, and responding quickly to my every move*).

5. **Cut, Cut, Cut:** Comb through your essay and cut as much as you possibly can. Try for fifteen words per page. Cut extra words that don't add meaning, such as *really, very, basically, thing, it, it is, it was, there is, there were, this is,* and *that*. Example: *My brother's constant whining is one of those many characteristics that really frustrates me to no end* can be cut to *My brother's constant whining frustrates me*. Cut wordy phrases that don't add meaning, such as *on the other hand, due to the fact that, needless to say, in my*

personal opinion, in this point in time. Cut redundant words, such as in *big tall skyscraper.* The words *big* and *tall* have similar meanings, and using the specific word *skyscraper* tells your reader that the building you're referring to is a large building.

6. **Sentence Variety:** Readers appreciate a change of pace, and varying sentence lengths and structure can add that sense of texture to your writing, and help you better emphasize key pieces of information. Comb through your draft and focus in on your sentences. Count the number of words in each sentence. How many sentences are the same length? Look at the structure of your sentences. How many include introductory phrases, conjunctions, or dependant clauses? Read your essay out loud, listening to the rhythm, noting places where you stumble over a word or strive to emphasize something that's not being emphasized by the writing. Then revise, using short sentences for emphasis, long sentences for depth and description, moving important pieces of information to the ends of sentences for added emphasis.

Third Week

Students read about literacy and discourse communities, both theoretical readings by Deborah Brandt (Brandt, 1998), and David Bartholomae (Bartholomae, 1985), and personal literacy narratives by authors such as Mike Rose (Rose, 2005), Perri Klass (Klass, 1987), Amy Tan (Tan, 2004), and Richard Rodriguez (Rodriguez, 1982). Students then write and revise snapshots based on the writing prompts they've selected from "Writing about Discourse Communities" and "Writing about Literacies":

Writing about Discourse Communities

1. **Exploring a Discourse Community:** Think about a discourse community that you are very familiar with (i.e. a

workplace, a social circle, an academic discipline). What words are specific to this community? Why are there words that are specific to this community? What are the speaking and/or writing practices of members of this community? Who generally gets to speak/write? How can people enter this discourse community? What would gain a person entry? What would keep a person out? Develop a brief narrative that highlights some of the language practices specific to this discourse community.

2. **Entering a Discourse Community:** Think about a time when you were aware of entering a discourse community. How did you feel before you were fluent in this discourse community? How did you enter the community? Did anyone act as a sponsor? How did you learn the discourse practices of this community? How do you now stand as a member of this community? Develop a brief narrative that illustrates a key experience you had when you entered an unfamiliar discourse community.

3. **Moving between Discourse Communities:** Think about a time when you were aware that you were moving between discourse communities. How would you describe each of these communities? What was the relation between these communities? Did they clash against each other or blend together? How did your discourse practices change as you moved between these communities? Do you feel like a different person in each of these communities? Develop a brief narrative that illustrates a key experience you had when moving between discourse communities.

4. **In Conversation:** Think about the conventions of conversation in one of your discourse communities. Who gets to talk? How are turns taken? How do speakers signify that they want a response? How do listeners know when to jump in and speak? How do listeners signify that they are listening, following the conversation? How is silence interpreted? How does body language figure into the conversation? Describe

a scene where members of this community interact so that someone from outside of this community has a look in.

Writing about Literacies

1. **Literacy Spaces and Artifacts:** Explore a room that is important to you (i.e. a bedroom, a lab, an office). What literacy artifacts do you see? What literacies are represented in this room? If you moved to come to school, what kinds of written pieces did you bring with you? Develop a brief narrative, exploring how artifacts in a particular space represent your literacies. Or, examine one artifact and write about it in detail, seeing where this takes you.

2. **Literacies of Someone You Know:** Think about the literacies of a family member or close friend. How do you know about this person's literacies? When you enter this person's space (i.e. house, room, office), what literacy artifacts do you see? How do this person's literacies affect your relationship with this person? How have this person's literacies affected your own? Develop a brief narrative that highlights the relevance of this person's literacies.

3. **Oral Literacy:** Think about the role of oral literacy in your family or one of your discourse communities. What stories are told? Who tells the stories? When are they told? Why are they told? How do these stories change over time, or change when different people tell them? Do these stories coincide with or contradict written histories? Are they written down anywhere? Develop a brief narrative that focuses on one of these aspects of oral literacy.

4. **Acts of Sponsorship:** Think about a time when you sponsored someone into a literacy, or when someone acted as a sponsor to you. What prompted this act of sponsorship? How did this sponsorship take place? How did this sponsorship play into your relationship with the other person? Have you or the other person retained this new literacy? Develop a brief narrative about an act of sponsorship.

Fourth Week

During this week, students read through the many pieces that they've written and revised and select snapshots that they want to include in their snapshot essays. We explain that snapshot essays are segmented, with white space or subtitles instead of transitions between each section of the essay, but that, like any essay, snapshot essays move the reader from one place to another, using narrative structure to carry the reader through the essay. We often provide students with Toby Fulwiler's useful definition of a snapshot essay: "Each individual snapshot focuses on one dimension of self the way a single photograph captures one particular scene. At the same time, a collection of such verbal episodes, carefully juxtaposed against others, tells a larger more complete story the way a collection of photographs in an album or exhibit tells a larger story" (Fulwiler, 1999: 105).[1] To help students understand this concept, we read several snapshot essays together, including Susan Toth's "Going to the Movies" (Toth, 1988); Geeta Kothari's "If You Are What You Eat, Then What Am I?" (Kothari, 2000); Annie Dillard's "Total Eclipse" (Dillard, 1988); and Nicole Lamy's "Life in Motion" (Lamy, 2005),[2] as well as former students' essays written from this project. Students workshop the first draft of the essay in their writing groups. During this workshop, the students not only discuss the crafting of individual snapshots and the overall organization of the essays, but also whether the writer needs to develop additional snapshots to emphasize larger themes or to create more coherence in the essay.

Fifth Week

This week, students workshop the second draft of the essay, in what we call a "Paperswap" workshop. Before the workshop, we create a feedback form focusing on the aspects of the project that we believe students would most need to consider during revision, such as using details, creating a focus, and coherence. We ask students to bring three copies of their draft to class. Students place the copies in three distinct piles on our desks and then we hand out the feedback forms, asking each student to take three. Meanwhile, we remove two piles of drafts and spread the rest across the desk. We ask the students to come up and select one essay from a student outside of their writing group (the goal is to provide more critical feedback at this point in the drafting process). Then, we spread the second pile across the desk and ask students to hold onto the first essay when they are finished commenting, and then to select a second essay to continue the process. (When the second pile is gone, we spread out the third.) At the end, students return the essays and completed forms to the writers.

If there is time for another workshop during the drafting of this essay, we sometimes ask students to try a "cut-and-paste" revision. Students bring a printed copy of their snapshot essay, cut up by section,[3] and then they ask one other student who has not read their essay to put the draft together in the order that s/he feels makes most narrative sense. The goals of this workshop are to help writers see other possibilities for the essay's narrative trajectory and places where they might fill gaps or make clearer connections in the narrative itself. While, quite often, the reader reorganizes the snapshots, sometimes, the reader reorders the snapshots in the very same order, offering a confirmation to the writer about the current narrative direction. We make it clear to the writers that they do not need to retain the order that the readers selected; this exercise allows writers to see new possibilities, and, at times, this workshop opens up a revised or new storyline for the writers to explore.

The projects are due at the end of the fifth week. To retain the focus on writing process, we ask students to hand in mini-portfolios – folders containing all drafts, peer feedback, the final draft, and a cover letter. Here's this part of the assignment description:

Turn in a folder containing the following pieces:

- *Snapshot Essay*: must contain 5–7 snapshots; use 12-point font, Times New Roman, with 1" margins; each snapshot should be well-crafted and well-edited, and contribute to the essay as a whole.
- *Paper Trail*: drafts, revisions, worksheet from Paperswap workshop
- *Cover Letter*: Tell me the story of your writing of the essay, answering the following questions:
  o What have you learned about your literacies and the writing process during this project?
  o How did revision help you to explore and further develop your writing? How did you use feedback from readers (i.e. classmates, teacher, or writing studio consultant) during the writing of different snapshots? Choose a snapshot that you feel taught you the most about writing and revision, and tell me the story of your writing it.
  o If you had more time, how would you further develop this essay? Choose one snapshot, and tell me how you would revise it further.

III. Implementation

Evaluation and advice are not what writers need most. What writers need (and fortunately it's what all readers are best at) is an audience: a thoughtful, interested audience rather than evaluators or editors or advice-givers. In the long run, you will learn the most about writing from feeling the presence of interested readers – like feeling the pressure or weight of a fish at the end of the line.
– Peter Elbow and Pat Belanoff, *Sharing and Responding* (Elbow and Belanoff, 1999: 5)

As indicated by the above assignment description, the class is run primarily as a writer's workshop during this project. During each class meeting, students engage in peer review, write to additional prompts, and begin the work of revising. As instructors, we move among the writing groups, listening into conversations, providing feedback to drafts, and answering questions that arise.

The questions that students have often arise from the differences between this writing project and others they have experienced in high school, English language institutes, or other college courses. Revision as a process for refocusing and developing meaning is often new to them, as they often have experienced revision only as "error fixing," or, at most, as exchanging a word or phrase for a new one. In Massachusetts and New Hampshire, as in many states, high-stakes testing has prompted language arts teachers to return to a focus on five-paragraph essays. Residential second language students who experienced part of their education in U.S. high schools may have been tracked into low-level language arts classes that focused on sentence-level writing (Fu, 1995). International second language students have reported to us that the English language institutes they studied at to achieve TOEFL scores for college admittance focused exclusively on five-paragraph essays and error correction. Students from similar educational landscapes may have difficulty moving away from conventional essay structures to those such as the snapshot essay described above and from revising as editing to more substantive revision. To address these concerns, we discuss with our students the history of the five-paragraph essay as a school genre, and we talk about our own writing processes and those of published writers. Fixed notions of genre and writing process are hard to undo, and we recognize this project as a first step in a course that seeks to address these concerns throughout the semester.

Other questions that students raise focus on the difficulty of moving from individual snapshots to a cohesive snapshot essay. As they draft each snapshot, students often are uneasy about whether they are "wasting their time" writing about something that might not be included in the final snapshot essay. Students also raise concerns about whether they will ever find a theme amid pieces that feel disparate, disconnected from one another. As instructors who have experience hearing and dealing with these concerns, we offer reassuring words to our students: "Don't worry. Just write to the prompts and trust this process. Later on, I know that you will find ways to link some of these pieces into a story." In their reflective cover letters accompanying this project, students often note their initial skepticism about this process, and their fear that they would never find an essay amid the various pieces they'd written. Inevitably, through revision and through their conferences with one another and their teacher, they find the connective tissue that brings the pieces together into a cohesive narrative with a clear theme. Past students have developed stories with themes that discuss their growing love of reading, their fear of writing, and their proficiency in a particular literacy, such as a sport or cultural tradition.

Students also raise questions about how the project will be evaluated. To answer these questions, we provide a marking guideline, or rubric, with the elements of the rubric aligned with the questions developed for the Paperswap Workshop feedback form. As part of the rubric, students are evaluated on the paper trail (the particular drafts that illustrate their revision process) and the cover letter reflecting on the writing process. It is important that the final draft be evaluated as part of a larger project, so that such elements as revision and students' growing knowledge of the writing process can be considered during assessment.

Despite these questions, most students find this project to be freeing. The project design relies on "enabling constraints" (Summerfield and Summerfield, 1986), as the writing prompts and structured revision process provides room to roam, but not so much room that students get lost, wasting time spinning their wheels in trying to figure out what is expected of them and how to proceed in their writing. Once students experience freewriting to the prompts and then using the revision prompts to craft a more focused and detailed snapshot, they start enjoying the process of writing and creating pieces of writing that they feel proud of, writing some of them didn't think they were capable of producing. Once they experience peer review as encouraging and generative, they start to enjoy writing workshops, even looking forward to seeing how readers will respond to their newest drafts. And, once they begin to see the focused theme and stories emerge within their snapshot essays, they become more invested in sharing that story more clearly with their readers.

IV.   Reflections and Recommendations

We have used this writing project for a long time, adapting it as we've moved across teaching contexts, because it is the most effective project we have tried for introducing students to revision and writing workshops. Even though the first-year courses we teach do not focus on personal experience writing but rather on persuasive and researched writing, the writing processes used during this project and the language we've developed for discussion about revision continue to serve as a foundation for writing projects throughout the rest of the semester. Students are proud of the writing they produce during this project, a pride that comes through when we ask students to select their best work for a class magazine published at the end of the semester or a final portfolio "best essay" section; students often choose this project.

When we moved this project across institutional settings, we adapted the project according to the focus of the first-year composition programs in each setting. For example, at the University of New Hampshire, the first-year writing course focuses on personal experience writing, persuasive writing, and researched writing. At Bridgewater State University, there is a two-semester first-year writing sequence, with researched writing reserved for the second semester. So, research writing prompts were included when the course was taught at UNH, but not at BSU. At Keene State College, the first-year writing course focuses on a fifteen-week sustained research project; however, the initial part of the course focuses on writing process, and so this project becomes an essential part of the work in those first few weeks. We recommend that instructors wishing to try our ideas adapt the writing prompts to best fit the first-year composition curriculum at their own institutions, as this project creates the foundation for the course.

As we moved the course across institutions, we discovered the extent to which students' previous experiences with writing in school affected their comfort levels with nontraditional essay structures and the revision process. We recommend that those who want to try out our ideas investigate writing instruction in local high schools, so that they as writing instructors can be prepared for those conversations with their own students.

However instructors adapt this project, we hope that all will find, as we have, that this project will set the stage for students to draw on their multiple literacies, multiple linguistic experiences, and multiple educational experiences when writing and reading, resources they can then draw on throughout their writing course, and throughout their lives as writers.

Notes

1. Other resources listed in the bibliography with chapters or sections defining/describing snapshot essays are Sondra Perl and Mimi Schwartz, "Taking Shape" (Perl and Schwartz, 2005); Robert Root, "Collage montage, mosaic, vignette, episode, segment" (Root, 2005); and Brenda Miller and Suzanne Paola, "Collage/Braided essay" (Miller and Paola, 2004).

2. Other snapshot essays that we have found useful are Will Baker, "My Children Explain the Big Issues" (Baker, 2004); Charles Simic, "On Food and Happiness" (Simic, 1994); and Alice Walker, "A Thousand Words: A Writer's Pictures of China" (Walker, 1989).

3. If the technology is available, students can also bring an electronic version of their essay to class. In this case, we recommend that the writers mix up the snapshots so that they are not in any particular order, and then the reader can reorganize the snapshots in the order that s/he thinks is best.

References

Baker, Will (2004) My children explain the big issues. In Brenda Miller and Suzanne Paola (eds.) *Tell it Slant: Writing and Shaping Creative Nonfiction* 205–207. Boston: McGraw Hall, Inc.

Ballenger, Bruce (2007a) Chapter 1, Writing as inquiry. *The Curious Writer* (2nd edition) 1–31. New York: Pearson/Longman.

Ballenger, Bruce (2007b) Chapter 2, Reading as inquiry. *The Curious Writer* (2nd edition) 33–67. New York: Pearson/Longman.

Bartholomae, David (1985) Inventing the University. In Mike Rose (ed.) *When a Writer Can't Write* 134–65. New York: Guilford Press.

Bauer, Eurydice (2009) Informed additive literacy instruction for ELLs. *Reading Teacher* 62: 446–448.

Berthoff, Ann E. (1981) Recognition, representation and revision. *Journal of Basic Writing* 3: 19–32.

Bloom, Lynn Z. (2006) *The Essay Connection* (8th edition). Belmont, Washington: Wadsworth Publishing.

Brandt, Deborah (1998) Sponsors of literacy. *College Composition and Communication* 49: 165–85.

Canagarajah, A. Suresh (2002) *Critical Academic Writing and Multilingual Students*. Ann Arbor, Michigan: Multilingual Matters.

Cox, Michelle and Tirabassi, Katherine E. (2008) Playing with revision. In Anne Doyle, Kathryn Evans, Michelle Cox, Evelyn Pezzulich, and Benjamin Carson (eds.) *Embracing Writing: First-Year Writing at Bridgewater State College* (2nd edition) 44–48. Boston: Kendall-Hunt.

Cummins, James (1991) Interdependence of first and second language proficiency in bilingual children. In Ellen Bialystok (ed.) *Language Processing in Bilingual Children* 70–89. Cambridge: Cambridge University Press.

Dillard, Annie (1988) Total eclipse. *Teaching a Stone to Talk: Expeditions and Encounters* 9–28. New York: Harper-Perennial.

Elbow, Peter and Belanoff, Pat (1999) *Sharing and Responding* (3rd edition). New York: McGraw-Hill.

Fu, Danling (1995) *"My Trouble Is My English": Asian Students and the American Dream*. Portsmouth, New Hampshire: Heinemann.

Fulwiler, Toby (1999) *The Working Writer* (2nd edition). Upper Saddle River, New Jersey: Prentice-Hall.

Gere, Anne Ruggles (1994) Kitchen tables and rented rooms: The extracurriculum of composition. *College Composition and Communication* 45: 75–92.

Klass, Perri (1987) Learning the language. *A Not Entirely Benign Procedure: Four Years as a Medical Student* 73–78. New York: Penguin Books USA.

Kothari, Geeta (2000) If you are what you eat, then what am I? In Alan Lightman (ed.) *The Best American Essays 2000* 91–100. Boston: Houghton-Mifflin Company.

Lamy, Nicole (2005) Life in motion. In Robert Root and Michael Steinberg (eds.) *The Fourth Genre: Contemporary Writers of/on Creative Nonfiction* (3rd edition) 115–19. New York: Pearson/Longman.

Miller, Brenda and Paola, Suzanne (2004) Collage/Braided essay. *Tell it Slant: Writing and Shaping Creative Nonfiction* 151–154. Boston: McGraw Hall, Inc.

Murray, Donald M. (1996) *Crafting a Life in Essay, Story, Poem*. Boston: Boynton/Cook.

Perl, Sondra and Schwartz, Mimi (2005) Chapter 4, Taking shape. *Writing True: The Art and Craft of Creative Nonfiction* 46–63. Stamford, Connecticut: Wadsworth Publishing.

Roberts, Cheryl A. (1994) Transferring literacy skills from L1 to L2: From theory to practice. *Journal of Educational Issues of Language Minority Students* 13: 209–221.

Rodriguez, Richard (1982) *The Hunger of Memory*. New York: Bantam Books.

Root, Robert L., Jr. (2005) Collage montage, mosaic, vignette, episode, segment. In Robert Root and Michael Steinberg (eds.) *The Fourth Genre: Contemporary Writers of/on Creative Nonfiction* (3rd edition) 371–382. New York: Pearson/Longman.

Rose, Mike (2005) *Lives on the Boundary: A Moving Account of the Struggles and Achievements of America's Educationally Underprepared*. New York: Penguin.

Simic, Charles (1994) Food and happiness. *The Unemployed Fortune-Teller: Essays and Memoirs* 6–12. Ann Arbor, Michigan: University of Michigan Press.

Summerfield, Judith and Summerfield, Geoffrey (1986) *Texts and Contexts*. New York: Random House.

Tan, Amy (2004) Mother tongue. In Robert Atwan (ed.) *Best American Essays* (4th edition) 147–154. Boston: Houghton-Mifflin Company.

Toth, Susan (1988) Going to the movies. *How to Prepare for Your High School Reunion and Other Mid-Life Musings* 108–112. Boston: Little Brown and Company.

Walker, Alice (1989) A thousand words. *Living By the Word: Essays* 99–115. San Diego: Harcourt-Brace Publishing.

4   Empowering Basic Writers Through "This I Believe" Essays

Molly Hurley Moran

I.   Background

In the perennial debate over whether personal writing has a place in the first-year college composition course, I side with those who favor its inclusion. My own experience as a writer, as well as my witnessing of student writing over several decades of teaching, has caused me to acknowledge the truth of Peter Elbow's (e.g. Elbow, 1995), Donald Murray's (e.g. Murray, 1991), Robert Brooke's (e.g. Brooke, 1991), and other composition theorists' assertions that all good writing is grounded in personal experience and beliefs. I agree with the late Robert Connors that while the proper goal of freshman composition is academic writing, i.e. exposition and argument,

> [l]earning that one has a right to speak, that one's voice and personality have validity, is an important step, an essential step. Personal writing, leaning on one's own experience, is necessary for this step. (Connors, 1987: 181)

Being encouraged to explore and find meaning in their personal experiences is especially important for under-prepared first-year college student writers (commonly referred to as "basic writers"), the population I largely teach, because these students are less sure of themselves and of their place in the academy than are other college students.

With these thoughts in mind, for the past several years I have built my basic writing course at the University of Georgia (USA), Introduction to Academic Writing, around personal writing, making heavy use of journaling, assigning several personal essays, and encouraging students to develop topics for their expository and argument essays out of insights and opinions they discovered in their journaling. I have been generally pleased with this approach except for one thing: prior to Fall semester 2008, whatever reading text I used in the course tended to undermine my approach. If I chose one of the standard first-year composition readers, students were generally bored with or daunted by the essays. They couldn't relate to, or often even understand, classics like "Once More to the Lake" (White, 1941), and they were not interested in topics related to diversity and multiculturalism, which they had been force-fed since middle school and which figure heavily in today's college reading and rhetoric texts. Further, the authors of most of the essays in the standard texts are professional writers, a fact that only reinforced my students' belief that essay writing is something people like themselves are incapable of. However, if I chose a text designed for remedial writing courses, containing short model essays written by students rather than longer, more complex essays by professional writers, I feared I was perpetuating the five-paragraph-theme formula that many of my students had learned in high school and that I was trying to pry them away from. Finally, in Spring semester of 2008, I found the reader I'd been searching for: the 2007 publication of selected essays from the American National Public Radio (NPR) "This I Believe" series (Allison and Gediman, 2007a).

For those who are not familiar with it, this series is a project launched by NPR that invites people from all walks of life to submit statements of a few hundred words expressing a core belief or personal credo. Selected submissions are read over the air by the authors during the NPR programs "All Things Considered" and "Morning Edition". The series was originally broadcast in 1951 and ran for five years, with Edward R. Murrow hosting and with well-known public figures being invited to write essays. It was revived fifty years later, with one change: the general public may now submit essays. Otherwise, the modern version takes the same approach as the original: the series emphasizes the importance of heeding one's own inner voice in the midst of the noisy opinion-mongering that pervades our culture, and essayists are asked to express beliefs that grow out of personal insight and experience and to avoid doctrinaire statements. The editors of the published collection put it this way: "Aim for truth without accusation, patriotism without political cant, and faith beyond religious dogma" (Allison and Gediman, 2007a: 3).

Reading these guidelines in the introduction to the anthology, I became excited, because they express in concise yet compelling terms what I would like my students to do, and to avoid doing, in the essays they write: express beliefs that they have arrived at through their own reflection rather than spout the politics and religious credos of their parents and preachers or the herd-like thinking of their peers. I therefore decided to adopt *This I Believe* as the reader for my University Academic Writing course, and I re-designed the course around that material.

The intended outcomes for using *This I Believe* as the reader in a basic writing course are as follows:

- Students will gain a deeper understanding of their own beliefs and values.
- Students will see the act of writing as a way to express these beliefs and values rather than as something they have to do to satisfy a teacher's requirements.

- Students will develop respect for and attentiveness to others' beliefs and values.
- Students will develop a surer sense of their own voice.
- Students will develop an appreciation of concrete, vivid, precise language and images, and hence will be inspired to improve their own prose style.

II.   Description of Activity

This is a description of a 15-week basic writing course whose purpose is to lead students from personal writing to academic writing that is grounded in their personal beliefs and reflections. The course meets three days a week for 50-minute periods and comprises five cycles, each lasting approximately two and a half weeks. For the first three days of each cycle, students read essays for homework (essays in *This I Believe* for Cycles 1–4, and newspaper opinion essays for Cycle 5) and write a journal response; the class periods following these homework assignments are devoted to discussion of the readings. For the next four or five days of each cycle, students work both in and out of class on the various drafts of their paper assignment for that cycle. Each paper is approximately 500–750 words, or two to three pages, and the final draft (to be graded) is turned in on the last day of the cycle (hence, a total of five papers written during the 15-week semester).

Before outlining the five cycles, I will describe aspects of the course that are ongoing throughout the semester.

Journaling

Journaling is done both to increase students' fluency and to help them cultivate the habit of reflection. Students do both in-class and out-of-class journaling. They write in their journal for the first five minutes of every class in response to a thought-provoking prompt the teacher puts up on the overhead projector screen. These prompts are usually maxims or philosophical statements that teachers are familiar with or can pick up from Internet lists of famous or inspirational sayings. Here are a couple of typical examples:

> "There is a Zen saying that goes, 'The way we do one thing is the way we do everything.' Reflect on the truth of this statement as it pertains to your own behavior or the behavior of someone you know."

> "The famous 'Peace Prayer' begins, 'Make me an instrument of peace.' Do you believe that it is possible for one individual to help spread peace in the world?"

Students also do out-of-class journal writing in response to the *This I Believe* essays and, in Cycle 5, newspaper opinion essays which they read for homework. The instructor gives students the guideline that each out-of-class journal entry be at least 200 words and take at least ten minutes to write. At the beginning of the semester, the instructor gives students a handout containing generic prompts they can select from to spur their reflection on any essay they read; some examples are:

> "Why did this essay move/inspire/anger/etc. you?"

> "What in your own experience supports this author's belief?"

> "If you could talk to this author, what would you want to say to or ask him or her?"

> "Has this essay caused you to re-think a particular view or belief you hold?"

Journals are collected at the mid-point and at the end of the semester and rated as "exceptional" if there are no missing entries, if all entries meet the length requirement and some exceed it, and if all entries are reflective; "adequate" if there are no more than a couple of missing, sketchy, or purely narrative entries; or "inadequate" if several entries are missing, are too short, or are more narrative than reflective. The journal rating received at the end of the semester (which reflects the quality of the journal over the entire semester) determines the number of points added to or subtracted from the student's final course average: five points are added for "exceptional"; two points are added for "adequate"; and five points are subtracted for "inadequate."

Discussion of Homework Readings

During the reading and discussion phase of each cycle, the bulk of each class (following the in-class journaling) is devoted to discussing the homework readings. For the first four cycles, the readings are essays in *This I Believe*. The class discussion of each of these essays begins with the class listening to a recording of the author reading the essay (a five-CD audio-book version of the anthology is available from Audio Renaissance; Allison and Gediman, 2007b). Then the class discusses the essay's content – the belief it expresses and the details, examples, narratives, and reasoning used to support the belief – and students' reactions to the content. If the discussion lags, individual students are called upon to read their out-of-class journal responses to the essay (students are notified on the course syllabus that each of them will be called upon at least once to do this), and points made in this response usually trigger further class discussion. After addressing the content, the class turns to the essay's structure, looking closely at how the essay is organized and weighing in on whether this is an effective arrangement.

The final aspect of the essay to be considered is its style. Students are asked to point out particular language, images, sentences, and passages they like, and the class discusses why these are effective. The instructor frequently draws attention to concrete nouns, strong verbs, and rhythmic sentences. This part of the discussion sometimes spawns style exercises, such as having students compose imitative sentences or rewrite vague sentences (made up by the instructor) using concrete, vivid language. This part of the discussion can also be used as an opportunity for a grammar lesson, for example, pointing out how the meaning of a particular sentence in the essay would be changed if the commas were removed from a non-restrictive clause, or how the pleasing rhythm of a certain sentence is the result of the author's use of parallelism.

Peer Feedback During the Writing Process

At the start of the writing phase of each cycle, the class is divided into small groups, each consisting of three or four students. For the duration of each paper assignment, students give feedback to one another at every stage of the writing process, usually with each stage covering one class period. In the first stage, planning, each student explains his or her essay topic and tentative plan for development to the group, who in turn offer suggestions or raise helpful questions. In the next stage, each student reads aloud his or her first draft to the group, who subsequently offer (orally) validating, affirmative statements and constructive suggestions about content and arrangement. In the third stage, each student brings in enough copies of his or her revised draft to give to all group members. Group members silently read one another's drafts and write comments in the margins concerning content, arrangement, and style. Students are encouraged to point out what works and what is effective as well as to point out (kindly and constructively) coherence or development problems, awkward sentences, and imprecise language. In the last stage, students bring in their revised-again drafts and work on editing and polishing them, consulting with their group members about points of grammar and mechanics.

Instructor Feedback During the Writing Process and on Final Drafts

Students turn in a copy of every draft to the instructor, but the instructor writes comments only on the final draft, the one that receives a grade. The reason for collecting every draft is for the instructor to be able to check, if necessary, to make sure a student is doing conscientious revisions and to have a student's work on hand if the student wants to confer about an essay while in the process of writing it. Students are required to set up at least two such conferences with the instructor but may drop in during office hours whenever they feel the need to. If a student is having serious problems with grammar and usage, the instructor will refer that student to a writing center tutor.

During each essay-writing cycle, the instructor participates in a different small-group feedback session each day. Since class size is typically sixteen or seventeen students, there are usually five groups of three or four students each, which means the instructor can spend one class session per group per essay. Students can receive additional feedback on their drafts in conference with the instructor, as explained above.

The instructor assigns a grade to the final draft and writes comments about the paper's content, organization, and style. These are geared towards helping the student see how s/he could make the paper more effective, because at the end of the semester students select two of their essays to revise during exam week, in lieu of taking a final exam. The instructor's tone is encouraging and the suggestions constructive. In order to avoid aggravating students' tendency to feel defeated by their difficulties with grammar, only the most frequent and most bothersome errors in a paper are addressed. The instructor points out one or two instances of each of these errors in the adjacent margin and then explains the relevant rule or convention in the comment sheet attached to the paper; it is up to the student to look for further instances of a particular error and to figure out how to correct it. When editing an essay, students are urged to consult their prior papers' comment sheets to remind them of their particular error tendencies.

Lesson Cycles

What follows is an outline of the five cycles. The homework readings whose titles are listed in Cycles 3 and 4 can all be found in *This I Believe*. The writing phase of each cycle is spread over approximately four or five days, as explained above.

Cycle 1, Culminating in Paper 1: A "This I Believe" Essay

The first night's homework is to look through *This I Believe* and select two or three essays whose titles or openings intrigue the student. In the next class, the selections are pooled and the class decides on three to read, one for each of the following three nights' homework assignments and subsequent class discussions. Following the reading phase of the cycle, students try their hand at composing their own "This I Believe" essay. They select a core belief and show how they arrived at it and how it operates in their life, using vivid details, examples, and images.

Cycle 2, Culminating in Paper 2: A Response to an Essay in This I Believe

For each of the three homework assignments in this cycle, students are instructed to read an essay in *This I Believe* whose title or opening intrigues them. In each class, two or three of these essays are discussed. (Although all students won't have read each essay discussed, they will have exposure to each from listening to the recording preceding the discussion.) Following the reading and discussion phase, students write a formal response to an essay in *This I Believe* that resonated with them. Although the course's paper assignments from this point onwards are not "This I Believe" type essays, they are spawned by essays and ideas the students encounter in *This I Believe,* and the focus of the course continues to be plumbing one's own beliefs in one's writing. This second paper assignment moves students from an exclusive focus on their own ideas to engagement with another's ideas, an approach which forms the basis of most of the kinds of writing they will do in college. It also challenges them to go beyond merely summarizing these ideas; they must discuss why the ideas are important or valid, supporting their opinions with details and examples from their own experience.

Cycle 3, Culminating in Paper 3: A Comparison-Contrast Analysis of "This I Believe" Essays that Touch on Similar Ideas

The first night's reading homework is the following three essays from *This I Believe*: "In Giving I Connect with Others," "The People Who Love You When No One Else Will," and "The Power of Love to Transform and Heal." The second night's reading is three more *This I Believe* essays: "The Connection between Strangers," "The Power of Presence," and "Always Go to the Funeral." The third night's reading is a final trio of selected essays: "A Shared Moment of Trust," "Mysterious Connections that Link Us Together," and "We Are Each Other's Business." For the third paper, students take two or three of the assigned readings that touch on a similar belief and discuss the authors' variations on this belief as well as their own attitude towards it. For example, three of the essays – "We Are Each Other's Business," by Eboo Patel (Patel, 2007); "Mysterious Connections That Link Us Together," by Azar Nafisi (Nafisi, 2007); and "The Connection between Strangers," by Miles Goodwin (Goodwin, 2007) – all express a belief in the need to overcome our separateness and forge connections with others, but each author emphasizes a different way to do this: Patel feels compelled to fight ethnic discrimination by means of activism; Nafisi sees the path to empathy as lying in the reading of the great literature of different cultures; and Goodwin believes that small gestures of compassion are the most powerful way to unite strangers and spread peace. This assignment gives students practice in comparison-contrast analysis, a mode common in academic writing, while also calling on them to explore their own views and experiences with regard to the belief.

Cycle 4, Culminating in Paper 4: A Critical Analysis of "This I Believe" Essays That Touch on Similar Ideas

The first night's reading homework is "The Making of Poems," "The Artistry in Hidden Talents," and "Jazz Is the Sound of God Laughing." The second night's reading is "An Athlete of God,"

"Seeing in Beautiful, Precise Pictures," and "Creative Solutions to Life's Challenges." The third night's reading is "An Honest Doubter," "Growth that Starts from Thinking," and "A Balance between Nature and Nurture." The fourth paper of the course is somewhat similar to the third paper in that students discuss an idea that is expressed in two or three of the essays, but they select an idea that they do not agree with or that they have reservations about. This assignment thus continues to give them practice in engaging with others' ideas and in weaving their own ideas into their discussion, but it also challenges them to think critically about what they read, an approach which of course is a mainstay of good academic writing.

Cycle 5, Culminating in Paper 5: An Argument Concerning a Current Controversial Issue

The homework and discussion readings for this cycle are opinion pieces taken from newspapers rather than essays from *This I Believe* because the latter are not issue-oriented and this cycle teaches students to reflect on their stand on current controversial issues. The discussions focus on students' own responses to the issues and on the way the opinion-piece authors construct their arguments. For this assignment, the first night's readings are "For Once, Blame the Student" (Welsh, 2006), "Reading Muscles Rarely Flexed" (Moses, 2006), and "Make the Grade and Make Money" (Colavecchio-Van Sickler, 2007). The second night's readings are "Don't Urge Gym Time; Require It" (Bell, 2006), "Strong School P. E. Programs Have Ripple Effect" (Moag-Stahlberg, 2006), and "Make Room for Arts, P. E. at School" (2006). The third night's readings are "Use of Crack Should Not Make Me a Felon" (Jackson, 2006), "Mere Recreation Can Kill You" (Bohn, 2006), and "Enhanced Athletes? It's Only Natural" (Miah, 2008). Following the reading cycle, students write an argument paper in which they assert their stance on one of the controversial issues raised by the homework readings. They are required not only to cite from the assigned article(s) they address, but also to include at least one outside supporting source.

This assignment gives students practice in argument and in the use of research to support their thesis – two more mainstays of academic writing – while continuing to encourage them to develop their thesis out of reflections on their own beliefs.

Exam Week: Two Paper Revisions

Students revise two of their five graded essays and submit them to the instructor during the exam time scheduled by the university for the course (they do this in lieu of an examination). If the grade on a revision is higher than the original, it replaces the original; if it is the same as or lower than the original, it does not count. The final grade for the course consists of the average of the five essay grades (80%), the grade on class participation (20%), plus or minus the points reflecting the quality of the student's journal.

III. Implementation

The Value of "This I Believe" Essays

I implemented the approach described above in my basic writing course at the University of Georgia during Fall semester 2008. This is a course in the Division of Academic Enhancement (a learning support program) that incoming students who make below a certain score on the English Department's placement essay are recommended to take (until 2003 they were mandated to take it). The students in the course are usually an ethnically diverse group; my Fall 2008 course consisted of ten American students along with one German exchange student, two South Koreans, and one Indian (the families of the last three students moved to the U.S. when the students were in middle school). There were nine females and five males. What the students had in common was a generally negative attitude towards academic writing, either disliking it or feeling they were no good at it. Many had done very little writing in high school, and many had had bad experiences with writing, such as routinely having their papers returned covered with red ink pointing out grammar errors. Most of the students also admitted to not liking reading or not reading much.

The first indication I had that my decision to build the course around *This I Believe* was successful was the rich, enthusiastic class discussions the readings spawned. As far as I could tell, all of the students read all of the assigned essays all of the time – a first in my experience of teaching a first-year writing course. Several students asked me how they could find NPR on the radio so that they could listen to more essays, and one student told me she was going to buy a copy of the reader to give to a friend as a Christmas present – another first in my teaching experience. One reason the students were drawn to the anthology seemed to be that most of the essays are written by ordinary people like themselves and are of the length that my students feel capable of producing (short, 500 to 600 words). It was therefore inspiring to them to realize that they too might be able to write a publishable essay; they did not feel the chasm between themselves and the authors that students feel when confronted with a more traditional anthology.

Another reason for the students' attraction to *This I Believe* was the audio-book supplement. The class loved starting the discussion of each homework reading by first listening to its recording, and I discovered that doing this helped them to better grasp the notion of "voice." We English teachers are always stressing the importance of students' developing their own voice or a fresh voice, but voice is something that is very hard to teach. Those of us who love to read develop an ear for it, but my basic writing students are usually not great readers; some even have such difficulty with reading that they butcher an essay's prose when they have occasion to read a sentence or passage aloud. Therefore, hearing the authors read their essays, with their own speech patterns and rhythms, seemed to make the idea of voice more real to my students. I urged them to pay attention to the voice they were producing in their own writing by reading their drafts aloud to themselves. The recordings also helped make more concrete to my students the notion of audience. They could picture people like themselves – students listening to the audio-book in a writing class or people driving home from work listening to NPR – as being a possible audience for their own essays.

In addition, I found that the *This I Believe* reader provided helpful models for teaching style. Students were required to point out at least one thing they liked about each essay, and this usually turned out to be a concrete detail, an apt word or phrase, or a precise description. While these features are true of most good writing, they are especially true of *This I Believe* essays because their characteristic homely wisdom is best conveyed in concrete language and imagery. Two examples of students' choices of effective language use in *This I Believe* essays were Colleen Shaddox's use of the metaphor "Jazz is the sound of God laughing" (Shaddox, 2007) to explain her life-long attraction to jazz and Sarah Adams' dictum "Be cool to the pizza delivery dude" (Adams, 2007) to express her philosophy that we should respect those who perform low-paying, unglamorous jobs. Such examples helped the students appreciate the power of concreteness and conciseness and the need to fight their tendency to use vague, general language.

Finally, *This I Believe* proved to be a good tool for considering effective essay structure. Although the essays are short, they do not adhere to the rigid five-paragraph introduction-body-conclusion formula that most students come into my course thinking is *de rigueur* for thesis-support essays. We looked closely at the way each essay we discussed was organized, and we discovered a wide variety of methods of development. I was able to use these examples to drive home the idea that an essay's structure should grow out of the author's purpose rather than be a mold into which the author forces his or her material. However, since I knew that some of my students felt the need for structural guidelines for the first writing assignment, I pointed out that some of the *This I Believe* essays do adhere to the same general pattern – a movement from personal narrative, to insight into the experience narrated, to illustration and analysis of the way this insight has influenced the author's life. I told them that if they were flailing when trying to organize their own "This I Believe" essay, they could try using that approach.

The Writing Assignments

The students loved writing the first assignment – a "This I Believe" essay of their own. They seemed primed for it after having immersed themselves in inspiring examples of this genre. I received some delightful submissions for this assignment, revealing that students had taken to heart our discussions about concrete details, vivid language, striking imagery, sentence variety, and paragraph-length variety. Although some of these attempts resulted in strained metaphors or "purple prose," I was pleased to see that at least students were showing an interest in developing their prose style.

Students were also enthused about the second assignment because they all had an essay from *This I Believe* that resonated strongly with them and that they had written about in their journals. The only unforeseen problem with this assignment was that some students turned in their journal response as their essay, with only cosmetic changes made in each stage of the writing process. As a result, I had to explain more clearly that the journal is a place to explore ideas that can be honed into an essay but that an essay is more structured and polished than a journal entry; the problem did not occur again in later essays.

Most students did a good job of the third paper because in their journaling they had explored the similarities and differences between the ways the assigned readings of this cycle addressed certain themes. Since their essays grew out of these reflections, the result was not the pointless, mechanical exercise I often receive when I assign a comparison-contrast paper. Although a few students did just point out the ways two or three essays were similar and the ways they were different, most did a more significant discussion of the variations of a common theme running through three essays and their own stance on that theme.

The fourth paper proved to be a problematic assignment because most of the students were hard put to find points in the assigned readings that they disagreed with or had reservations about (this is understandable, since *This I Believe* essays are generally non-controversial and non-dogmatic). As a result, most of the essays ended up being essentially a comparison-contrast analysis with a paragraph tacked on stating minor, insignificant ways in which the student's attitude or experience was different from the author's. My rationale for this assignment had been that I wanted to build increasing complexity into their papers, but I think now that this criterion would be met even if the fourth paper had the same instructions as the third paper because the readings assigned in this cycle were on more complex topics (the growth of cognition, the need for art in one's life, the question of whether nature or nurture determines one's development).

Students produced good arguments for the fifth paper assignment. Although the controversial issues they read about and wrote their arguments on were topics they'd heard a lot about in the popular media, most students did not produce the kind of parroting of talking heads' views that I often get when I assign an argument paper. The lesson they'd ingested from *This I Believe* about the importance of heeding one's own perceptions and responses, coupled with the habit they'd developed of reflecting on their views in their journals, resulted in fresher, more original arguments.

IV.   Reflection and Recommendations

Using *This I Believe* as the reader for and focus of my basic writing course proved on the whole to have been an excellent decision. It effected a marked improvement in students' attitudes towards both reading and writing. My class loved reading and discussing the pieces in the anthology. They were itching to compose their own "This I Believe" essay, and they took that and every subsequent writing assignment seriously; the small-group feedback on one another's drafts was consistently thoughtful and earnest. Indication of the interest students were taking in their writing is that several hands would shoot up whenever I asked for volunteers to read their final draft to the whole class.

Not only their attitude towards writing but also the quality of their writing improved. Although students made roughly the same number of grammar errors as did students in prior classes, they produced more interesting content and fresher language. I attribute this improvement to their realization – from studying *This I Believe* essays – that what makes for good writing is not dramatic or unusual experiences but rather paying close attention to whatever experiences one has. Students tend to assume that a personal essay is interesting only if it describes a sensational event, like being abused as a child or losing a close friend in a car fatality, but *This I Believe* essays usually recount small, quiet experiences, such as a dejected soldier's gratitude at being handed a magazine to read by a little girl on a plane (Goodwin, 2007) or an engineer's mid-life discovery of the satisfaction of piano-playing as a hobby (Rusnov, 2007). The authors plumb such experiences for their deeper meaning, and so students see that even though their own lives may be uneventful, they harbor rich topics for essays, and this realization motivates students to cultivate the habit of reflection, a habit which is crucial for writers. On the whole, then, my students' essays last semester contained deeper and more original thought than did students' essays of previous semesters.

I plan to follow the same approach in Fall 2009 (the next time I will teach this course), but with two modifications:

- I will provide sample essays for writing assignments in cycles 2–5, since *This I Believe* does not contain essays of the type students are assigned to write in these cycles. (I can compose some of these myself or use selected ones from previous classes, with students' permission.)
- I will change the instructions for Paper 4, making them the same as those for Paper 3 – but referencing

different readings – for the reason explained above in the Implementation section.

Eventually, I will begin varying the readings assigned in *This I Believe*. Teachers adopting this reader will find that it contains a wealth of essays to choose from and that essays can easily be grouped thematically. Some teachers may also want to look at additional essays housed in NPR's online archives (<www.thisibelieve.org>). And teachers will find the op-ed page of their local or regional newspaper to be a good source for essays on controversial issues to assign for Cycle 5.

Although the curriculum described in this chapter is intended for a basic or developmental writing course, it could be adapted for a regular first-year composition course. In the latter kind of course, the instructor could supplement the course's regular reader with either the *This I Believe* anthology or with selected "This I Believe" pieces which students can access. The first one or two essays students write could be the same as their counterparts in the basic writing course described above; then after gaining the increased confidence and sense of a personal voice that these writing experiences would give them, they could turn to their regular course text and begin writing longer, more conventionally academic papers.

Two final suggestions I offer are that instructors have their students compile a class audio anthology, comprising recordings of their own essays, and that they urge their students to submit their "This I Believe" essays to NPR. Writing with these goals in mind will no doubt inspire students even further.

References

Adams, Sarah (2007) Be cool to the pizza dude. In Jay Allison and Dan Gediman (eds.) *This I Believe: The Personal Philosophies of Remarkable Men and Women* 7–9. New York: Holt.

Allison, Jay and Gediman, Dan (eds.) (2007a) *This I Believe: The Personal Philosophies of Remarkable Men and Women*. New York: Holt.

Allison, Jay and Gediman, Dan (eds.) (2007b) *This I Believe: The Personal Philosophies of Remarkable Men and Women* [CD]. New York: Audio Renaissance.

Bell, Katherine (2006, March 21) Don't urge gym time; require it. *Atlanta Journal Constitution* A11.

Bohn, Meghan (2006, April 4) Mere recreation can kill you. *Atlanta Journal Constitution* A11.

Brooke, Robert E. (1991) *Writing and Sense of Self: Identity Negotiation in Writing Workshops.* Urbana, Illinois: National Council of Teachers of English.

Colavecchio-Van Sickler, Shannon (2007, June 10) Make the grade and make money. *St. Petersburg* [Florida] *Times* 1P.

Connors, Robert (1987) Personal writing assignments. *College Composition and Communication* 38: 166–83.

Elbow, Peter (1995) Response. *College Composition and Communication* 46: 87–92.

Goodwin, Miles (2007) The connection between strangers. In Jay Allison and Dan Gediman (eds.) *This I Believe: The Personal Philosophies of Remarkable Men and Women* 81–83. New York: Holt.

Jackson, Charles (2006, March 28) Use of crack should not make me a felon. *Atlanta Journal Constitution* A11.

Make room for arts, P. E. at schools. (2006, March 14) *Atlanta Journal Constitution* A8.

Miah, Andy (2008, August 3) Enhanced athletes? It's only natural. *The Washington Post* B01.

Moag-Stahlberg, Alicia (2006, March 14) Strong school P. E. programs have ripple effect. *Atlanta Journal Constitution* A9.

Moses, Jennifer (2006, May 15) Reading muscles rarely flexed. *Atlanta Journal Constitution* A15.

Murray, Donald M. (1991) All writing is biography. *College Composition and Communication* 42: 66–74.

Nafisi, Azar (2007) Mysterious connections that link us together. In Jay Allison and Dan Gediman (eds.) *This I Believe: The Personal Philosophies of Remarkable Men and Women* 171–73. New York: Holt.

Patel, Eboo (2007) We are each other's business. In Jay Allison and Dan Gediman (eds.) *This I Believe: The Personal Philosophies of Remarkable Men and Women* 178–80. New York: Holt.

Rusnov, Mel (2007) The artistry in hidden talents. In Jay Allison and Dan Gediman (eds.) *This I Believe: The Personal Philosophies of Remarkable Men and Women* 204–06. New York: Holt.

Shaddox, Colleen (2007) Jazz is the sound of God laughing. In Jay Allison and Dan Gediman (eds.) *This I Believe: The Personal Philosophies of Remarkable Men and Women* 214–16. New York: Holt.

Welsh, Patrick (2006, March 8) For once blame the student. *USA Today* A11.

White, E. B. (1941, October) Once more to the lake. *Harper's* 553–56. Reprinted in Laurie G. Kirszner and Stephen R. Mandell (eds.) (1996) *The Blair Reader* (2nd edition) 41–46. Upper Saddle River, New Jersey: Prentice Hall.

5   Local Heroes, Local Voices

Pauline Burton

I.   Background

The idea for the activity described in this chapter – and the thematic sequence of which it forms a part – was prompted by a paper by Kieran Egan (1991) on the value of the Romantic imagination in teaching high school students. Egan (1991: 67) argues that three aspects of the Romantic imagination are particularly appealing to present-day adolescents: an intense focus on reality through detailed observation, the figure of the Romantic hero (exemplified by Byron and Napoleon), and an emphasis on myth, fantasy and "wonders." He proposes incorporating these perspectives – combined with a storytelling approach – into a "Romantic planning framework" (Egan 1991: 67) for teaching. Egan is dealing with a younger age group than college students, and his illustrative lesson plan is for teaching history rather than writing, yet his idea (and the humanism of the pedagogical philosophy supporting it) lends itself to adaptation.

Two out of three of Egan's Romantic features – the intense focus on reality through detailed observation, and the figure of the hero – are particularly appropriate for the college writing classroom, since they address both the skills of higher-level writing and the issue of emotional engagement with the subject matter. The first feature sounds remarkably like a definition of original research, which university students are expected to undertake in most (if not all) academic disciplines. The second feature – the figure of the hero – can still (as Egan argues) catch the students' imagination, especially through the medium of storytelling; it also lends itself to discussion, exemplification, and critical thinking, all of which are central to writing at university level.

The Romantic hero is a solitary creature, and is almost always male. To appeal to older students, and to create rich input for a whole-semester writing theme, the concept needs to be broader. Hence, my decision to add "role models" to "heroes" in the overall theme; there is some overlap between the two concepts, but they are not identical. Role models are often female, and prompt consideration of the subtler forms of heroism; in addition, they link the hero to the self, requiring students to write and think about their own heroic qualities and aspirations. Further, the idea of a hero can be connected to a wider context, yet one within which first-year university students can reasonably be expected to conduct original research: the local community or the community on campus.

The central requirement for the task outlined in this chapter – to conduct, record and write up an interview with a "local hero", working in pairs – is a new experience for most first-year college students. As such, it stretches their abilities, moving them into Lev Vygotsky's "zone of proximal development" (Vygotsky 1978: 86) with support from the instructor, from peers in whole class discussions and writing workshops, and from collaboration through pair work in the task itself. Dialogue is thus a key part of the writing process, outside the classroom as well as within it, between the paired students and their interviewees. The idea of dialogue as a source of creativity (Bakhtin 1934/1981) has been influential in numerous accounts of language development and use (Carter 2004; Halliday 1978; Mercer 1999). A key purpose of the "local heroes" assignment, therefore, is to help the students develop their own voice as writers by hearing, recording, and responding to "local voices."

The main aims of the activity can be summed up as follows:

- To engage and sustain first-year students' interest in the writing process
- To introduce the principles and techniques of primary research
- To help develop good writing habits (close observation, accuracy, honesty, redrafting, peer review, editing, and proofreading)
- To provide an authentic purpose and audience for student writing
- To help develop a sense of "voice" in writing – both personal voice and the voices of others – through dialogue and storytelling.

II.   Description of Activity

This is an activity designed for university students in their introductory, first-year writing class as the second assignment out of four in a sequence of tasks organized around the theme of heroes and role models. The syllabus description of the assignment is as follows:

Paper 2: Local Heroes, Local Voices
This paper will involve you in a small-scale primary research project, and will practice your ability to collect, synthesize and order information and write persuasively. Working in pairs, you will find someone in your local community or on campus that you regard as a hero, interview them, document their achievements, and explain why you have chosen them. The person concerned need

not be well known (though they might be known locally). The interview must be audio-recorded. You do not need to transcribe the entire interview, but you do need to summarize and interpret your interviewee's views as faithfully as you can, and give any direct quotations accurately. This paper will be about 8 pages long, and will be co-written with a partner. (Weeks 5 to 8).

As the time scale in this description indicates, work on this project starts after the first month of the semester. Making this the second assignment in a linked sequence is not an essential part of the activity, but it has several advantages:

- There is sufficient input time, before the activity begins, for students to read a variety of texts – literary and fact-based – related to the theme, and to discuss the nature of heroism;
- Since this is a fairly complex task, first-year students have the opportunity to cut their college writing teeth on a short (2- to 3-page) individual paper first;
- The topic of the first paper – writing about a role model in the student's own life – starts with the self and its immediate environment, while the "local heroes" paper moves outwards to the campus and the local community;
- Subsequent papers can build on this by considering the claims to heroism of notable figures in history and current events, and by asking the students to take on the stance of community leaders and argue the case of under-represented or misrepresented groups (thus becoming heroes themselves).

The length of time up to final submission of the "local heroes" paper – around four weeks – is designed to provide enough time for the students to contact prospective interviewees, write up the interviews, critique each other's work, redraft, edit and proofread. The project is carried out in stages, inside and outside of class, as detailed below. Each stage in the classroom corresponds with one class period (50 minutes), so the total time taken in class for this activity is six class periods (including two writing workshops), plus two rounds of consultations with each pair. Assuming a class size of about 20, consultations takes roughly another four hours of the instructor's time.

Stage 1 (Week 1): Class Discussion of Possible Local Heroes and Pair Formation

What kind of person on campus, or in the local community, could be regarded as a hero, and why? The students are asked to discuss this question in small groups, after which each of them needs to make at least one suggestion of a potential interviewee – either a specific person or a type of person. The students are encouraged to discuss the reasons for their choices and to link them to definitions of heroism arrived at through reading and discussion earlier in the semester. Based on their suggestions and interests, the students are asked to stand up, move around, and form pairs to choose and contact a potential interviewee. The instructor helps unpaired students find a partner (in an odd-numbered class, a group of three can be allowed, in preference to one student working alone). The students work together in pairs to create a shortlist of possible interviewees, and to consider strategies for identifying and locating them. Finally, they report their ideas back to the class as a whole.

Stage 2 (Week 1): Class Discussion of Interview Etiquette and Practicalities

The instructor asks the students about their previous experience of interviewing (e.g. for high school projects) and elicits their ideas on issues such as getting in touch with interviewees, being prepared, confidentiality, recording the interview, and the ethics of interviewing. The instructor sums up the students' ideas and supplements them where necessary. Working in pairs, the students draft an email message to a prospective interviewee asking for an interview and giving the reasons for their request. Students review the email message of another pair: the instructor moves around making suggestions for improvement. Draft emails are saved and included in a project file, along with the final version (completed outside class).

Stage 3 (Week 1): Arranging the Interview and Carrying Out Preliminary Research

The students get in touch with their prospective interviewees and fix an interview date. Meanwhile, they carry out as much research as possible (e.g. by reading published accounts, if any, of the person's life and work and/or by researching background information about people in the same category), and write it up as the first draft of a background section in the paper. In practice, the amount of time students take to contact their interviewee and receive a response will vary: students need to be allowed some flexibility in this, provided they are prepared for the interview. They should also be ready to call on an alternative interviewee if need be. Drafts of the background material are submitted by the beginning of the second week.

Stage 4 (Week 2): Drafting the Questions

The students report back to the class on their progress. With input from the instructor and from each other, they draft the questions for their interviews. They are asked to prepare six or seven open-ended questions (for a thirty-minute interview) with supporting prompts if the interviewee is slow to speak, to link their questions both to the purpose of the interview and what they already know about the interviewee, and to arrange them in a logical sequence. Expecting the unexpected, and responding flexibly to what the interviewee has to say, is also discussed. The proposed questions are handed in to the instructor at the end of class.

Stage 5 (Week 2): Consultations

The instructor meets with each pair separately, either outside class time or during class while others work, to ensure that they are prepared for the interview with appropriate questions and a clear division of labor. Possible problems, such as missing interviewees or interpersonal difficulties, can be addressed at this stage. The students may need help in borrowing recording equipment, or the instructor may be able to secure equipment for the class and then students can sign up to use it for their interviews. In addition, students sometimes have their own portable audio or video recording devices capable of making reasonably good voice recordings.

Stage 6 (Weeks 2–3): Interviews

The students conduct and record their interviews, making an extra copy of the recording immediately to make sure that it does not get (wholly or partially) erased inadvertently and that the instructor will get a copy, and write up the first draft of their paper within a week of the interview. They are each expected to contribute half of the writing up, to indicate which of them is primarily responsible for which part, and to work together to produce an accurate and cohesive account.

Stage 7 (Week 3): Writing Workshop

First drafts are brought into the computer lab in soft copy for peer review (with twinned pairs) and further development. The drafts and copies of recordings are submitted to the instructor at the end of the session (in hard copy or electronically). If time permits and playback capabilities are available, at Stage 7 a class session can be added for students to share a selected 3-minute segment of their recording in front of the class.

Stage 8 (Week 3): Consultations

The instructor consults (during or outside of class) with each pair
to give feedback on the first draft.

Stage 9 (Week 4): Writing Workshop

Second drafts are brought into the computer lab in soft copy for
editing and peer review (with emphasis on effective linking, use
of direct quotations, accuracy, and mechanics). The final paper is
submitted at the end of the fourth week, along with the interview
questions, drafts, and supporting information, in an interview
project file.

Stage 10 (Week 5): Reflecting on the Project

The students discuss the experience: what they learned, what difficulties they encountered, and how they overcame those difficulties. A read-around of extracts from students' work leads into a
concluding discussion of the nature and importance of local heroes
in local communities, including the university.

   As soon as possible after the final class, the project files are
graded and returned. The students are reminded to thank their
interviewees (via email) and share their final paper with them.

III. Implementation

This activity was carried out with three classes of first-year composition students (60 students) at Georgia Southern University in
the fall semester of 2007. Almost all of the students had come to
university directly from high school; typically, they were eighteen-
year-olds (there were only four mature students, all women, aged
between their mid-twenties and their mid-forties). There were
roughly equal numbers of females and males (with slightly more

males); eleven of the students were African American, one was Asian American, one Hispanic, and the rest were White.

Some of the groundwork for the activity was laid during the first four weeks of semester. Preparatory reading included an interview with the first female chief of the Cherokee Nation, Wilma Mankiller (Nelson 2006); an article on the nature of courage by a gay male rugby player (Stahl 2006); and Mark Haddon's novel "The Curious Incident of the Dog in the Night-time" (Haddon 2004), about the responses of an autistic teenager to a family crisis. In response to these readings and in response to each other's writing in the first paper, the students discussed the nature and characteristics of a hero. Writing techniques were also discussed; for example, the students worked in small groups examining Andrew Nelson's article, to discover how a skillful writer can use background information, summary, interpretation, direct quotation, and physical detail to bring an interviewee to life.

The implementation of the activity itself followed the stages given above, though there were some modifications in timing: the mid-term break came partway through the activity, thus giving the students another week to track down their interviewees and catch up on writing their first draft. This extra flexibility was an advantage as some interviewees proved elusive and cancelled earlier appointments. In addition, some students wanted to interview people in their own communities and were only able to do so when they returned home for the mid-term break.

Most of the writing workshops were held in computer labs. However, these labs were available only in alternate weeks, and the three classes were not on the same schedule. Accordingly, some writing workshops were held in ordinary classrooms, with the students bringing in drafts in hard copy for peer review.

Most of the input for the task is in the first week; this involves not only teacher input, but demands on the students to express their views. All of the students were expected to speak in class (an expectation reinforced by a seminar-type seating arrangement), and some of them appeared unused to this. Most, however, came up with practical suggestions of possible interviewees. In one class, a student enquired, somewhat dismissively, "Why not just ask a guy who flips hamburgers?" Somewhat to this student's surprise, his suggestion was taken seriously, and a lively discussion ensued on the qualities that might make a hamburger-flipper a worthy local hero. Subsequently, a few of the papers did feature working-class heroes, including a cleaner in one of the student residences and a Mexican illegal immigrant.

The main objection raised by students at this stage was that they might not have time to identify, contact, and interview prospective interviewees (in the event, all of them did, though one or two pairs trailed in late). Some of them even asked how they could possibly identify interviewees, given that they were new both to the campus and the town. I encouraged them to consider interviewing senior faculty in their chosen majors, leaders in local charities and churches, and key figures mentioned in university publications and in the local newspaper. Several students raised the idea of interviewing sports coaches on campus, senior figures in the university counseling service and in the intercultural student center, and resident advisers in their dormitories. One enterprising pair interviewed the president of our university, while another contacted a rising local politician who was courting the student vote. One pair went out into the countryside to interview a farmer, and returned with an interview with a farmer's widow instead.

As the interviews went ahead, out-of-class consultations became important. There were crises: a few partners were unavailable or uncooperative (leading to solo papers), interviewees deferred or disappeared, and one interviewee responded so concisely that the pair concerned had very little to write up (though they turned the relative failure of their interview into an interesting piece of writing). Somehow, in the end, it all came together; and the reward for the students (and for me) came when they realized that they were able to write something that was of real interest to an audience of their peers, and that the redrafting process could help them achieve something to be proud of.

IV. Reflections and Recommendations

In terms of the quality of writing produced, I believe that this was the most successful activity in the semester's work, and that the original aims were met for most of the students. A few did less work than their partners; the majority, however, remained on task, active, and enthusiastic. They accomplished something many of them had openly doubted they could achieve: to complete a live interview with their own choice of interviewee and turn it into a polished piece of writing.

An additional benefit for some students was that the interviews connected them with potential mentors on campus and in the community. I received an email from one faculty member who had been interviewed by two students in his subject area, pointing out the potential career benefits of the assignment through encouraging students to engage with the academic and professional communities they aspire to join. Though this was a benefit for only a few, their final class discussions showed that the "local voices" in the stories they shared gave them a fresh understanding of the nature of heroism in everyday life.

This was the first cycle of an activity that I plan to use again, with the following recommendations for improvement:

- To alert the students more strongly, at the beginning of the semester, to the need to consider and begin contacting interviewees;
- To add more background readings of interviews from magazines and encourage students to compile their own collection;
- To use a web-based bulletin board for students to post and review their draft writing as a supplement to classroom work;
- To encourage and facilitate students to use multimedia recording – for example, video recording, pod-casting, and photographs – to supplement written text;

- To compile the students' work online and seek a wider audience for it.

With appropriate adaptations, this activity could be used in a variety of teaching and learning contexts, such as the following:

- With learners of English as a second language, such as international students in an English-speaking country;
- With younger students, such as senior high school students;
- With adult education students;
- In other subjects besides English, such as history, social studies, business, cultural anthropology, journalism and media studies;
- In other languages besides English.

Whatever the context, the common factors would be the use of the "local heroes, local voices" theme to engage the students' interest and of the research and writing process to discover new worlds and communicate their discoveries to an audience of their peers.

References

Bakhtin, Mikhail (1934/1981) *The Dialogic Imagination* (ed. Michael Holquist; trans. Michael Holquist and Caryl Emerson). Austin: University of Texas Press.

Carter, Ronald (2004) *Language and Creativity: The Art of Common Talk.* London and New York: Routledge.

Egan, Kieran (1991) Relevance and the Romantic imagination. *Canadian Journal of Education* 16(1): 58–73. Retrieved on 8 November 2005 from http://www.csse.ca/CJE/Articles/FullText/CJE16-1/CJE16-1-5Egan.pdf.

Haddon, Mark (2004) *The Curious Incident of the Dog in the Night-Time.* New York: Random House.

Halliday, Michael A. K. (1978) *Language as Social Semiotic: The Social Interpretation of Language and Meaning.* London: Edward Arnold.

Mercer, Neil (2000) *Words and Minds: How We Use Language to Think Together.* London and New York: Routledge.

Nelson, Andrew (2006) Wilma Mankiller. In Joan T. Mims and Elizabeth M. Nollen (eds.) *Mirror on America: Short Essays and Images from Popular Culture* (3rd edition) 65–71. Boston/New York: Bedford/St. Martins.

Stahl, Christopher (2006) I ruck, therefore I am: Rugby and the gay male body. In Joan T. Mims and Elizabeth M. Nollen (eds.) *Mirror on America: Short Essays and Images from Popular Culture* (3rd edition) 72–76. Boston/New York: Bedford/St. Martins.

Vygotsky, Lev S. (1978) *Mind in Society: The Development of Higher Psychological Processes* (eds. Michael Cole, Vera John-Steiner, Sylvia Scribner and Ellen Souberman). Cambridge, Massachusetts: Harvard University Press.

6 A Funny Thing Happened To Me

Martha C. Pennington

I. Background

Humor as Theme for a Writing Class

I have long had a hobby of collecting and writing humorous pieces, which I have occasionally performed or used as material in my academic work (teaching as well as academic presentations). Over many years, I have used or developed humorous material for teaching points of language, including grammar, spelling, and punctuation, as well as other course content, gradually accumulating a large store of exercises. Last year, I decided to use my long-term interest in humor as the theme of my first-year writing courses. Out of this grew an especially successful writing assignment, the Personal Funny Story.

Humor has the natural advantage of increasing the enjoyment of learning. Moreover, humor provides a wealth of material spanning all types of communications media and many different rhetorical forms and purposes of writing. It also touches on theories and practices in a range of disciplines, from *science* (e.g. psychology, biology) to *humanities* (e.g. language, literature, culture), *business* (advertising, management), and *communications* (e.g. public speaking, theater, television).

Much has been written on the topic of humor, which has attracted the attention of many of the world's great thinkers, from Plato and Aristotle to Freud. Theories of humor are reviewed in a seminal work by Paul McGhee, *Humor: Its origin and development* (McGhee, 1979) and in later discussions by others (e.g. Cohen, 1999; Gulas and Weinberger, 2006; Holt, 2008). Three theories or mechanisms of humor figure prominently in the literature:

Incongruity	Humor results from the resolution of information that conflicts with expectation, logic, or rationality.
Superiority/Disparagement	Humor results from a sense of superiority in disparaging others.
Arousal/Relief	Humor results from the arousal and subsequent sense of relief when repressed aggression or forbidden feelings are released.

Humor has been considered in terms of the types of functions it fulfils (Ziv, 1984), generally classified into the following categories:

Intellectual	Humor fulfills the need to exercise the mind.
Psychological	Humor helps work off repressed aggression and fears and is a form of self-expression.
Social	Humor is a means of socializing and bonding and of commenting on and seeking to change society.

As suggested by this list of functions, humor is a basic human response and a central feature of human cognition, emotion, use of language, communication, and interaction with others.

Humor is omnipresent on television in the form of current and classic situation comedies (*sitcoms*), cartoon series aimed at children or adults, and both daytime and late-night talk shows. Stand-up comedians often have a presence both on television, generally in late-night time slots, and on the internet, where routines performed on television or in clubs can be viewed at YouTube or other online sites. Humor is also present in the articles, stories, and cartoons of magazines and books, in poetry and song, in plays and musical theater, and in the ubiquitous advertisements that saturate our present-day environment.

Humor may be entirely frivolous, as in many cartoons or the physical humor of the *Three Stooges* or *America's Funniest Home Videos*, or may attempt to influence thought and behavior, as in a humorous advertisement geared to selling a product or a satire geared to raising awareness of social injustice and changing people's minds and behaviors. Good humor is challenging to write and may involve narration, dialogue, and dialect; chronological order, description, and comparison/contrast; persuasion and argumentation; hypothetical situations and projections of potentials and future scenarios; imagination and creativity. All of these require a strong command of language, both word choice and sentence structure.

Humor offers many opportunities for delving into theory and empirical research as well as use of sources. Any library will have a wide selection of humorous books in addition to books on different aspects of humor. In a one-hour on-site browse in our university library, my students found several edited collections of scholarly articles on humor as well as numerous compilations and joke books, theoretical treatises on humor and scholarly books on specific types of humor such as puns and satire, and handbooks for using humor in teaching and public speaking. In a one-hour browse on the internet, they found a wide range of sources, from humor websites to articles about humor in over a dozen journals available online. There is at least one scholarly journal (e.g. *Humor: International Journal of Humor*) devoted to the study of humor, and articles on humor commonly appear in scholarly journals in fields such as management, counseling psychology, child development, linguistics, and literature.

Goals and Assignments

Beyond the general outcomes of a first-year writing class, this class has the following theme-related outcomes:

- Improve your writing and use of English through humor;
- Apply principles learned about humorous writing to other forms of writing;
- Sharpen critical and analytical skills through comparison and contrast of different forms of humor and humorous writing;
- Develop a personal perspective on and theory of humor through reading, discussion, class presentation, and research on humor.

Within the humor theme of the course, students complete five assignments, three of these short papers, one of which is the Personal Funny Story. Two of the short papers are persuasive pieces involving description, analysis, comparison and contrast, and argumentation. In one of these short assignments, students write on a favorite type of humor, specific piece of humor, humorist, or comedian; the other requires them to write about their favorite story from among a provided selection of humorous stories. In addition to the three short papers, students write a longer paper involving humor theory and research and give a group presentation on a type of humor. The first draft of each written assignment is first reviewed by peers and then given input by the instructor towards revision in one or more further drafts.

The Personal Funny Story asks students to craft a funny story in order to entertain and also to show something about the writer's nature or character by drawing a generalization or moral from it. The immediate audience is the teacher and the other students. In addition, students are encouraged to think of other audiences such as family, friends, and colleagues. We discuss the value of humor in social relationships and its use in casual conversation as well as speech-making and in leadership functions such as building teams and running meetings. They are encouraged to aim to write a story that they can keep and use on multiple occasions and with multiple audiences.

The Personal Funny Story assignment, though originally designed as a first writing assignment for a composition course with humor as the theme, can be used as a first assignment in any writing course. This assignment has a number of goals. First, it helps to familiarize the instructor with the students and the students with each other. In addition, the assignment generates a first piece of writing in an enjoyable and self-motivating way that others can also enjoy. In this way, it builds camaraderie and interest in the course and provides a first assignment students want to share that can be used as a basis for introducing the expectations and format of peer review. The assignment also establishes a baseline of the students' writing to help the instructor plan teaching content and approaches. Finally, it offers a motivating context for learning from teacher feedback and redrafting to a highly polished product.

II.   Description of Activity

Step 1: Models and Response (Weeks 1–2)

Students view and read samples of humor from television, movies, and stories, and discuss their responses to these. (The two persuasion-argument papers draw on these samples, which may also give ideas for the Personal Funny Story.)

Step 2: Systematic Analysis and Guidance (Week 2)

Students characterize the model stories in relation to instructor-developed handouts (Handouts 1 and 2 in Appendix), visit story-writing and humor websites and discuss their advice, and consider how funny stories are told and designed.

Step 3: Getting Ready to Write (Week 2)

Students are given the Personal Funny Story assignment and try to come up with one or more funny incidents that might work for their funny story. Some students quickly get ideas. Others who do not are advised to consult their friends and family members. In the next class, we discuss ideas for the stories and help students decide on what they would use as their funny story, based on a step-by-step procedure (Handout 3).

Step 4: Peer Review and Read Around of First Drafts (Week 3)

Groups of 3 students read and comment on each others' drafts (Handout 4). Volunteers read their stories aloud to the class.

Step 5: Individual Conferences (Week 3)

Students and teacher conference on the story drafts, which are graded based on the story criteria (most students receive 3/5 or 4/5) with advice given towards improved structure, content, and language.

Step 6: Further Drafts (Weeks 4+)

Students hand in revised drafts.

III.   Implementation

I have used "Rip Van Winkle" as a model of a good story that is also humorous and as a base for comparison and contrast of other stories and story types, such as the regional, often absurdist humor of stories in *Laughter in Appalachia* (Jones and Wheeler, 1987) or some of the shorter and sillier, though often quite sophisticated, absurdist stories of Woody Allen, Steve Martin, or *The New Yorker*. Developing a good base of humor and story types, though not necessary for the Personal Funny Story assignment, supports the assignment by providing models as well as motivation in the way of humor and entertainment.

Once they have decided on the story they want to write, students may need help with one or more of the following aspects of the assignment:

1. Story structure
2. Having a point about their nature or character grow out of the story
3. Making their story funny

Occasionally, students have trouble with the story structure, either the order of information or some missing information that interferes with coherence. Reading the story aloud to peers will often help to pinpoint and rectify these problems.

Most students are able to tell their personal funny story in a reasonably clear, coherent, and well-structured manner but may have trouble with the opening and closing strategies. This problem is often tied to the second problem, i.e. making sure that a point about their nature or character comes out of the story. Sometimes students have crafted a funny story that does not make any obvious point about their nature or character. In this case, peers as well as the instructor can help find a generalization about the author that can be taken from his or her story. Often that point is implicit and can be made more explicit in the first and last paragraphs or sentences. Here are examples from two different stories:[1]

In an opening paragraph	I am a person who, just when it seems that things can't get any worse, makes them worse.
In a concluding paragraph	I don't have it in me to be anyone's enemy – and especially not a person who is his own worst enemy.

Students are aided by thinking of their story as a *snapshot* of themselves that can be improved by explicit *framing* at the beginning and the end to make a point about their nature or character stand out more sharply. To aid in this framing, they can try completing statements such as:

For the opening   "I'm the kind of person who…"
"I never thought I would …, but in fact I …"
"I'd like to give you an example of how I …"
"This is a story illustrating a key feature of my nature, which is …"

For the ending   "From this story, you can see that I …"
"This story shows me as …"
"This story is an example of how I …"
"This story illustrates my character in …"

These explicit story starters and enders often serve not as final text but as transitional to the final revised text of the story.

Most students write about incidents involving themselves, but sometimes the story focus is on another person or persons. In such cases, the conclusion can include reflections on the other person(s) as well as on the author, as in the following example:

I was in my early twenties before I realized how much having Andrew as a father figure has affected my views on life and my personality. He definitely shaped some of my musical tastes, for which I am grateful. More than that, he taught me that it doesn't matter what other people think about you, especially when it comes to outward appearances. If I don't feel like ironing my shirt one day, what does it matter what some stranger thinks about it?… Andrew taught me to be comfortable with the person I am, and there's no greater freedom than that.

It is common for students to have some difficulty making their story funny. In such a case, I help them to find places in their story draft where they can make humorous comparisons (What is it like? What does it remind you of?) or exaggerations that stretch a point, perhaps to an absurd degree, on the model of other humor and funny stories. For example, a student began a story about an incident of spontaneous combustion in his front yard as follows: "The weather was extremely dry in Atlanta last year, so much so that we did not have the usual number of flies, and the pine needles in our yard were even drier than usual. Since the lawn was dead, there was no need to mow it. And so instead of chopping up the pine needles in the lawn-mower, I raked them around the trees. Little did I realize that I was creating a fire hazard." As I pointed out, this description, although clear, was simply not funny. I suggested that the student consider the following exaggerations in "Tucker's Knob and the Weather" by Ernest "Doc" McConnell as inspirations:

 It got so dry, people at the Baptist Church started sprinkling and the Methodists just used a damp cloth.
    Didn't rain but one drop of water all summer. John Malt had walked out and looked up at the sky…that one drop hit him right between the eyes. He fainted. Had to pour two buckets of dust on him to revive him. (Jones and Wheeler, 1987: 135–136)

The student studied this input in the light of his original text and eventually came up with the following revised opening:

Atlanta was so dry last year that the flies decided not to come, and all the lizards and frogs had to move out to the country or go on an involuntary crash diet. It was so dry that the grass stopped growing and turned brown in the middle of June. Except for the fact that it was 98 degrees Fahrenheit, you coulda been fooled into thinking it was the Australian winter.
    The grass being dead, there was no point in mowing the lawn. So instead of the pine needles being chopped up in the mower, I raked them up like I do in the winter and pushed the piles up around the tree trunks and the bushes as mulch. Although this seemed like a good idea at the time, in fact it was like piling too many wool blankets on a person when the heat is turned up full blast – just as likely to kill them as to do them any good!

Often the changes students make to increase humor add colorful and original language. Thus a student who wrote about her pet fish traveling in the car with her in a gallon zip-lock bag, encouraged to stretch for humorous images and language, came up with "my little grouper-trooper." As tends to happen to kept fish, this one eventually was found floating lifeless in its bowl. Brainstorming images and comparisons to keep her description humorous, the student came up with "my fish…my little buddy…was doing the dead man's float…." Besides using humorous examples as models, students can recycle and adapt famous phrases to humorous effect, as one student who wrote about surviving being stung by dozens of bees did, ending his story, "O sting, where is thy death?"

IV.   Reflections and Recommendations

In my fourth time teaching the Personal Funny Story, I am now planning to give this as a two-stage assignment in which students write a snapshot personal funny story as their first draft and then explicitly add another "layer" to the story in their second draft in order to build a frame around it that draws an explicit generalization about themselves which is introduced at the beginning and then raised again in the light of the story at the end. The idea of having students first focus on writing the story and then focus on drawing a lesson, principle, or generalization from it and framing the original story within that "higher layer" of meaning has evolved out of the conferences I had with students about how to improve their first drafts.

Draft 1 *Snapshot Story*
Tell about a funny incident that you were involved in.

Draft 2 *Framing Your Snapshot Story*
Draw a generalization, implication, or moral from your snapshot story about your nature or character. Add this as another "layer" to your story in the way of a conclusion and an introduction that sets up your story to foreshadow the generalization, implication, or moral in your conclusion.

With models and guidance, even students with only basic writing skills can have fun with and also stretch themselves in the Personal Funny Story assignment. However, there is a caution for anyone wanting to incorporate humor into college teaching: Humorous material and readings must be carefully selected, as off-color or otherwise potentially offensive humor (e.g. ethnic jokes) are everywhere, including examples in several of the more serious treatments of humor. I advise addressing up front, as I now do, people's widely varying tastes and sensitivities in humor (as in other things) and the potential offensiveness of many types of humor to some specific audience or person. Raising these matters for consideration and discussion early on will solve many problems related to differing student values and sensitivities in advance.

Note

1. Students agreed in writing to allow their personal funny stories to be used as examples.

References

Cohen, Ted (1999) *Jokes: Philosophical Thoughts on Joking Matters*. Chicago and London: The University of Chicago Press.

Gulas, Charles S. and Weinberger, Marc G. (2006) *Humor in Advertising: A Comprehensive Analysis*. Armonk, New York and London: M. E. Sharpe.

Holt, Jim (2008) *Stop Me If You've Heard This: A History and Philosophy of Jokes*. New York and London: W. W. Norton & Company.

Jones, Loyal and Wheeler, Billy Edd (1987) *Laughter in Appalachia: A Festival of Southern Mountain Humor*. Little Rock: August House.

McGhee, Paul (1979) *Humor: Its Origin and Development*. San Francisco: W. H. Freeman and Company.

Ziv, Avner (1984) *Personality and the Sense of Humor*. New York: Springer Publishing Company.

Appendix

HANDOUT 1   **Comparing Funny Stories**
               For each story we read, complete the chart below.

1. *Characterize*   Characterize the story in terms of story structure and
                    language.

Story Structure   What techniques are used for each part?

Opening

Progression

Closing

Language   What type of language is used? Give examples.

Vocabulary

Spelling

Grammar

2. *Revise*   How could you revise the story to improve it or create
                   a new story?

3. *Rank*   Give reasons for your ranking of this story compared
                   to the others.

HANDOUT 2   **What Makes a Good Story**
For each story we read, consider these features.

A sense of time and place, given by:
- Descriptive detail
- Specific events/locales

A memorable character at its center, who should be:
- An original and/or a recognizable type
- Flawed but in some way sympathetic

A sequence, which should include (usually in this order):
- Setting/background
- Conflict/trouble
- Resolution/climax

A theme or moral, which should:
- Be a universal or enduring truth
- Grow out of the story

Plot focus, as shown by the features of:
- Direction and cumulative build-up of tension and interest
- Revelation through showing not telling
- Parsimony: no wasted words or information

Narrative elements of:
- Action
- Dialogue

Use of language to create:
- Vivid images
- Mentally visualized scenes

Connection to the reader, who should feel:
- A sense of recognition
- An emotional response

Some useful websites:
http://www.creativekeys.net/StorytellingPower/article1004.html
http://www.aaronshep.com/youngauthor/elements.html
http://thinkingwriter.com/?p=76

HANDOUT 3   **Workshop on Writing a Funny Story**
Read and complete each starred* exercise.

Story Structure

Your assignment is to tell a funny story in a way that is entertaining and shows something about your nature or character. If you do a good job, the story can help your teacher and classmates get to know you better and can also be told on other occasions, such as at a gathering of family, friends, or colleagues at work, or as part of a speech. A good personal funny story comes in handy on many occasions. As we have seen in the funny stories we have read, a funny story, like any good story, usually has a memorable central character (or characters) and is built up in stages that include:

Explicit Story Introduction (*optional*)	*Once upon a time*; *I'm going to tell you about…*
Background (may or not be funny)	on the story's place, time, and/or characters
Story Narrative or Event(s)	chronological order, dialogue (*typical*)
Story Point	resolution or moral

In addition, funny stories may include:
• Funny images
• Funny language
• Jokes
• Hyperbole or exaggeration
• Implausibility, impossibility, or absurdity
• A punchline

In your Personal Funny Story, you will want to tell a story with some or all of the above elements in which you may or may not be the central character. If you are not the central character, then as narrator you will be an additional character whose thoughts and nature intrude on the story by your reflections on the story and on yourself.

Direct Approach

You may want to take a direct approach in which you start by introducing yourself and the point you want to make about your nature or character. If you start this way, you will construct your story to reinforce what you have told the reader about yourself by an illustrative story. You may then add a resolution or draw a conclusion from the story. This may "revisit" the point about your nature or character in a new way, or it may be a totally new point e.g. a general moral about human nature or some kind of punchline.

Indirect Approach

You may want to lead up to something about your nature or character in-directly, through the telling of your story, rather than through introducing it explicitly in the beginning. If so, you can start off with some other kind of background to your story and not get to the point about your nature or character until later, or even not till the very end of the story.

Which approach do you want to try?   Direct   Indirect   Other:

Getting Started

Two ways to get started in developing your story are to start from personal characteristics or to start from an event.

Starting from Personal Characteristics

One approach is to start from your own characteristics. Make a list of words or phrases that you think describe your true nature or character or that others have used to describe you.

e.g.   shy, quiet   *Self:*
         thoughtful, serious
         a good friend, loyal

One way to develop your story is to poke fun at yourself by a narration of something that happened in which you come off as silly or are in some sense "the loser". Another way is to exaggerate something about yourself to the point of humor or even ridiculousness.

e.g.   shy and quiet to the point of not responding to questions in a job
       interview
       such a sound sleeper that you slept right through an important
       event

* _Self:_

Another way to develop your story from your own personal characteristics is by contrast with someone else you know well and spend a lot
of time with.

e.g.   a brother or friend who is very easy-going vs. you who worry about
       everything

* _Contrast:_

Instead of contrasting yourself with another person, you could use that
person as the basis of a character that you develop, perhaps as a representative type of human being.
e.g.   someone sweet but lazy: a lovable but inefficient person (Rip Van
       Winkle type)

* _Self or Other Character Type:_

You could then describe and comment on the person in a way that reflects
something about your own nature or character. If you talk about yourself
or select a memorable person or someone important to you that you know
well to write about, you will be able to use yourself or the other person
to make a good story that involves a moral, life lessons, human foibles,
and/or typical human behaviors and that is also funny.

* _Who will be your main character?_   _Self_   _Other:_

Once you decide on a person to write about—yourself or another person
you know well—you will need to think of a funny event which can show
your own true nature, with yourself or the other person as a character in
the event. Review the list of types of events below to get ideas for what

could be a memorable event that might be the basis of a good story. If the story is not funny in itself, you might be able to poke fun at yourself through the story or otherwise make a funny point about yourself in relation to it.

* *<u>Idea for event:</u>*

* *<u>Write out your event in chronological order:</u>*

Next, you need to think about how to connect your event to your nature or character in your story structure. Sketch out your idea for the story structure:

* *<u>Opening:</u>*

* *<u>Progression:</u>*

* *<u>Ending:</u>*

Now you are ready to write out your whole story. Once you have done that, review "What Makes a Good Story" and think about how you might embellish the description of the person and of the relevant event to make it a better story.

* *<u>Ideas for Embellishments:</u>*

<u>Starting from an Event</u>
A different approach to getting started on your Personal Funny Story is to begin with a real event and then develop it into a funny story by adding in details and giving it humorous elements. If you select a memorable event, something-out-of the-ordinary, you will probably have a lot to

say about it, and because it is unusual, it can be the basis of a good story about you and your character involving a moral, life lessons, human foibles, and/or typical human behaviors as well as humor.

To start writing your story this way, first, think of a memorable event of one of the types below. If possible, it should be something that happened to you, but if you can't think of anything that happened to you, the next best thing is to use something that happened to someone you know well and that you can use to talk about yourself through your response to what happened. If the story is not funny in itself, you might be able to poke fun at yourself through the story or otherwise make a funny point about yourself in relation to it.

A time of danger or trouble – a time when you thought, "I am in really big trouble now!"

An amusing event – something funny when you (and/or others) laughed a lot.

A major event which taught you a lesson – something that happened to you that made you learn or change (preferably, for the better).

Something very unexpected or surprising that changed the way you think or act.

Something that happened or happens to you repeatedly – the fact of this happening repeatedly helps to tell something about you and can be funny.

* *Idea for event:*

* *Write out your event in chronological order:*

Next, describe yourself (or the person involved, if not you) in the event in a way which suggests why the event had the effect on you that it did. In your description, try to get at something significant about your nature or character.

* *Description of self (or other) in relation to event:*

Now, think about how to connect the event to your nature/character in the story structure. Sketch out your idea for the story structure:

* ***Opening:***

* ***Progression:***

* ***Ending:***

Now you are ready to write out your whole story. Once you have done that, review "What Makes a Good Story" and think about how you might embellish the description of the person and of the relevant event to make it a better story.

* ***Ideas for Embellishments:***

Additional Considerations
You may want to consider building your story:
• By analogy to another story
• By changing the context of something (e.g. describing a school like a prison)
• By using a format (e.g. one-liner hyperbole jokes: NOUN *is so* ADJ *that* joke-clause)
• By using aspects or parts of other stories (e.g. opening strategy, background format, overall story structure)

You may want to try adding some dialogue as characteristic things the main character is likely to say or things s/he would say in the action of your story event. Then think of how others would respond to the character's words and build some dialogue, considering:
• Would they be talking face to face or on the phone?

- Where they are from, e.g. Do they speak colloquial or standard English?
- How old they are, e.g. Do they use youth language or old-fashioned expressions?
- Would they ask a lot of questions or make mostly statements?
- Would they be excited or upset when they spoke?
- Would they tend to talk a lot or a little?

To try adding dialect, review other stories to get some ideas or even some exact language to use (if appropriate for your story).

Some useful websites:

http://www.humorwriters.org/Maryemma.html
http://www.krisneri.com/writingtips2.html
http://www.writerswrite.com/journal/may02/hornung.htm

HANDOUT 4   **Peer Response Sheet for Personal Funny Story**

Writer's Name _____   **Responder's Name** _____

Work in a group of 3. Each one exchanges their paper with 1 groupmate and then the other to give written feedback on the peer response sheet items below. Once all 3 readers have finished writing their feedback on the 2 papers they read, they each read the 2 sets of feedback for their **own** paper and then ask the 2 responders to clarify or elaborate on their feedback as needed, and to give additional feedback if wanted. Turn in peer response sheets in your folder with your draft.

1. Is the story funny? Did it make you laugh?
2. What was funny about it?
3. Which of the following techniques did the writer use to generate humor?
    — Funny event
    — Funny character (self or another person)
    — Funny language
    — Hyperbole, exaggeration, or absurdity
    — A punchline or unexpected ending
    — Make fun of a characteristic of the writer him/herself
    — Make fun of a certain type or category of person
    — Contrast of people
    — Joke(s)
    — Other _____
4. Does the story succeed in making a point about the writer's nature or character? How and where in the story is this done?
5. Can you think of any person or group that might not find this funny and if so, why not?
6. Do you think the story structure could be improved by shortening or lengthening any part (opening, progression, ending), and/or changing the order? If so, make a suggestion.
7. Give the writer one or more pieces of advice as to how s/he might revise the story or sharpen the humor in terms of its content (what it is about).
8. Give the writer one or more pieces of advice as to how s/he might revise the story or sharpen the humor in terms of its language.

Part 2
Argumentation and Writing from Sources

7   The "Delayed Thesis" Essay: Enhancing Rhetorical Sensitivity by Exploring Doubts and Refutations

Sara Hillin

I.   Background

The assignment described here asks students in an advanced composition course[1] to write a brief "delayed thesis" essay in which they explore the angles of opposition to their own claim before introducing their own thesis. Such an essay is structured so that the bulk of the piece (generally, at least two-thirds of it in this course) is devoted to supporting claims that the writer has considered but ultimately plans to refute or partially concede to. For example, a student who feels that Melville's "Bartleby the Scrivener" is a critique of capitalism might write a delayed thesis essay in which s/he covers other valid interpretations first (such as the notion that the tale is autobiographical), considers their merit, and then illustrates her/his own claim. The idea of having students explore the opposing sides of their own arguments is, of course, not new. Aristotle, for example, felt that giving attention to one's opposition through carefully predicting what that opposition might be was key to effective persuasion. In his *Treatise on Rhetoric* he terms this element of argumentation the "refutative," defining it as the "consideration of contradictions; if there occur any contradiction under all the circumstances of time, conduct, sayings, and the like" (Aristotle, 1995: 189). Likewise, in the 1970s, Peter Elbow popularized the "believing and doubting game," stating in *Writing without Teachers* (Elbow, 1973) that in order for him to change his mind, something had to happen to make him admit to mistakes. That "something," he explains, happens when the opposition "lets up on his guns a little, stops trying to show that I'm an idiot, and in fact shows some glimmer of understanding for why *I* believe what I do believe" (Elbow, 1973: 185, emphasis in original). This sense of a "letting up on the guns" is one reason that I have students write these essays largely based on their own investigation into potential opposition; I want them to anticipate and respond civilly to criticism rather than relying on me to expose the lingering questions or holes in their argument.

Elbow (1973: 190) also explains that the ability to, among other things, "be combative and thrusting, to be fiercely stubborn, to have a hunger for certainty, to doubt everything, to have a dug-in and unmoving self..." is immensely useful. Although doubting should, in my view, be given just as much attention as believing, I find that most students are woefully under-prepared in the skills of: (i) locating ideas that oppose their own, and (ii) responding to them with rhetorical sensitivity.

As Erika Lindemann comments in *Rhetoric for Writing Teachers*, in reference to the believing/doubting game, "...assuming the role of doubters, they [students] produce all the evidence that they can think of against the writer's position" (Lindemann, 2001: 197). She adds that "'believing and doubting' responses can help strengthen certain kinds of writing, especially arguments" (p. 197). The delayed thesis exercise allows students to use doubting as a tool to discover refutations and strengthen their claims.

Finally, Sharon Crowley and Debra Hawhee state in *Ancient Rhetorics for Contemporary Students* that "attention to invention should disclose arguments that need to be anticipated and refuted"

(Crowley and Hawhee, 2004: 270). Because this assignment focuses on doubting and the creation of a refutation, it is a perfect platform for students to focus on a practice that I find (as a teacher of both first-year and advanced college composition) is underdeveloped in most students.

II.   Description of Activity

This assignment is the third in a series of short essays I assign to my advanced expository writing students, all of whom, by that point in the term, are deep into drafting their major research-based argumentative essays. Because I know they are finally at the point of gaining confidence in their own knowledge base and claims, I like to add this assignment as the final "twist" that shakes them out of complacently presenting their own perspectives without giving more than marginal consideration to their potential opposition. The assignment given to students reads:

Short Essay #3
English 3326.01
Length: 1½–2 pages
Delayed Thesis Essay

For this paper, I want you to construct a delayed thesis argument. This means I want you to prepare the argument as if you were presenting it to a potentially hostile audience (and you will have to imagine exactly what your audience's opposing viewpoints are to make this successful). Your thesis will appear nearer the end of the paper, and your beginning paragraphs will explore the opposing views and explain whatever common ground you may see between their views and your own.

The topic of your argument:
You have some freedom to decide exactly what you wish to write about. It may be helpful for you to rework and condense the argument you are beginning to work on for Major Project 2 for this

assignment. It may, in fact, give you some more ideas for organization (or ideas for how to better appeal to your audience) to make the major project the basis for this assignment. If you decide to use your major project as the basis for this paper, you will have to imagine how you would construct the argument if your audience had *reservations* about some aspect of your topic (and you may use first person).

Those of you who do *not* wish to use your second major project as the basis for this argument may look to pretty much anything else (literary or nonliterary) as the basis for the argument. In either case, make sure to use appropriate rhetorical means to identify with the audience.

Evaluation criteria:

- Obvious attempt to appeal to readers who oppose the claim
- Identifiable claim
- Mastery over spelling/grammar
- Cohesion among and within paragraphs
- Conciseness

I demand conciseness in this essay – it is to be one and a half to two pages long, and no more (or penalties will be imposed). This assignment also emphasizes attention to voice (I allow students to use "I" in any of their work): as Lizbeth Bryant points out in *Voice as Process*, "as writers build voices, the construction zone becomes a third space in which new voices are taking shape as writers integrate voices at varying intensities" (Bryant, 2005: 97). I do not want my students to cower behind their insecurities – rather, I want them to discover a voice that is confident even as it acknowledges potential problems with internal logic.

I give the students the choice of using this assignment either to develop the refutation aspect of their major research essay or to write a delayed thesis about a topic of their choice. I like the assignment to be *kairos*-based,[2] so that students who are tired of using their research essay topic as a springboard for many of our lower stakes writing assignments may write in the delayed essay assignment about whatever is moving them at the moment. Most do, however, use their same research essay topic for the delayed thesis assignment. Such was the case with one student (Student E from the discussion excerpts under "Implementation"), who was so enraged over a report about GM and Ford executives flying in private jets to petition for financial assistance at the nation's capital that she wrote the essay on this topic; she was simply passionate about the issue. In addition, this student chose to do a delayed thesis format for her research essay on Charlotte Perkins Gilman because of what she learned about audience and organization during the process of creating the delayed thesis argument.

III. Implementation

This essay is something the students are aware of all semester long, but we do not actually discuss delayed thesis arguments until the last third of the semester. The time between when the actual assignment is distributed and when it is due is usually about three weeks.

We have quite a bit of discussion of audience during the production of the essay, as the *audience* is what drives the content and organization of a piece based on opposition. Because these students are advanced, I try to get them thinking of potential outside audiences (such as journal editors). The primary audience addressed, however, is still me, their teacher.

When I implement this assignment in a face-to-face class, the first day is a discussion of "invitational rhetoric" with an emphasis on Sonja Foss and Cindy Griffin's conception of the term as referring to an attempt to eschew the drive to change and control one's audience through heavy-handed means (Griffin and Foss, 1995). Griffin and Foss (1995:4) explain that invitational rhetoric, rooted in feminist concepts of "equality, immanent value, and self-determination," creates an "invitation to the audience to enter the rhetor's world and to see it as the rhetor does" (p. 5). The goal is a nonhierarchical dialogue in which both rhetor and audience listen to and understand each other's perspectives. Students are genuinely intrigued by this form of rhetoric that positions the writer and her/his audience as equals.

The second day, I ask students to take two minutes to consider potential arguments against some aspect of their essays. This exercise gets us talking out in the open about their arguments' shortcomings. Invariably, several students will say they simply do not have a clue as to how to see opposition to their own work. At that point, I ask them to present their claims and evidence, and gently prod them on one or more issues. Classmates will join in and raise questions, helping their peers invent and respond to opposing views. The discourse never takes on an accusatory tone. Rather, the questioning clarifies for students just what they can use as a starting point rather than asking them to create opposition in a vacuum.

On the third day, I generally model the creation of the delayed thesis with my own work and a few examples of their emerging drafts of the major essay. I explain how I have come to detect my own blind spots in my arguments. I also identify a few of their own gaps and offer ideas for how they could be filled. For example, one student planned to research the question of why Herman Melville wrote such "non-boring" books in an otherwise "boring" time in which his contemporaries produced "boring" work (an interesting premise but a shaky one because of the clearly loaded term *boring*). Since the operative word or concept of "boring" seemed to be the crux of her exploration, I modeled an audience response in which I opposed the idea that Melville's contemporaries were boring and asked how she might even define the term without offending me as a reader. Wrestling with this question helped her see the problems involved in calling works "boring" and also helped her clarify her argument's purpose in the longer research essay.

The fourth day is a workshop in the computer lab in which I work with each student as s/he creates the delayed thesis. The fifth day is a kind of debriefing discussion on what was learned in the process of creating these essays. The sixth day, the essays are due, and we move on to discussing the organization of the major research essay.

After students complete the delayed thesis essay, I ask that they articulate their emerging organizational plan for the longer researched argument and explain their decisions/justifications about where their claims will appear. The following is the discussion prompt on this topic for one of the online classes:

> For Major Project 2 [the researched argument], what kind of organizational pattern did you use? Did any of you choose to go the delayed thesis route? Did you feel it was most effective to put the claim upfront? Did you use any subheadings? What is it about the way you organized the presentation of your evidence that contributed to the effectiveness of your work?

When specifically asked to consider and talk/write about these critical issues of arrangement, students reveal in their online posts (or discussion responses, if the class is face-to-face) a greater sensitivity to their audience rather than merely their own personal preference for closed form, thesis-driven prose. The discussion that follows also functions as part of my evaluation of the effectiveness of the assignment. Student feedback and reflection is crucial for me to determine what they have learned. Here are a few excerpts from students' online posts responding to the above discussion prompt (the italics for emphasis are mine) that show students' engagement with the question of thesis placement, with particular reference to the delayed thesis assignment:

> Student A: *I rather liked the challenge of the delayed thesis but I haven't completely settled with it. I think directly addressing the thesis can be effective, but I'm too picky to stop poking and prodding until the very last minute.* At this point, I still feel that my entire paper is extremely susceptible to drastic changes.

> Student B: I enjoyed doing the delayed thesis. I am not sure if I will use it in Major Project 2 or not. I think it is easier to put the claim up front and work from there. *I plan to start in the earlier*

years and work my way to present time, I think it is the only way to prove my point.

Student C: Being a person that likes to let know people where I stand, I chose the more classical approach to the thesis, and present it right up front. Whether or not this is effective is to be seen, *but I believe that my topic allows for this type of arrangement.*

Student D: It's been, so far with me, like I'm taking off on a sprint. Just getting through it. I'm trying not to get bogged down. *If anything's been helpful, it's been that I'm approaching James's The Beast in the Jungle (fairly) chronologically, as Marcher's condition in the story is one of deterioration (in my opinion–though he's somewhat unware [sic] of it). [Some may not believe The Beast in the Jungle is a story of deterioration. I tried to explore this is in my delayed thesis.]*

Student E: *I did choose to use the delayed thesis in my paper. I thought it was effective because I could present my argument, then evidence, give my thesis, and lastly give my thoughts on the argument. I wanted to organize it that way so that the reader could form their opinion before my standpoint is present.* I have written it in chunks at this point, but I am putting it together in a flowing manner. This is my weakness, trying to get each paragraph to flow from one to the other. I find this delayed thesis a better way for me to present my information up front and then give my take on the subject in the end. I find it very striking for my reader, and easier for me to keep my thoughts organized throughout the paper.

Student F: I presented my thesis rather early in my paper, because I wanted to allow the reader to form their own opinions as they read. *I often feel that with a delayed thesis, the reader may not fully understand the argument until the thesis is presented.* At the same time, I like to inform the reader about the statement I'm attempting to make early on, so that they may read the rest of the paper from my standpoint, so to say.

Student G: For me the organizational method that seems best is that of an "Info-commercial". That is, I felt it would be best to restate the statistical and historical points upfront. In this manner, I can lead the reader in the direction that leads to my research findings, with fewer difficulties in using so other method. I see this as providing a used 'road map', which the reader is already familiar with and is accustomed to its legend.

Using this method of association provides a suitable vehicle for – yes – the "Delayed Thesis" approach to my research argument. Considering my topic; it is a case where rhetorical sensitivity must be employed, I expect a great deal of adversity from the reader when first reading my argument, but when they look back at the 'road map', they can understand my position better than if I had not provided the map.

These comments illustrate the generative nature of the delayed thesis exercise; students clearly made several of their decisions about audience, organization, and content in light of their experience in playing the "doubting game" to discover and respond to a hesitant audience.

IV.   Reflections and Recommendations

I evaluate the students' essays in terms of how well they use rhetorical sensitivity to engage with their opposition and smoothly lead into a claim – rather than simply drafting a traditional argument and then moving the thesis to a later ("delayed") position in the last draft, a move which does not allow them to think through and construct the necessary metadiscourse and overall coherence. Concerning assessment and returning the essays to the students, I found that audio podcasts in conjunction with written comments are quite useful in personalizing the commentary.

Although this description of the activity focuses on advanced students, I also believe it can be adapted for use in a composition course at any level where persuasion comes into play. I find that even advanced students have tremendous trouble <u>extensively</u> acknowledging their opposition's side, and so this exercise gets them out of their comfort zone. And because the essay is so concise, there is no room for them to hide behind the padding that many advanced English majors are so deft at creating.

The reason I do not demand that all students use their major essay topic to develop their refutation is that, regardless of whether or not they do, they will, through this experience, learn a tremendous amount about audience. I have taught this essay for three semesters, and the process of sifting through and addressing opposing views is always an eye opener for students; the exercise has ramifications beyond the essay itself that relate to how they see writing in general. For example, most students come away with a much better understanding of *choice* in argument structure: whereas before, they were convinced that presenting the thesis up front was the only way to effectively argue, they now understand that a delayed thesis can be just as effective, depending upon one's subject matter and audience. Several students have cited this exercise as the reason they chose to pursue a delayed thesis format in their final long essay. And even those who do not use the delayed thesis format have made a conscious choice to stick with a classical, early-thesis format for their long research essay, given that they have experience arguing with a different organizational pattern.

I have taught the delayed thesis exercise in both face-to-face and online formats (in two online courses and two face-to-face courses). In the online format, in which I found that the assignment was just as successful, the building up of an interactive rapport with students (and between students) far in advance of introducing this essay is key; otherwise, students might feel detached and perhaps even threatened by the thought of a hostile audience or the idea that I, as the instructor, am going to play the role of that hostile audience. I have found that active online discussion threads (approximately two per week) which ask the students to engage in increasingly complex acts of reflective analysis – i.e. going from prompts such as "write a humorous story about a time in which you procrastinated on your writing," borrowed from Lisa Ede's *Academic Writer* (Ede, 2007), to "articulate your claim for the major essay and explain a bit about the thinking that led you to it" – build a lasting sense of community. I also answer these self-reflective questions along with the students and comment, in a lighthearted manner, on their own contributions, which levels the playing field even more.

Some students are resistant to the delayed thesis assignment, and, even in their final drafts, show traces of the thesis too early on. But even in their struggles with the task, I can see their attempt both to invite the reader into the conversation and to acknowledge their own doubts about their own arguments. The form is the traditional essay, and although other instructors might prefer to integrate multimedia forms into this assignment, I feel that students need the safe, familiar structure of the essay in which to test the waters of opposition.

The following email from a student (who feared she would not get credit for the essay because it was turned in a little after the due date) shows the generative power of this exercise; in it, she cites this exercise as the catalyst for discovering just what her claim was for the major research essay (again, the italics are mine):

> "*I'm not sure if you'll agree to grade it, but regardless I REALLY appreciated this assignment. Initially I found it a pain to force myself to argue against what I wanted to be fighting to prove, but upon finishing it (the first time) I managed to narrow down my argument and finally figure out what point I really want to make.* My problem now is my rough draft. I still have time to play with it I'm sure but it needs much more work now that I have a better idea of what I want to come out of it. I need to cut out a lot of useless information and insert more relative material to meet the 8 page standard.
>
> Please excuse this rant, but I'm getting gradually more and more excited about this paper. I'm going to get back to reconstructing this essay in hopes that it will do me some good, and even if it isn't a grade it would be nice to have the short essay on file for my progress."

The delayed thesis essay has become an integral part of my composition course because of its power to make students anticipate and actively engage with potential opposition, while strengthening their skills in analyzing audience, organizing information/ideas, and developing claims. The primary value of this assignment is that it gets students thinking about their audience in ways they have not before, instead of pigeonholing consideration of the "other side" to the arbitrary, obligatory paragraph or two tucked away in the body of a long argumentative essay. As a result of this assignment, students' longer research-based arguments show more sophisticated refutations. It is one activity through which I can actually see my students growing as writers.

Notes

1. At my university, we have one general advanced writing course (English 3326: Advanced Expository Writing), and it is required of all English majors and minors. Students from other disciplines often take the course as well. All students enrolled in the course have had at least two semesters of sophomore level literature courses, and many have also taken several upper level literature courses that focus on close study of genres, critical theory, and literary periods. Although most of our upper division English courses involve a writing component, the Advanced Expository Writing course is the only one that focuses heavily on argumentation, thesis development, and research. The course is given in both face-to-face and online formats.

2. *Kairos*, as William Covino and David Joliffe explain, refers to "the right or opportune time to speak or write" and also "connotes the right measure, the appropriate move in a rhetorical situation" (Covino and Joliffe, 1995: 62). Although in truth grades are often at the forefront of students' minds, I give these writers as much choice as possible in topic selection so that they can devise those appropriate rhetorical moves and measures based on an actual engagement with something they feel passionate about.

References

Aristotle (1995) *Treatise on Rhetoric* (trans. Theodore Buckley). Amherst, Massachusetts: Prometheus Books.

Bryant, Lizbeth (2005) *Voice as Process*. Portsmouth, New Hampshire: Boynton/Cook.

Covino, William A. and Joliffe, David (1995) *Rhetoric: Concepts, Definitions, Boundaries*. Boston: Allyn and Bacon.

Crowley, Sharon and Hawhee, Debra (2004) *Ancient Rhetorics for Contemporary Students* (3rd edition). New York: Pearson and Longman.

Ede, Lisa (2007) *The Academic Writer: A Brief Guide*. Boston: Bedford St. Martins.

Elbow, Peter (1973) *Writing Without Teachers*. London: Oxford University Press.

Foss, Sonja K. and Griffin, Cindy L. (March 1995) Beyond persuasion: A proposal for an invitational rhetoric. *Communication Monographs* 62: 2–18.

Lindemann, Erika (2001) *A Rhetoric for Writing Teachers* (3rd edition). New York: Oxford University Press.

8 Literature-with-Exposition: A Critical Thinking and Writing Assignment

Gita DasBender

I. Background

While most first-year writing programs consist of either a one-semester writing course or a two-semester sequence of expository writing, the practice of teaching imaginative literature in composition courses still thrives in some programs today. In 1993, Erika Lindemann argued against literature-based writing courses, claiming that such courses "focus on consuming texts, not producing them" (Lindemann 1993: 313) and criticized programs that perpetuated this practice. Lindemann's central concern was that literature-based writing courses did not provide students with an opportunity for "evaluating sources, reading critically, interpreting evidence, [and] solving problems in writing" (p. 313). In addressing this disciplinary divide between rhetoric and literature, Gary Tate responded to Lindemann by proposing that writing courses include all types of resources – literature and non-fiction – that would help us "adopt a far more generous vision of our discipline and its scope…that would exclude *no* text" (Tate, 1993: 321). For those of us in writing programs where literature is valued, the task of re-imagining ways of teaching literary texts in the composition class is a challenging one indeed. How do we align the goals and purposes of expository writing with literary interpretation and analysis?

While the disciplinary debate between literature and composition is well established, there is also the view that "despite the historically aggrieved, yet symbiotic relationship of composition studies to English studies," a movement that brings the two closer is perhaps inevitable (Berkenkotter, 1991: 157). Composition studies is a "hybrid field" (p. 165) that reflects interdisciplinarity, and if we are to embrace this marriage of disciplines pedagogically, then we need "to articulate the models of knowing that inform our practice" (p. 166). At first glance, the goals of literary interpretation seem to be far different from, if not opposed to, those of expository writing. While literature demands that writers experience, appreciate and interpret literary texts, expository writing demands that writers engage with ideas and arguments in non-fiction texts so as to be able to pose well-reasoned and carefully-evidenced arguments of their own. The gap between appreciation and exposition, however, can be bridged not by excluding literature or essays but by including both in the writing class as long as the "model of knowing" that underlies such practice is clearly understood. When non-fiction essays are used as a reference point or as framing texts for understanding and interpreting "imaginative literature" (Steinberg, 1995) students can produce essays that meet the expository goals of developing coherent, compelling, and well-supported arguments by analyzing literature.

Though the goal of first-year writing is to improve academic writing skills in general, the course and assignment this chapter addresses also expects students to develop critical thinking and analytical writing abilities. It is possible to foster critical thinking in the composition class by developing an interdisciplinary curriculum taught by teachers who emphasize reading, writing, and discussion (Comley, 1989; Brookfield, 1987; Meyers, 1986; Shor, 1987). By reading and responding to short stories and poetry alongside essays that are thematically connected to the literature, students not only learn to interpret literature but also to draw larger conclusions about their *meaning* in the context of the essays which serve as perspective-generating texts. In effect, students learn to engage with literary texts by critically analyzing them but ultimately write expository essays that reflect universal ideas.

The subject of this chapter is an assignment sequence designed for a first-year writing course that uses works of literature along with non-fiction essays to help students develop strong ideas in their writing. The central purpose of the assignment is two-fold: (1) to introduce students to literature so that they can experience, analyze and interpret these texts in the context of related non-fiction essays and (2) to help them write compelling analytical essays which use literary interpretation for expository purposes.

The main goals of the assignment are:

- To appreciate, analyze and interpret works of literature;
- To engage in critical thinking through close-reading and interpretation;
- To draw connections between and integrate ideas from fiction, poetry and non-fiction texts;
- To generate ideas and writing in stages and to address one complex writing task at a time;
- To revise by synthesizing pieces of writing to form a complete essay;
- To develop strong, compelling, and original arguments.

II.   Description of Activity

This essay is taught in the second semester of a first-year writing sequence as the second writing assignment of three. It is a writing course that uses literature, and the general theme of the course is "Literature and the Natural World." While the three assignments are not interrelated, the first essay sets the tone for the course and the level of textual engagement students will need to succeed in the class. The assignment is described as follows in the course syllabus:

Essay Progression 1: Of Man and Beast

In this essay, I expect you to explore an interesting idea about our place in the natural world so that your readers can understand something new and different about how we interact with other creatures. For the assignment, you will read several short stories, poems, and essays and learn to draw interesting connections between texts of your choice. The goal of the assignment is to read and analyze literature and non-fiction essays so that you can write about what the texts mean and how the ideas from one can deepen our understanding of another. In particular, you will use ideas from an essay to illuminate our understanding of a short story and use a poem as a piece of evidence for your developing argument. Keep in mind the topic of the essay – "Of Man and Beast" – as you approach the assignment; your central ideas need to reflect this topic. You are also required to summarize the texts and to incorporate quotations into your writing as supporting evidence. The essay should be about six pages in length and should include a Works Cited page in the MLA format.

Readings

Fiction: Franz Kafka's "The Metamorphosis," Gabriel García Márquez's "A Very Old Man with Enormous Wings."

Essay: Loren Eiseley's "Judgment of the Birds" and Charles Darwin's "The Struggle for Existence" from *The Origin of Species.* (These are available online in Blackboard.)

Poetry: Henry Reed's "Naming of Parts," Paul Muldoon's "Hedgehog," Marge Piercy's "A Work of Artifice," Emily Dickinson's "I dreaded that first Robin, so" and "'Nature' is what we see," D. H. Lawrence's "Snake," and May Swenson's "The Universe."

The assignment sequence begins in the second week of classes after the department diagnostic test has been administered to ensure proper placement and to gauge the level of writing proficiency, and after students have been introduced to the course and to each other. The class meets twice a week for an hour and 15 minutes, and the entire sequence – including discussion of readings and completion of the final draft of the essay – lasts for approximately four weeks.

Week 1 (Day 1)

For this first week, students are assigned the short story, "The Metamorphosis," by Franz Kafka (Kafka, 2007) from their textbook, *Literature: Approaches to Fiction, Poetry and Drama* (DiYanni, 2007). Since students need to be oriented to the ways of approaching fiction as they read the story, they are also assigned a section from the textbook entitled "Understanding Literature: Experience, Interpretation, Evaluation." The instructor begins class discussion by first going over this section so that students begin to get a sense of the processes involved in reading and responding to literature and also to provide them with the specific vocabulary associated with these processes. Students then write an informal response to two questions "What is interesting to you about Gregor Samsa's character? What does his transformation represent to you?" for about ten to fifteen minutes. This allows them to do some pre-liminary thinking about the main character, Gregor Samsa, before the class moves on to a large group discussion where students are encouraged to read from their responses.

Week 1 (Day 2)

The discussion of "The Metamorphosis" continues on the second day but becomes more in-depth as students explore details and try to grapple with how the details contribute to the overall meaning of the story. The following is used to generate responses for a large group discussion:

> Identify five or six details that struck you as interestingly related while you were reading the story and write down what inferences you make from these details. For example, you may select sections of the story where Kafka describes Gregor and explain how these details help create a portrait of the character and his deepening alienation from the world. Or you may gather details about Gregor's father to examine the sort of relationship he has with Gregor and how (or why) this affects Gregor's transformation. Focus primarily on Gregor's physical and mental condition and attempt to interpret his transformation.

Week 2 (Day 1)

Students come to class having read Gabriel García Márquez's short story, "A Very Old Man with Enormous Wings," which is a shorter text than "The Metamorphosis" so the entire class period is devoted to discussion of the story. Small groups of students (no more than three in a group) work together on a prompt that helps them both discuss and write about the story. The prompt is as follows:

> Gabriel García Márquez's short story is written in the style of *magic realism*, a form of writing that fuses commonplace details of everyday life with fantasy and blurs the line between the real and the imagined. As complex and confusing as the story might be, upon close examination, certain clear themes about human behavior emerge from this vividly written tale. What do you think these themes are? Consider the details of the story that struck you most (quote briefly from the text) and write about some of the issues that García Márquez tries to emphasize.

Since this is a group project, students are required to first talk about the story so that they can begin to get a sense of the plot ("what happens") and then to come to some agreed-upon understanding of the meaning ("why" it happens) of the text. After the discussion, each group collaboratively writes a response to the prompt which is then shared with the whole class. A whole class discussion of the short story then follows.

Week 2 (Day 2)

This is when non-fiction essays are introduced to the class. Students are familiar with the non-fiction genre having already taken the first-semester writing class focused on expository writing. Nevertheless, some have difficulty comprehending complex ideas and arguments and the assigned essay, "The Judgment of the Birds" by Loren Eiseley, is not an easy read. To make the transition from one genre to another, the instructor reviews some basic characteristics of non-fiction and clarifies the distinction between fiction and non-fiction before moving on to discussing the essay. By writing an informal response to the essay, students begin to develop an understanding of parts of the essay as a basis for eventually making sense of the whole. The instructor assists in this reading comprehension task by creating a question that focuses on a central idea and its relation to the rest of the text. Students focus on what an abstract idea such as "see[ing] from an inverted angle" means by explaining it in reference to concrete examples that Eiseley uses throughout the essay. As they engage in this task, students develop a deeper sense of Loren Eiseley's main point, and they are encouraged to use the informal writing they produce in the actual writing assignment in a revised form. Students write a short response in fifteen to twenty minutes and then share their responses, which leads to a group discussion of the essay.

> Interpret the following from "The Judgment of the Birds" and state how it relates to the rest of Eiseley's essay. What idea is Eiseley talking about?

> "To see from an inverted angle, however, is not a gift allotted merely to the human imagination. I have come to suspect that within their degree it is sensed by animals, though perhaps as rarely as among

men. The time has to be right; one has to be, by chance or intention, upon the border of two worlds. And sometimes these two borders may shift or interpenetrate and one sees the miraculous."

Week 3 (Day 1)

Students come to class having read an excerpt (the first eight paragraphs) from the chapter titled "The Struggle for Existence" from Darwin's *Origin of Species*. They have also read all of the assigned poems. Discussion begins with the Darwin selection and the instructor guides the conversation by asking what students had the most difficulty with. Central points about the struggle for existence and the need for interdependence among species are discussed in reference to the two short stories. Students brainstorm connections between Darwin's essay and the stories and then begin to test arguments from the essays to see if they apply to the works of fiction. Finally, each poem is discussed briefly so that students get a sense of their meaning and relevance to the essay assignment. The goal of this lesson is to introduce students to the notion of intertexuality; although individual texts are meaningful in themselves, putting texts in conversation with each other can help students develop powerful original ideas.

Week 3 (Day 2)

Students now begin to write short assignments that gradually lead to a draft of the essay. The instructor spends some time in the previous class explaining this method of essay writing and helps students understand how the essay will be written in steps. The essay is produced gradually, progressively, so that the various writing tasks – summary, analysis, connection, and development of ideas – are attempted one at a time and focused on individually. Each prompt is assigned for homework and is reviewed in class before the day it is due. The assignment due on this day is Writing Exercise 1:

Choose a short story as the primary text that you will analyze for the essay you are writing. Focus on character development, symbolism, or any other aspect of a short story you find worthy of analysis. Your writing should try to get to an interesting interpretation of the story by examining specific parts of the text that serve as evidence. Make sure you quote directly to support your points. Limit yourself to two double-spaced pages.

This course consistently used Blackboard for all coursework, so all writing assignments were submitted into Blackboard's Discussion Board, which is viewable by all. Homework is required to be submitted into Blackboard before class so that all responses are available for discussion and feedback in class.

Week 4 (Day 1)

The essay progression now moves to the more complex stage where students focus on creating connections between texts. This homework assignment (Writing Exercise 2) explains what students need to do and also provides some guidance on how to approach making connections between texts.

Explore the connection or pattern of ideas that you believe brings two texts together, **a short story and an essay**. Look deeper into this connection by reflecting upon specific aspects of the pieces. Consider how the ideas of the essay explain or illustrate the message and meaning of the short story. The goal of your essay is to develop an idea about the relationship between humans and the natural world. Limit yourself to two pages. Here are some questions you may consider:

1. What does Gregor Samsa's transformation symbolize? How does it represent a struggle for existence? At what levels does Samsa struggle to survive (Darwin)?
2. Who exactly is the very old man with enormous wings? Use specific details from the short story to support your argument. What is the man's purpose in the story and what does his struggle represent (Darwin)?

3. How is the presence of the old man "miraculous" (Eiseley)?
4. How does García Márquez employ irony to convey his message? How does this message resonate with the essays you've read?
5. Eiseley claims that sometimes "the mundane world gives way to quite another dimension" for those "who have retained a true taste for the marvelous." How does this idea apply to the situation in either "The Metamorphosis" or "A Very Old Man with Enormous Wings?"

In class, students work in pairs reading their writing to each other and gathering feedback on how their writing is developing. This is a critical stage for peer review and instructor feedback because the central idea or argument of the essay depends on the ideas students begin to develop in Writing Exercise 2. As they formulate the relationships between an essay and a short story, students are required to use brief direct quotes from the texts, and are encouraged to incorporate them within their own sentences. Block quotes are generally discouraged because when students quote extensively in this form, they expect the quote to speak for itself and often fail to elaborate on or explain the quotations. Instead, they are taught to infuse crucial words and phrases from the text into their own sentences to demonstrate that they not only understand the text but that they are able to engage with it to articulate their own ideas.

Week 4 (Day 2)

Students have completed Writing Exercise 3, which requires them to use evidence from a poem that enhances their developing argument:

> Select a poem whose ideas provide evidence for the essay you are writing. For this assignment choose a quote or two from the poem and write a page reflecting on the relevance of the quotes to the ideas you're developing.

Class time is spent on examining the use of a poem as evidence. Students work in groups of three reviewing the main connection drawn in Writing Exercise 2 and the new piece of evidence that the poem affords. The essay progression is complete with Writing Exercise 3 so the instructor discusses the process of putting the pieces together in draft form. While students are tempted to copy and paste the individual exercises, the instructor carefully explains that the essay should not be viewed as a math formula in which the exercises add up to the final product. Rather, the instructor uses the metaphor of a puzzle to explain how the pieces (the writing exercises) need to fit together in a particular way in order for the essay to be a coherent whole. Transitional sentences (and perhaps even short paragraphs) may need to be created, and a thoughtful conclusion needs to be written. Students work on these elements of their writing for the latter half of the class. For their reference, the instructor posts a sample student essay culled from a previous class in Blackboard so students can have access to a model essay as they draft their own. On the rough draft due in the following class, the instructor provides detailed written feedback which students refer to as they revise for the final essay. In class, students review and respond to each other's rough draft by using the following peer-review prompt:

Read your partner's draft and respond to the questions below:

1. How clearly has the writer interpreted the short story? How accurate is the representation of the story? What is missing from the interpretation?
2. What is the connection that the writer draws between the short story and the essay? What idea about "man and beast" is the writer trying to develop?
3. Does the draft have enough evidence in terms of direct quotations and paraphrase? Which parts of the draft do you think need more direct evidence?
4. How does the writer incorporate the poem into the essay? Do the quotes from the poem fit well with the overall argument of the essay?

5. What suggestions for improvement do you have for the writer?

III. Implementation

This assignment sequence has been taught for several years in the second (College English II) of a two-semester sequence of first-year writing at Seton Hall University. While College English II is not a true Writing in the Disciplines course, four theme based versions of the course are offered with readings from other disciplines. The four versions of the course are: Literature and the Humanities, Literature and the Natural World, Literature and Public Life, and Literature and the Human Psyche. The assignment sequence presented here was developed for Literature and the Natural World.

Since this was the first writing assignment of the semester, careful attention was paid to introducing students to literature. In the first two weeks when students were immersed in readings, we not only discussed textual details, trying to get a handle on the plot, but we also talked about how to make sense of the text as a whole. Often students were asked to think about the message or meaning of a story or poem by focusing on direct evidence from the texts themselves. Speculation was highly encouraged. Students could have hunches about what was happening in the text as long as the hunches were accompanied by reference to specific parts of the text that seemed to support the hunch. This often opened up the conversation and allowed students to take risks with interpretation. Still, the message and meanings of literary texts seemed elusive. It was difficult for students who were still novice readers to grapple with the sophisticated literary techniques of Kafka, García Márquez, or Muldoon. The instructor emphasized a dual approach in textual interpretation: keep the central idea (or the meaning) of the text in mind as you work your way though the details, while making sure the details support the idea.

After students started writing the exercises the instructor read each student's work so as to know the level of engagement and to ensure students were headed in the right direction with the assignment. However, no written feedback was provided on the exercises. Instead, students were encouraged to read their writing out loud in class and received verbal feedback from their peers and the instructor. Although initially daunted, students quickly learned to shed their self-consciousness and take pride in reading their work to the class. Also, without written feedback from the instructor, students became more self-reliant and reached out more assertively to their peers for comments. Writing was shared for many reasons: to demonstrate what the student was able to do well, to discuss and get help on what the student struggled with, and to get reassurance that the writing matched the instructor's expectations.

The level of interest in sharing new writing intensified as the students moved on to the more complex task of connecting texts. Essentially, the idea of making textual connections has to do with how the observations of an essayist (Eiseley) or his arguments (Darwin) speak to the development of plot, action or characters in the short stories. The texts in this course were selected because they illuminate each other and allow readers to learn how the ideas in the non-fiction texts help us understand the meaning of literary works. Since the goal of the writing assignment is exposition and not literary criticism, making sense of literature through the lens of observations about the human condition or discipline-specific theories allows students to make interesting claims and arguments about both genres of writing. Indeed, the act of literary interpretation may become more purposeful when students attempt to understand literature in relation to profound ideas, concepts and theories that illuminate human action and our place in the world.

Much time was devoted to peer-review that helped students understand how others approached the task of connecting texts and provided new ideas about how to improve their own. The drafting stage was perhaps the most frustrating primarily because students tended to see each writing exercise as a complete "essay."

To disabuse students of this idea, the instructor reviewed a sample student essay (from a previous class) as a model that demonstrated how each writing exercise was a part of the essay and needed to be seamlessly incorporated into the developing whole. The metaphor of "play" was used to encourage revision, a true re-seeing of the exercises so that students could learn the following: that writing is not linear but recursive; that pieces of writing are not static but can be moved around depending on the effect one tries to achieve; and that the final product is often greater than the sum of its parts. To demonstrate this notion of play, the instructor helped students read through and rearrange sentences and paragraphs from the writing exercises to teach them how to "play" with their writing so that they could develop a desirable and compelling structure for their essay. In doing this students not only realize the necessity of reorganizing writing for structural reasons but also learn the benefits of good revision. This sort of play helps them rethink what they have written, and to add and delete, all necessary steps in revision.

Overall, students produced thoughtful, analytical, well-supported, and compelling essays that went far beyond the requirements. More importantly, new and unique ideas emerged from the in-depth examination of literature and non-fiction essays. Because of the focus on generating writing for every exercise, most students were able to produce at least five to six pages of writing, if not more. In general, the structure of the student essays reflected the assignment, that is to say, the writer started with the analysis of a short story, drew a connection between the story and the ideas of an essay which was then further supported by evidence from a poem, and concluded by reiterating general ideas about human nature. Some writers were more inventive and considered the writing exercises to be enabling constraints; they were constrained by the tasks assigned but took creative control over how they responded to the exercises and constructed their essay. Here are the last three paragraphs of an essay where the student is able to integrate her observations from two texts – a short story and a poem – to articulate the general ideas about human interaction that she's been developing throughout her essay. Her essay is titled "Learning about Humanity."

Although our environment, rule and norms of the society influence our actions, like in the case of father Gonzaga in "A Very Old Man with Enormous Wings", we are also influenced by our education. This fact makes us act irrationally because we just follow our fears without listening to what our heart and minds tell us. For instance, society imposes upon us the idea that snakes are bad, that "black snakes are innocent [while] the gold are venomous" (Lawrence 1151) and that they have to be killed before they kill us. As such, D. H. Lawrence in his poem "Snake" tells us that once he met with a snake and he listened to "[t]he voice of [his] education" (Lawrence 1151) that said to him: "He must be killed.../if you were a man/ you would take a stick and break him now, and finish him off" (Lawrence 1151). He has this idea in his head, although he confesses: "how I liked him/ How glad I was he had come like a guest in quiet, to drink at my water-trough/ And depart peaceful, pacified, and thankless/ Into the burning bowels of this earth" (Lawrence 1151).

One can appreciate how Lawrence is afraid of the snake, but, at the same time, he enjoyed looking at it, showing his love for nature. Consequently, the reader can realize how people feel afraid of interacting with living beings that are different from us even though they are not harmful. In "A Very Old Man with Enormous Wings", we see that the old man is different from the rest of the people and, because of that, he is rejected and mistreated although he is a peaceful being. In the poem "Snake", we see how Lawrence rejects the snake although it is not harmful. For these reasons, sometimes it is important to put aside what our education and traditions force us to do and follow what our mind and our feelings tell us.

As we can see, our humanity and the nature that surrounds us are beautiful. Each of us, just because of the fact that we are humans, deserves respect, consideration and love. It is very important to observe our attitudes when we interact with our fellow beings and not to allow ourselves to be influenced by tradition, laws or prejudices because they only drive us far away from what our humanity and heart tell us to do. More important, one should not ever forget that, as the world rotates every single day, our lives are rotating also and our destiny might change drastically from one day to the other, either in a positive or in a negative way. As such, one should treat the other, as one wants to be treated.

The student is able to develop these conclusive ideas because in analyzing Loren Eiseley's essay and connecting it with García Márquez's short story, she wrote:

> The conditions of suffering and misfortune which many of us might be living should not make us unhappy and pessimistic, but we should change our negative perceptions and see life from an "inverted angle" (Eiseley). We should also convince ourselves that each difficulty we might experience, should be an opportunity for learning and growing personally because, finally, the beauty of life "will come to the eye of those who have retained a true taste for the marvelous" (Eiseley) and those "who are capable of discerning in the flow of ordinary events,…another dimension" (Eiseley). Unfortunately, in the story, "A Very Old Man with Enormous Wings", the people who surround the angel do not appreciate that he is a marvelous human being who needs their help. If they had seen life from an inverted angle, meeting with the angel would have been an opportunity of fortifying and nourishing themselves internally. If they had treated the angel in a different way, they would have been happier with themselves and they would have felt internal satisfaction. If they had followed "another dimension" (Eiseley), they would have enjoyed the miracles of life.

As evident, this student is not just able to notice deep connections between non-fiction, fiction and poetry but express her own understanding of the meaning and relevance of these texts in elegant, compelling language.

While mainly designed for native speakers of English, this sequence was also adapted for non-native speakers in the ESL sections of College English II that I taught. Generally speaking, international students who are not native English speakers come with strong backgrounds in reading and interpreting literature, and are often very excited about working with fiction and poetry. They seem to be more accustomed to literary analysis than to expository writing and often adjust quickly to interpreting literary works. However, reading these complex texts in English poses a problem for those who are still in the process of learning English. Small group assignments where two to three students (with varying English proficiency) work on specific reading and interpretive tasks often helps these students develop reading competence, gain confidence to ask questions about a text, and to have some preliminary hypothesis about the meaning of the text. The key here is to encourage students to speak up and to have confidence in their reading ability. Also, when reading non-fiction texts, ESL students are given substantial time to discuss abstract or complicated ideas (for instance, the Darwin essay) that may be new to them. Some background information on the discipline that the course is linked to, whether it is the natural sciences, psychology, or political science, is helpful in clarifying and contextualizing the non-fiction essays.

Writing about complex ideas from non-fiction essays and their connection to literature also poses a difficulty for English language learners. They struggle with both content and form, that is, they have a hard time comprehending and responding to difficult texts in a coherent and structured way. A lot of time is spent in class reading student writing aloud so that whole class gets a sense of what the writer has accomplished, what still needs to be worked on, and what good writing looks like. It is particularly important to show students a model essay written for the specific assignment sequence so that the assignment seems accessible and not a burdensome task. I often show sample essays written by other ESL students so that the class is not intimidated by the polished writing of some of my native English speakers. However, there is also good reason to show essays by non-ESL students as examples of proficient writing. Ultimately however, grammar and mechanical errors, though they can be distracting, often recede into the background when students recognize the strength of interpretation and critical thinking in the sample writing and aspire to model their own writing in the same vein.

IV.   Reflections and Recommendations

As an assignment that uses literature for expository ends, the combined literary and expository writing assignment was particularly gratifying to teach. Literature has so often been seen as a constraint in composition studies that teachers rarely use it in writing courses. However, as this assignment demonstrates, creative use of literary works can not only expose students to different genres of writing as resources for critical thinking but also engage them in producing extraordinary writing. That said, it is important to recognize that students found it difficult to respond to the literary texts chosen for the assignment, perhaps because such response required a level of sophistication in reading skills that they did not possess. The instructor had to remind students that no work of literature is "easy" and that the easier a text seems, the harder it is to make sense of it. Because of the students' lack of interpretive ability, the instructor also had to teach literary concepts such as symbolism, irony, allegory, and magical realism in greater depth.

More time had to be spent in class modeling and discussing writing strategies than the assignment sequence reflects. Although there was always a well-conceived lesson plan for each class, teaching became intuitive in practice because the processes of reading and writing had to be constantly unpacked. Because students were always reading, writing, or interpreting texts, they had to juggle with several cognitive tasks and they often had unpredictable questions. This is not necessarily a negative thing; indeed, it sharpened students' sense of the relationship between reading and writing and forced them to organize their writing carefully.

While the assignment sequence can easily be adapted by focusing on a different discipline and by changing the theme and the readings involved, it is important to keep the organizing principle in mind. The discipline-specific non-fiction essays need to be philosophically (or socially, politically, environmentally) tied to the fiction so that students can work on illuminating the threads of thought that hold them together. Literature is not primary here; it is used in service of ideas inherent in the essays that students are required to build upon by using literary texts as evidence. Also, the instructor must help students stitch the essay together by modeling how the pieces of writing produced in the exercises can be organized into a cohesive whole. Students are most confused at the rough draft stage because they are usually unfamiliar with the form of the essay, and they do not understand writing as discovery. It is the instructor's responsibility to help students organize their ideas, develop a coherent structure, and generate compelling ideas.

As with any classroom practice, a good sense of what students are capable of achieving, and how far they can be challenged, is necessary for this assignment to be successful. A careful selection of texts that are not only enjoyable but also have underlying relationships is of prime importance because the assignment sequence hinges on textual connections. Regular and in-depth discussion of literature and non-fiction is also crucial to strong writing, and the instructor would do well to facilitate stimulating, guided discussions to help students develop new strategies for reading, understanding, and writing about texts. It is our duty, after all, to engage students in assignments that do not merely serve as course requirements but that allow them to discover a new world of ideas.

References

Berkenkotter, Carol (1991) Paradigm debates, turf wars, and the conduct of sociocognitive inquiry in composition. *College Composition and Communication* 42: 151–169.

Brookfield, Stephen D. (1987) *Developing Critical Thinkers: Challenging Adults to Explore Alternative Ways of Thinking and Acting.* San Francisco: Jossey-Bass.

Comley, Nancy R. (1989) Review: critical thinking/critical teaching. *College English* 51: 623–627.

Darwin, Charles (1859) *The Origin of Species*. New York: P. F. Collier & Son. Retrieved on 5 May 2009 from www.bartleby.com/11/.

Dickinson, Emily (2007) I dreaded that first Robin, so. In Robert DiYanni (ed.) *Literature: Reading Fiction, Poetry and Drama* 923–924. New York: McGraw Hill.

Dickinson, Emily (2007) "Nature" is what we see. In Robert DiYanni (ed.) *Literature: Reading Fiction, Poetry and Drama* 931–932. New York: McGraw Hill.

DiYanni, Robert (ed.) (2007). *Literature: Reading Fiction, Poetry and Drama*. New York: McGraw Hill.

Eiseley, Loren (1959) The Judgment of the birds. *The Immense Journey* 173–78. New York: Random House, Vintage Books.

Kafka, Franz (2007) The Metamorphosis. In Robert DiYanni (ed.) *Literature: Reading Fiction, Poetry and Drama* 612–641. New York: McGraw Hill.

Lawrence, D. H. (2007) The snake. In Robert DiYanni (ed.) *Literature: Reading Fiction, Poetry, and Drama* 1150–1152. New York: McGraw Hill.

Lindemann, Erika (1993) Freshman composition: No place for literature. *College English* 55: 311–316.

Márquez, Gabriel García (2007) A very old man with enormous wings. In Robert DiYanni (ed.) *Literature: Reading Fiction, Poetry and Drama* 399–403. New York: McGraw Hill.

Meyers, Chet (1986) *Teaching Students to Think Critically*. San Francisco: Jossey-Bass.

Muldoon, Paul (2007) Hedgehog. In Robert DiYanni (ed.) *Literature: Reading Fiction, Poetry and Drama* 1163. New York: McGraw Hill.

Piercy, Marge (2007) A work of artifice. In Robert DiYanni (ed.) *Literature: Reading Fiction, Poetry and Drama* 1169. New York: McGraw Hill.

Reed, Henry (2007) Naming of parts. In Robert DiYanni (ed.) *Literature: Reading Fiction, Poetry and Drama* 785–786. New York: McGraw Hill.

Shor, Ira (1987) *Critical Thinking and Everyday Life*. Chicago: University of Chicago.

Steinberg, Erwin R. (1995) Imaginative literature in composition classrooms? *College English* 57: 266–280.

Swenson, May (2007) The universe. In Robert DiYanni (ed.) *Literature: Reading Fiction, Poetry and Drama* 823. New York: McGraw Hill.

Tate, Gary (1993) A place for literature in freshman composition. *College English* 55: 317–321.

9 Paraphrase Integration Task: Increasing Authenticity of Practice in Using Academic Sources

Zuzana Tomaš

I.   Background

It is a truth universally acknowledged that plagiarism poses a significant threat to the academic success of many undergraduate and graduate students. Or perhaps I should credit the great Jane Austen for the borrowed opening from *Pride and Prejudice* and say: "It is a truth universally acknowledged" (Austen, 2003: 3) that plagiarism poses a significant threat to the academic success of many undergraduate and graduate students. What if I failed to realize that it had indeed been Austen's book that inspired the opening phrase? Could I not argue that it is simply a result of an unfortunate coincidence that the British author happened to start her renowned novel the same way I did this chapter? To avoid any possible accusations by Austen enthusiasts and to adhere to the established conventions of the genre within which I should be producing this text in the first place, I may simply choose to say "It is commonly believed" that plagiarism poses a threat to the academic success of many undergraduate and graduate students.

The above example illustrates how easy it is to fall prey to inappropriate textual borrowing, given that the boundaries between acceptable and unacceptable use of published sources are often blurred (Pennycook, 1996; Swales and Feak, 1994). However, despite the existing confusion, the stakes in the Western academy are high because writers caught plagiarizing may fail their courses or face expulsion from the university. International university students who write in English as their second language (L2) are particularly at risk when incorporating academic sources within their own writing. Research has shown that the development of appropriate textual borrowing practices (e.g. paraphrasing) in L2 writers is complex (Howard, 1995; Keck, 2006; Pecorari, 2003, 2006; Shi, 2004). Some of the reasons for this complexity include: (a) cultural differences in the notion of plagiarism (Bloch, 2001; Bloch and Chi, 1995; Pennycook, 1996); (b) developing language proficiency (Angelil-Carter, 2000, Dudley-Evans, 2002; Howard, 1995; Liu, 2005; Spack, 1997); (c) lack of experience with using academic sources (Dudley-Evans, 2002; Tomaš, 2006); and (d) the fact that citations are largely occluded aspects in academic writing (Pecorari, 2006).

Instructional interventions specific to citation practices can lead to significant gains in students' use of sources. For example, Tomaš (2006) found that L2 writers who struggled with citation in summary writing at the beginning of an academic writing course significantly improved by its end because of the instruction they received. Specifically, undergraduate L2 writers in the study made more significant lexical and syntactic changes to the original and included more devices signaling attribution (e.g. reporting verbs or phrases such as *according to*). Extending the frequently used summary task, Hsu (2003) examined the development of L2 writers' source use in an essay task. In the post-test conducted at the end of a writing course, she reported gains in L2 writers' inclusion of more sources and reduced amount of copying and unconventional documentation. Additionally, she found L2 writers demonstrated an increased understanding of concepts related to plagiarism and were even able to recommend strategies for avoiding plagiarism in the end-of-the semester interviews. In addition, Wette (2008) examined the effectiveness of a seven-hour unit on plagiarism and source use. Among other modest gains, she showed improvements in L2 writers' knowledge of rules and general ability to use sources in their writing, as well as a decrease in direct copying. It is difficult to attribute the development suggested in the above studies to a particular variable because one can argue that L2 writers enrolled in academic writing courses tackle all four factors in avoiding plagiarism: they conceptualize what plagiarism entails, improve their language proficiency, develop appropriate techniques in the use of academic sources, and pay closer attention to how sources are used in academic writing.

Although several L2 writing scholars have warned against oversimplifying instruction in source use (e.g. Jones and Freeman, 2003; Pennycook, 1996), writing teachers are likely to agree that explicit instruction in ways to avoid plagiarism – namely, quoting, paraphrasing, and summarizing – facilitates the development of the use of academic sources by student writers. I believe that writing teachers would also readily agree that they are unable to rely on the existing published materials when teaching about effective citation practices.

One inadequacy related to citation practices found in existing textbooks lies in the inconsistency of recommended strategies for avoiding plagiarism. In an evaluation of 27 writing textbooks available as reference materials to writing instructors at the University of Utah, Tomaš and Rosenberg (2005) found that six of the 27 did not mention paraphrasing at all, and 12 allocated a maximum of two pages to it, allowing students virtually no opportunities to practice paraphrasing. The textbook analysis also revealed the conflicting nature of paraphrasing, showing that what one author considers a characteristic of a good paraphrase, another sees as an inappropriate strategy for avoiding plagiarism (e.g. synonym use).

Additionally, most instructional resources teach paraphrasing as rephrasing isolated and decontextualized sentences that are often too obscure to understand (Yamada, 2001), thus failing to engage students in an authentic practice of source use. To illustrate, the majority of textbook exercises call for judgments of acceptable and non-acceptable paraphrases. Although such consciousness-raising is useful as the first step to a successful use of academic sources, it is not sufficient in helping L2 writers integrate sources as they produce their own original academic assignments (Barks and Watts, 2001; Whitaker, 1993).

While consistency of paraphrasing guidelines remains an issue to be addressed by researchers in writing pedagogy and authors of writing texts and reference books, the *Paraphrase Integration Task*, as described in this chapter, increases authenticity in instruction and practice of citation. It engages students in the type of practice that resembles what writers actually do in the process of using academic sources in their writing. Instead of simply asking students to rephrase isolated sentences, students are required to use an academic source in a task that is contextualized in real discourse. This task is more challenging than rephrasing a single sentence, but less complex than having to use multiple sources in an academic essay – an assignment students are often expected to do in academic writing courses as well as in mainstream university courses. In other words, the *Paraphrase Integration Task* serves as a bridge between the initial, consciousness-raising approach to source use practice and the fully authentic composing of source-based academic assignments. I view this frequently omitted learning phase as a necessary step to the mastery of citation practices in academic writing.

The value of this task lies not only in that it resembles the actual process of paraphrasing, but also in that it forces students to be critical about academic sources. The task requires students to use critical thinking skills as they match the source-based evidence with a corresponding idea in an academic paper. They are further challenged to rephrase and integrate this evidence effectively in the paper.

II.   Description of Activity

The unofficial name of the *Paraphrase Integration Task* used when working on source use with my students is *Helping Jun*. Students are told that "Jun" is an L2 writer who needs their help. The activity takes from 20 to 50 minutes, depending on how many of the steps below are incorporated. Prior to the activity, the instructor should discuss with students the purpose of citation in academic writing and the ways of integrating sources into their writing.

Step 1: Selection of Source Text and Its Integration into Student's Text

Each student is given the introduction to a research paper excerpted from Jun, an ESL university student (Appendix 1) and the excerpt from David A. Walker's article "The International Student Population: Past and Present Demographic Trends", discussing current demographics of the international student body (Appendix 2). Students are told that Jun needs to support the information in his introduction with information from the journal article, but he does not know how; he needs their help.

1. The instructor tells the students to carefully read the excerpt from the journal article.
2. Students are then asked to read Jun's introduction.
3. The instructor asks students to discuss in pairs which information from the article supports the ideas in Jun's introduction.
4. The instructor asks students to add the information they selected from the article to an appropriate place in Jun's introduction.
5. The instructor reminds students to paraphrase, not quote.
6. The instructor also encourages students to provide an in-text citation and matching reference from the original source at the end of Jun's revised introduction in the APA

format to help students become accustomed to this standard practice.

As students work, the instructor should monitor how successfully students paraphrased the information from the article and incorporated it into Jun's introduction.

Step 2: Peer Assessment of Paraphrase Integration

The instructor has pairs exchange their papers with each other and compare whether they selected the same information from the source and paraphrased the original material appropriately. Students can also evaluate each other's effectiveness in incorporating the paraphrase in Jun's paper by using a rubric (Appendix 3). For students to use this rubric successfully, the instructor needs to explain the rubric and allow clarification questions. The teacher's modeling of the process of using the rubric to assess paraphrase integration before students do the task is also helpful.

Step 3: Reflection and Feedback

Depending on the timeline for this activity, the instructor can also encourage students to reflect on the process in which they did this task. For example, the instructor may ask the students if they paraphrased the selected information first and then incorporated it into Jun's paper or if they did these two tasks simultaneously. S/he may also ask the students if they used any additional strategies that helped them with this task (e.g. highlighting information, taking notes, etc.).

The instructor can then ask representatives of groups to present their observations from this task, commenting on whether they successfully strengthened Jun's paper by using the information from the article. Students generally also like to address points raised during the reflection on the process of doing this task. If the class size is too large, the instructor can either choose volunteers or ask each group to select the incorporated paraphrase that they consider most effective.

Finally, it is advisable that the instructor allow time for questions and clarifications and also provides positive feedback on areas of successful integration of the paraphrase and encouragement and support in areas where the majority of the students experienced difficulty with this task. If the students struggled to successfully integrate the paraphrase, the instructor needs to diagnose the source of difficulty and plan a future instructional intervention. For example, if students failed to select relevant information from Walker's text, the instructor may need to focus on reading strategies in her upcoming lessons. If students fell short of sufficiently modifying sentences that surround the paraphrase, the instructor can address grammatical strategies that may be useful in paraphrasing (Keck, 2006) or in modifying sentences preceding or following the paraphrase.

Step 4: Application

Provided students were able to integrate the paraphrase in a paper during the supported classroom activity described above, they may be ready to do it on their own, in a more authentic task. If they previously wrote a paragraph or an essay on the same topic, the instructor could give each student a relevant article. Mirroring the steps of the in-class *Paraphrase Integration Task*, students could be asked to select the most important information to support points they are making in their writing, integrate this information, perhaps even self-evaluate their paraphrase integration using the assessment rubric in Appendix 3. Alternatively, in the subsequent class, they could once again engage in peer review.

III. Implementation

The *Paraphrase Integration Task* has been used and adapted with university L1 and L2 writers in several academic writing courses.

Students who succeed at this task generally choose to support a statement in Jun's essay about the popularity of US universities by reinforcing it with the statistics reporting the number of registered students at US universities during the 1997 and 1998 semesters as presented by Walker (2000). They paraphrase this statement concisely while staying true to the original content. Similarly, successful students tend to accompany this newly incorporated paraphrase with a modification of the preceding and following sentence(s) in order to achieve a more effective text flow.

The sentences listed as a–c are the new, student-produced paraphrases of the original sentence from Walker (2000:77): *The demographic composition of today's international students shows that of the 481,280 students enrolled during the 1997–98 academic year, 279,142 (58%) were male and 202,138 (42%) were female.* The bolded sentences are sentences modified by students in order to increase the cohesion of the overall text. The first and the last sentence come from Jun's essay.

Examples of Successfully Inserted Paraphrases

...Studying in a country different from one's native country has become particularly popular. For example, a lot of students from Europe, Asia, and Latin America now choose to study in the United States of America. **In fact, the United States is arguably the most popular English speaking country for pursuing higher education**.

a. According to Walker (2000), almost half a million international students chose to study at American universities.

b. To illustrate, almost half a million international students choose the US for their university studies during the academic year of 1997–1998 (Walker, 2000).

c. The popularity of the US as a favorite country for university studies is clear in statistics provided by Walker (2000). Walker gives an example of the number of students registered in the US universities during 1997–1998, claiming almost half a million students took advantage of the high quality of university studies in the US.

One of the reasons why the US universities are so popular is in the convenience. Students enjoy the variety of degrees offered by American universities, the diversity found in American academia, and the personal freedom they experience when living away from home....

First, students who produced the above paraphrases were able to sufficiently rephrase and attribute the original source, thus avoiding potential accusations of plagiarism. The pair who produced *Paraphrase a* may have slightly overgeneralized Walker's claim by not including the time period (academic year 1997–98) for which the statistics were originally given. *Paraphrase b*, produced by another partnership, includes both the number of international students enrolled and the year for which the statistics were given. A similar amount of factual information (number of students and time for which the statistics were relevant) is captured in *Paraphrase c*. However, the success of this paraphrase may be brought into question, given its interpretative manipulation of the original source. Because students who produced this paraphrase comment on the quality of education in the US, an issue not originally mentioned by the author, this paraphrase may not be considered a true or even an appropriate paraphrase of the original source.

Instances such as those in Paraphrase *c* lend themselves to rich classroom discussions of what it means to rephrase someone's words and the rephraser's responsibility to capture the intended meaning of the original writer. Because we use others' writing to advance our own rhetorical purposes, this issue is more nuanced than students initially think. The question surrounding the paraphrasing of the phrase "academic year 1997–1998" can also lead to a thoughtful discussion among students about what requires or does not require rephrasing or quotation marks. Finally, those student writers who approach reading and writing tasks critically often comment on the need to find a better source to support Jun's introduction. For example, some students have suggested that they would try to find statistics showing how many international students choose the US versus other English-speaking countries. They complain that Walker's article does not provide Jun with the most effective evidence for what Jun is saying. This observation, whether offered or elicited, provides a pedagogical opportunity for teaching novice writers about appropriate academic evidence for supporting their writing.

Examples of Less Successfully Inserted Paraphrases

Even less proficient students are generally able to identify the appropriate evidence and insert it into the corresponding part of Jun's introduction. However, these writers struggle with appropriately rephrasing and citing the original source (Walker's article) and/or with integrating the paraphrase effectively with the surrounding text of Jun's introduction. These problems can be seen in paraphrases *d–g* below.

> …Studying in a country different from one's native country has become particularly popular. For example, a lot of students from Europe, Asia, and Latin America now choose to study in the United States of America. In fact, studying in the United States is probably more popular than studying in any other English-speaking country. International students find it very convenient to study here.

d. The composition of international students shows that of 481,280 students enrolled during the 1997–98 academic year 279,142 were male and 202,138 were female.

e. This is clear because 481,280 international students (279,142 males and 202,138 females) studied in the US in 1997–1998 (Walker, 2000).

f. For example, according to Walker (2000), 221,389 study as undergraduate students and 206, 950 as graduate students.

g. These varieties include research, doctoral, baccalaureate, two-year, and different kinds of university programs.

They enjoy, the diversity found in American academia, and the personal freedom they experience when living away from home...

Writing teachers tend to view *Paraphrase d* as problematic in that it is a near-copy of Walker's original article. The pair that produced this paraphrase exclusively employed a deletion strategy in his/her effort to modify the original text. The new paraphrase leaves out the words *demographic* and *today's* as well as the percentages originally included in the parentheses. Additionally, the paraphrase is not attributed to the original source. Generally, writing teachers tend to view the inadequate citation strategy demonstrated in *Paraphrase d* as a developmental phenomenon in novice writers' texts, and professors writing in the disciplines such as science or engineering often accept (attributed) near copies as a legitimate citation strategy (Hyland, 1999). However, if a student relies on a citation strategy demonstrated in *Paraphrase d* and fails to attribute the information to the relevant source, s/he risks being accused of plagiarism. Therefore, should examples such as the one in *Paraphrase d* arise in this activity, instructors should consider addressing unattributed near copy as a problematic citation strategy.

Paraphrases e and *f* are inappropriate in that they overly focus on details outlined by Walker (2000), thus causing the new text to lack cohesiveness. *Paraphrase g* is an example of information which, though it is accurate in terms of rephrasing content, adds irrelevant detail in relation to the rest of Jun's text. Finally, it needs to be mentioned that students who perform less successfully at the *Paraphrase Integration Task* often fail to modify the adjacent sentences, thus severely weakening the cohesiveness of Jun's introductory paragraph.

Modifications

Instructors can modify this activity according to the level of student writers. In classes for more advanced writers, excerpts from several different sources can be chosen to increase the difficulty. In line with differentiated instruction, when working with mixed groups, instructors can provide only one excerpt to the struggling writers, but have additional excerpts available for the more advanced writers. When working solely with struggling academic writers, it is essential that the instructor first prepare students carefully for this task. This preparation should be done in at least two steps. First, the instructor can share a sample essay into which a paraphrase from another source has been incorporated in several different ways. The difference can lie in the amount of original content captured in the paraphrase or in the type of signal phrase used to indicate the paraphrase (e.g. a reporting verb or a phrase such as *according to*). Additionally, modeling of the process that the instructor expects student writers to follow is also necessary. It is particularly effective to have an overhead transparency or a PowerPoint slide with an excerpt from an essay and a handout containing the excerpt from an academic source. The instructor can then show students how s/he would do this task, thinking aloud throughout the process.

Finally, in this task, the focus is on paraphrase, given that students are required to rephrase relatively specific information from a particular source to support a specific point in Jun's writing. However, instructors can adapt this task for incorporating summaries instead of paraphrases of academic sources. Adapting the task effectively requires the instructor to obtain a well-written research paper in which multiple academic sources have been summarized. The instructor then omits the parts containing the summaries from the paper and gives this new version of the paper, together with the academic sources originally summarized in the paper, to students. The instructor then directs students to read the academic texts, summarize them, and incorporate them in the paper. As with the paraphrase task, the instructor should first model this practice for students. To further increase accessibility, the instructor can limit the number of sections deleted from the original paper. Alternatively, in mixed ability classrooms, the instructor can adapt the requirement by assigning a specific number of summaries for specific groups of students.

IV.   Reflections and Recommendations

The *Paraphrase Integration Task* described in this chapter offers teachers of academic writing a more authentic way of helping students understand source use in the context of academic assignments. It mirrors what highly proficient academic writers do when they write: select and organize information from different sources, paraphrase and qualify it, and integrate it into actual academic papers. Additionally, the task often leads to important classroom discussions about the role of source use in the Western academy as well as about the process of paraphrasing. Also, more of the problems surrounding paraphrasing come to light during class discussions when the instructor uses the *Paraphrase Integration Task* instead of relying solely on traditional paraphrase instruction in which isolated sentences are judged as appropriate or inappropriate rephrases.

Some may worry that the task described in this chapter may be controlling the process of paraphrase integration too much, thus making the transferability of these skills from the task to the writing of an actual academic paper difficult. I would argue, however, that not including a task in which teachers have close oversight of students' developing skills before expecting them to use these skills in the context of more extensive academic assignments is, in fact, what causes much of the confusion, frustration, and oftentimes failure for students. The *Paraphrase Integration Task* is discourse-based and calls for active involvement between writers and texts, thus providing students with engaging authentic practice necessary for mastery of citation in academic writing. Writing instructors of both L1 and L2 writers should find this activity valuable in their academic writing courses.

References

Angelil-Carter, Shelly (2000) *Stolen Language? Plagiarism in Writing.* Essex (UK): Pearson Education.

Austen, Jane (1813/2003) *Pride and Prejudice.* Tony Tanner (introduction). Vivien Jones (ed.) Penguin Classics. London: Penguin Books, Ltd.

Barks, Debbie and Patricia Watts (2001) Textual borrowing strategies for graduate-level ESL writers. In Diane Belcher and Alan Hirvela (eds.) *Linking Literacies: Perspectives on L2 Reading-Writing Connections* 246–267. Ann Arbor, Michigan: University of Michigan Press.

Bloch, Joel G. (2001) Plagiarism and the ESL student: From printed to electronic texts. In Diane Belcher and Alan Hirvela (eds.) *Linking Literacies: Perspectives on L2 Reading-Writing Connections* 209–228. Ann Arbor, Michigan: University of Michigan Press.

Bloch, Joel G. and Chi, Lan (1995) A Comparison of the Use of Citations in Chinese and English Discourse. In Diane Belcher and George Braine (eds.) *Academic Writing in a Second Language: Essays on Research and Pedagogy* 231–247. New York: Ablex.

Dudley-Evans, Tony (2002) The teaching of the academic essay: Is a genre-approach possible? In Ann M. Johns (ed.) *Genre in the Classroom: Multiple Perspectives* 225–235. Mahwah, New Jersey: Lawrence Erlbaum.

Howard, Rebecca Moore (1995) Plagiarisms, authorships, and the academic death penalty, *College English* 57(7): 788–806.

Hsu, Angela Yi-ping (2003) *Patterns of Plagiarism Behavior in the ESL Classroom and the Effectiveness of Instruction in Appropriate Use of Sources.* Unpublished Doctoral Dissertation, University of Illinois at Urbana-Champaign.

Hyland, Ken (1999) Academic attribution: citation and the construction of disciplinary knowledge. *Applied Linguistics* 20(3): 341–367.

Jones, Alan and Freeman, Terrence. E (2003) Imitation, copying, and the use of models: Report writing in an introductory physics course. *IEEE Transactions on Professional Communication* 46(3): 168–184.

Keck, Casey (2006) The use of paraphrase in summary writing: A comparison of L1 and L2 writers. *Journal of Second Language Writing* 15(4): 261–278.

Liu, Dilin (2005) Plagiarism in ESOL students: Is cultural conditioning truly the major culprit? *ELT Journal* 59(3): 234–241.

Pecorari, Diane (2003) Good and original: Plagiarism and patchwriting in academic second-language writing. *Journal of Second Language Writing* 12(4): 317–345.

Pecorari, Diane (2006) Visible and occluded citation features in postgraduate second-language writing. *English for Specific Purposes* 25(1): 4–29.

Pennycook, Alastair (1996) Borrowing others' words: Text, ownership, memory, and plagiarism. *TESOL Quarterly* 30(2): 201–230.

Shi, Ling (2004) Textual borrowing in second-language writing. *Written Communication* 21: 171–200.

Spack, Ruth (1997) The acquisition of academic literacy in a second language: A longitudinal case study. *Written Communication* 14: 3–62.

Swales, John M. and Feak, Christine B. (1994) *Academic Writing for Graduate Students: Essential Tasks and Skills.* Ann Arbor, Michigan: University of Michigan Press.

Tomaš, Zuzana (2006) Textual borrowing and source attribution in second language writers. Paper presented at the American Association for Applied Linguistics Conference. Montreal, Canada. 19 June 2006.

Tomaš, Zuzana and Rosenberg, Amie (2005) Rethinking paraphrasing skills. Paper presented at the TESOL Convention and Exhibition. San Antonio, Texas. 30 March 2005.

Walker, A. David (2000) The international student population: Past and present demographic   trends. *Journal of Instructional Psychology* 27: 77–79.

Wette, Rosemary (2008) Evaluating a unit on writing from sources. Paper presented at the TESOL Convention and Exhibition. New York City. 2 April 2008.

Whitaker, Elaine (1993) A pedagogy to address plagiarism. *College Composition and Communication* 44(4): 509–514.

Yamada, Kyoko (2003) What prevents ESL/EFL writers from avoiding plagiarism? Analyses of 10 North-American college websites. *System* 31(2): 247–258.

Appendix 1

<u>Directions:</u> Read the introduction of an ESL student's essay about the challenges facing the international students in the United States. Then read an excerpt from an article written by Walker (2000). Think about how you could use the information from Walker's article to reinforce what the ESL student, Jun, writes in his essay. Finally, insert a paraphrase from Walker's article in an appropriate place in Jun's introduction. Remember to include an in-text citation as well as include the reference to the original article at the bottom of the introduction.

Advantages and Disadvantages of Studying Abroad

By Jun, an ESL student

Unlike in the past, nowadays students around the world have endless choices for pursuing higher education. Studying in a country different from one's native country has become particularly popular. For example, a lot of students from Europe, Asia, and Latin America now choose to study in the United States of America. In fact, studying in the United States is probably more popular than studying in any other English speaking country. International students find it very convenient to study here. They enjoy the variety of degrees offered by American universities, the diversity found in American academia, and the personal freedom they experience when living away from home. However, even if international students enjoy numerous benefits of the American educational system, which allows them to achieve good grades, gain knowledge, accomplish goals, and further their abilities, they also have to deal with culture shock, cost of living, homesickness, and difficulty to make American friends.

Appendix 2

"The International Student Population: Past and Present Demographic Trends" by David A. Walker (*Journal of Instructional Psychology*, June 2000)

Present Demographic Trends of International Students

As the American system of higher education enters upon the 21st century, the enrollment of international students continues to grow. The demographic composition of today's international students shows that of the 481,280 students enrolled during the 1997–98 academic year, 279,142 (58%) were male and 202,138 (42%) were female. The majority of these international students were classified as either undergraduates (221,389 or 46%) or graduates (206,950 or 43%) (Davis 1998).

International students were enrolled in six institutional types: Research I & II, Doctoral I & II, Master's I & II, Baccalaureate Colleges I & II, two-year institutions, and "other" institutions. Research institutions enrolled the most international students at 197,325 or 41%. Master's institutions enrolled 91,443 international students or 19%. Two-year institutions enrolled 72,192 international students or 15%. Doctoral institutions enrolled 67,379 international students or 14%. "Other" institutions enrolled 28,877 international students or 6.0%. Finally, baccalaureate institutions enrolled the least amount of international students at 24,064 or 5.0%.

Appendix 3: Paraphrase Integration Assessment Rubric

TASK: *Rate the success of your partner's paraphrase integration using this rubric.*

	2	1	0	Points
Content	The paraphrase builds well on the content of the surrounding text and provides relevant evidence for the point that the writer is making.	The paraphrase partly builds on the content of the surroundind text and provides some evidence for the point that the writer is making.	The paraphrase does not build on the content of the surrounding text and does not provide relevant evidence for the point that the writer is making.	
Flow/ transitions	The paraphrase transitions well and does not interrupt the flow of the text. It is easy to follow the logic of the point that the writer is making.	The paraphrase transitions with minor difficulty, causing a small interruption in the flow of the text. However, it is possible to follow the logic of the point that the writers is making.	The paraphrase does not transition well and/or the flow of the text gets completely interrupted. It is difficult to follow the logic of the point that the writer is making.	
Vocabulary	The level of formality in the paraphrase is the same as the level in the surrounding text.	The level of formality in the paraphrase differs somewhat from the level in the surrounding text (e.g. the writer may have used one non-academic synonym while paraphrasing).	The level of formality in the paraphrase differs significantly from the level in the surrounding text.	
Grammar	The paraphrase is grammatically correct.	The paraphrase makes the surrounding text ungrammatical in a minor way.	The paraphrase makes the surrounding text grammatically incorrect.	

TOTAL POINTS   __ / 8

COMMENTS

10 Teaching Critique Writing: A Scaffolded Approach

Nahla Nola Bacha

I.   Background

The writing activity outlined in this chapter is motivated by the need to help students write a critique based on a reading selection, which is one of the requirements in an advanced university English composition course. The objective of the critique is to develop students' critical thinking (cognitive) skills in understanding, analyzing, and evaluating the information they read – skills which they can apply to their major courses and in their life-long learning.

The activity is inspired by the success stories in the research on writing for academic purposes (Johns, 2001; 2008; Jordan, 1997; Kroll, 2001) and draws on the pedagogical implications of the three genre schools of thought on writing, the New Rhetoric School (e.g. Devitt, Reiff, and Bawarshi, 2004; Russell, 1997), the English for Specific Purposes School (e.g. Bhatia, 1993; Paltridge, 2001; Swales, 1990), and Systemic Functional Linguistics or the Sydney School (e.g. Eggins, 2004; Feeze, 1998; Halliday, 1994;

Hasan, 1985; Martin, 1992; see Johns, 2008, on their implications for writing pedagogy).

Systemic Functional Linguistics has been found to be better tailored to inexperienced writers than the other two approaches. Martin (1992) points out that this genre approach provides rhetorical structures such as narration, exposition, and description that contribute to learning the types of writing needed in an academic community, writing such as research papers and laboratory reports. The Systemic Functional model offers teachers a valuable explicit learning process through "linked stages" guiding students while withdrawing support gradually in developing their texts. Feeze's (1998: 28) teaching/learning cycle, which draws on work in Systemic Functional Linguistics and Genre, focuses on five stages in: (1) building the context of the purpose, audience and message of the text; (2) modeling and deconstructing the text; (3) joint construction of the text; (4) independent construction of the text; and (5) linking related texts. Furthermore, based on pedagogic learning theories, Feeze's (1998) model gives a great deal of weight to collaboration among peers and teachers to raise awareness of different genres and scaffold the learning process (teacher-supported learning) (Hyland, 2006; 2007; 2008). Most importantly, the model is based on Vygotsky's theory of the "zone of proximal development," where learners are able, through scaffolded learning opportunities, to move from no knowledge to realizing their potential and gaining knowledge (Vygotsky, 1962; 1978).

The critique writing activity described in this chapter provides a valuable framework for second-language and other novice writers to produce a text type found difficult for many in their first or second year of study at the university. The aim of the writing task is for students of diverse cultural and linguistic backgrounds to understand a contemporary reading selection and to write a five-part essay (adapted from the model of Behrens and Rosen, 2005) in which they: summarize the author(s)' main ideas; in light of the author(s)' purpose and intended audience, assess how well these ideas are presented according to defined criteria; evaluate the author(s)' main idea(s) by agreeing and/or disagreeing with one or two ideas; and provide reasons and evidence for their opinion. Even in contexts where group work in the writing classroom is not common, as in the Lebanese university context, it is thought that more learning will occur if students share ideas and interact. Hence, for the writing activity described here, group work is a central feature.

The students are divided into groups of five. Each member of the group writes one of the five parts of the essay individually, and then as a group they exchange papers, discuss the ideas, and dialogue on the responses. Such dialoguing or negotiation of meanings, based on Muldoon's (1991) response model, has been found to be successful and adaptable to the language classroom. In this approach, the students have to justify their ideas, consider alternative responses, and reconsider their own opinions. This interaction helps them to better understand the text and become sensitive to other viewpoints, and thus possibly also reconsider their initial assessments and opinions of it. This experience develops their critical thinking abilities, raises their threshold of tolerance for other views, and influences their perceptions and attitudes in a positive way, raising cultural awareness as students interact with classmates from different backgrounds. Further discussion and follow-up with their teacher and with other class members during the in-class oral reports at the end of the assignment provides an opportunity for students to gain confidence in their writing skills as well as develop their own writer's voice.

The main purposes of the writing activity are summarized below:

1. To help in the development of critical thinking skills;
2. To raise cultural awareness through selected readings and interactions with peers;
3. To provide an opportunity to engage in negotiating meaning, giving opinions, and providing evidence for these and to interact with others in a meaningful context;

4. To help in developing students' writing skills through the process of brainstorming, drafting, revising, and editing with peers;
5. To raise awareness of the diversity of genres (text types);
6. To help empower students as independent writers.

II.   Description of Activity

This activity is designed mainly for first-year entering L1 Arabic students of English at university level but can be adapted to other second or foreign language learners or any novice writers in any university context. The activity takes four weeks of class time, preferably after summarizing and paraphrasing have been dealt with, though, in the activity below, summary writing is integrated into the five-part critique essay. The activity is carried out over three hours per week of in-class instruction as well as through work done out of class during the four-week period. The activity takes place in five stages according to an adaptation of Feeze's (1998) teaching/learning cycle as described below:

Stage 1 (Week 1): Setting the Context for Writing

This stage provides students some background on what a critique is, where to find critiques, the purpose of critiques, and the possible audiences of critiques.

Students are informed in the first hour through PowerPoint projections that a critique is one way to evaluate weaknesses and strengths of a "text," such as a critique of a film, play, or book in the media, or a critique in academic writing. They are shown that in academic writing, critiques are found, for example, in research papers in establishing whether the sources are useful and credible and in examinations to show an understanding of the course material by assessing, interpreting, and evaluating. They are also found in the workplace in business plans assessing cost-effective approaches, in policies where strategies are assessed for weakness, and in performance reviews of work units and employees.

Students are then asked to read at home an article assigned by the teacher that relates to their life, to encourage high engagement in the subject matter. For example, "Too Much of a Good Thing" by Greg Crister (in Behrens and Rosen, 2005: 484–487), on how children should be guided in their eating habits, is of interest to young students, many of whom try to control their weight. The passage is discussed the second hour in class in terms of the author's purpose, audience, main idea(s), and supporting evidence. A possible outline of key themes is made together in class using the overhead projector and transparencies. Students are divided into groups of two and asked to put their outlines on the transparencies. Blank transparencies and marking pens are made available to the groups, and one of the students from each group with the help of his/her partner outlines the passage by hand on the transparency. Where computers are available, students may create their outlines as a word page or PowerPoint slide. Each of the groups presents the outline to the class. This may take more than one class period, but the aim is for the partners to work together and share their work with the others. For homework, students are given a different short passage to outline for individual practice.

During the third hour in class, students work with one of the outlines as a class activity and summarize the passage together. Criteria of **Conciseness, Organization, Objectivity, Language and the Thesis** (referred to as COOLT – "cool tea") are focused on. The acronym makes it easy for the students to remember the criteria and gives a pleasant break where students discuss what type of tea each one prefers (especially if the passage is on tea or a type of drink!). Students are then requested to summarize the article they have read (in our case, the one by Crister) for homework. Details of COOLT criteria are given to the students to help with the summary as follows:

Conciseness: focus on main points;
Organization: include appropriate transitions and correct order of main ideas;
Objectivity: emphasize main ideas as in original passage with no opinions of your own;
Language: use correct standard language of your own;
Thesis: begin the summary with author name(s), title of passage, source, a reporting verb (e.g. *argues*) that shows the purpose of the passage, and then the author(s)' argument(s) or main ideas.

Stage 2 (Week 2): Modeling and Deconstructing a Text

This stage involves showing models of critiques and discussing how well the writer critiqued the reading selection. Exercises can be given in re-organizing the text correctly, writing unfinished paragraphs, and improving on others.

During the first hour, a "good" student sample critique (referred to as Text 1, Appendix A) of a past semester's student work is projected and the five parts of the critique reviewed and explained: *Introduction, Summary, Analysis (or Assessment), Personal Response*, and *Conclusion.* Unsatisfactory sample student critiques can also be projected.

Part 2, the Summary part of Text 1 (Appendix A, 2. Summary), is projected first and evaluated together as a class activity as to how well it includes the criteria of COOLT (The introduction is dealt with later; see below.). Focusing on the summary first helps students to understand the passage so they are better able to analyze it and give their opinions. Also, this shows students that the parts of real texts are not necessarily written in the order they appear in the final product. Five points are given for each part of the summary; the sample summary was given a grade of 22 out of a total grade of 25 points.

Students then discuss the projected analysis (3. Assessment) paragraph of Text 1 and are informed that in analyzing a reading selection, there are five criteria (see Behrens and Rosen, 2005) they could consider in judging to what extent the author is successful in presenting the ideas: (1) the accuracy of the information (determined by relevant and credible supporting sources); (2) the definition of key terms (determined by clear and explicit of relevant connotative and/or denotative meanings); (3) the significance or relevance of the information to the topic (determined whether information given is relevant and/or necessary); (4) the interpretation of the information (determined by whether facts, statistics, examples etc. are fairly explained and clarified); and (5) the logic of the argument (determined by attention to avoiding fallacies or faulty reasoning). A grade of 23 out of a total of 25 points was given to the sample assessment paragraph.

Students are told that in their own essays, they will choose any two of these five criteria based on preference and relevance. Choice of two criteria gives them the time to focus and amply develop the assessment paragraph. They are also told that they are to support their two chosen criteria with two illustrations for each of the criteria chosen and with reference to the given passage. In Text 1, the student writer focuses on (a) *Significance of information* and (b) *Definition of key terms,* discussing and illustrating the extent of their effectiveness from the text itself.

In the third hour, students consider the Introduction, in which three parts are included:

- the author(s)' thesis statement, which includes the reference to the passage (author, publication date, source) and the author(s)' main idea(s);
- background information, which could include biographical information on the author(s) showing credibility to write on the topic and/or some current event or controversy on the topic; and
- the student's thesis statement agreeing and/or disagreeing with the author(s)' argument(s) and the reasons (two are sufficient) for agreement and/or disagreement.

A grade of 13 out of a total of 15 points was given to the sample Introduction for Text 1.

Also, in the third hour, the Personal Response paragraph is modeled using a text selected from students' work done in a previous semester (e.g. Personal Response of Text 1, Appendix A). In the Personal Response paragraph, students are made aware that their thesis statements (placed last in the Introduction) should be restated at the beginning of the Personal Response paragraph. Then, they are to deal with the author(s)' argument and one of their proposed reasons for their agreement and/or disagreement by giving evidence from the selected passage and from two outside sources which they are to research. They then deal with the second reason, supplying supporting evidence which can be the same two outside sources used when dealing with their first reason. They are also instructed to avoid faulty reasoning.

The modeling/deconstructing continues in the third hour, and perhaps part of the fourth, on the Concluding paragraph (see 5. Conclusion, Appendix A). Students are told that their thesis statements (e.g. the last sentence in the Introduction and first sentence in the Personal Response of Text 1) are also to be restated as the first sentence in the Concluding paragraph followed by a general reflection on the analysis or assessment of the selected passage and then a final remark (compare 1. Introduction and 5. Conclusion, Text 1, in Appendix A). A grade of 9 out of a total of 10 points was given for the sample conclusion.

To supplement the textual modeling and critique, logical fallacies are discussed, and exercises are given for identifying faulty reasoning and how fallacies can be avoided. The model critique is then linked to other related texts or variations of the same text type, specifically, the model critique in the required textbook (Behrens and Rosen, 2005: 61–63), which has a different organization and focuses more on personal opinion. Other texts, such as expository, narrative, and descriptive texts, are compared to the critique in order to raise student awareness of different rhetorical modes, and they are asked to infer the purpose and the audience of each. The modeling stage is for the purpose of showing the students the whole critique, the content necessary in each part of a critique, and the organization that focuses on the student's thesis.

Stage 3 (Week 3): Joint Construction of a Text

This stage involves student groups or pairs working together to produce a critique. The teacher may work with the students in writing a critique together using PowerPoint and/or transparencies before they start their group work.

An example of the teacher constructing the Introduction and Personal Response paragraphs along with the students before the student wrote Text 1 in Appendix A is presented as Text 2 in Appendix B. This includes students brainstorming together with the teacher while the latter writes the text on the computer projection or transparency for all to see the writing process. For example, in Text 2, the framework and the three main requirements of the Introduction are constructed, some brainstorming on the author's arguments are noted, and the main sections of the Personal Response paragraph are written together. The *thesis* (choosing one of the author's main arguments from the brainstormed list), is decided and two *reasons* for agreeing with the author's argument are found, and then the paragraph is developed by focusing on one reason at a time and providing evidence.

Students are asked next to develop the second reason. In this way, teacher guidance is gradually reduced supporting the genre approach in scaffolding. Teachers may wish to use some humor to keep the students engaged. On the topic of obedience, the following reason was brainstormed: "Students disobeying their teachers in not completing homework is not a vice as sometimes students need more time or have parties to attend to." Of course, the students would have to support this reason for agreement in a logical way, which can stimulate interesting discussion in class so that students can see the relevance of the personal opinion paragraph to their own lives. The citations in the sample Personal Response paragraph of Appendix B are hypothetical, used only for purpose of illustration.

A grade of 20 out of a total of 25 points was given for the sample Personal Response paragraph. The grading is done together with the teacher. In this case, the students felt that the writer did not give enough support and hence 5 points were deducted on Text 1.

In the second or third hour and after the teacher has constructed all parts of the critique together with the students, students are divided into groups or pairs. A leader is elected in each group who coordinates the work, puts the final product together, and presents it to the class. Each group selects a different passage under one theme from the required text, or all focus on one passage assigned by the teacher. Each student chooses the part(s) of the critique – Introduction, Summary, Assessment, Personal Response, or Conclusion – s/he is interested in and writes that part of the critique at home. If groups contain 5 students, this is optimal for assigning the different parts as homework.

Students in the third hour distribute their critique parts to their group, which puts together the completed critique and revises the parts for a good fit. The group leader coordinates the discussion to improve the critique, especially focusing on the author(s)' thesis and the student's thesis in the Introduction, which will affect the other parts of the critique. The leader, with the help of the others in the group, writes up a final draft of the critique outside of class time.

The teacher supports and helps the students in constructing and revising their final product during office hours and/or by track changes feedback inserted by computer. Each group in the first hour of the fourth week presents the essay (using a projection and/or handouts) and discusses its effectiveness with the class as a whole while the teacher monitors the class interaction.

Stage 4 (Week 4): Independent Construction of a Text

In the final stage, the first hour of the fourth week is spent choosing a reading selection from the required textbook under the same theme on which the group work was done, allowing the critiques from the group work done to be used as possible sources for the Personal Response paragraph. The selection is briefly discussed as in Stages 1 and 2 above. Students are requested individually to write Summary and Assessment paragraphs for the next class session.

In the second hour, a few student's individually written summaries and assessment paragraphs are projected, leading to discussion as to any improvements needed. Students are then requested to write the Introduction, the Personal Response paragraph, and the Conclusion, and to use two outside sources to support their ideas in the Personal Response paragraph for homework.

The third hour is used to project sample Introductions, Personal Response paragraphs, and Concluding paragraphs and to discuss their effectiveness. Students then conference outside of class with the teacher (as well as their peers) individually on the critique they are writing themselves, paying attention to language. Students are also asked to upload the final draft of the critique on <www.turnitin.com> for an originality report. The purpose of this is for the students to monitor their own work, checking whether they have over-quoted or need to paraphrase copied material and then to resubmit if necessary. In this way, using the electronic originality report has a learning aspect to it rather than a punitive one; students become aware of any plagiarism and how to avoid it.

III.   Implementation

The students who underwent this activity were 30 L1 Arabic students, the majority of whom had French as their second language and about 10% of whom had English as their third language. In the pre-university system in Lebanon, students learn two additional languages besides their national language, Arabic. School subjects are not taught in the national language; only the Arabic language courses are. If they attend a school in which English is the medium of instruction, students are referred to as English-educated and have French as their third language; if French is the medium of instruction, they are referred to as French-educated and have English as their third language. This is because a foreign language other than the one used as a medium of instruction is required in all public (Government-sponsored) schools as part of the new National Curriculum implemented in the early 1990's and as part of the reconstruction process after the civil war of 1975–1990. Even before the new National Language Curriculum was implemented, privately sponsored schools whether by the French, British, or Americans – were already offering a foreign language or two, the second being German, Armenian, or some other language, in addition to the instructional language. French, British, and American missionaries have greatly influenced the educational system, including in bringing with them their languages. Thus, Lebanese University students generally have a rich multilingual background that may give them a good foundation for academic literacy.

One important addition to the new language curriculum is the focus on acquisition of higher order cognitive skills such as critical and cultural awareness which were not focused on in the traditional curriculum. In the latter curriculum, rote memorization and the audiolingual approach were prevalent. Today, it has become important at the university level to emphasize the skills of the new curriculum. Activities such as the present one then take on significance in fostering the development of cognitive skills. (For a review of the new educational language system and its objectives at the pre-university level in Lebanon see Shaaban and Ghaith, 1997).

The activity was carried out in one of the advanced English composition classes in the English as a Foreign Language (EFL) courses at one English-medium university in Lebanon. The students were in their first year of university study, with an average age of 19, and were following different majors at the university, which gave discussion opportunities from different perspectives. The 15-week (3 hours/week) course which the students were attending focuses on two major writing assignments, critique and argumentative essays.

The critique was given one month after classes began and after the students had written summaries and paraphrases of some readings from the textbook and of student-selected articles on current topics of interest from magazines and journals.

This activity has been used for two semesters in the same course, and the qualitative text results show that the students do much better on the final examination, which is a critique, than they did before this approach was introduced. Although rigorous experimentation has not been carried out to reliably assess improvement, an initial result from the essays themselves and the informal interviews with the students after the activity was completed reinforced its value and the students' positive learning experience.

The activity has since been modified to include the following elements:

1. Forming groups of two or three, as five was too large a group for efficient work;
2. Allowing more time for the individual critique and an extension of one week for student-teacher conferences, which greatly helps improve writing, especially for the average and lower-level students;
3. Assigning shorter reading selections to save time in the reading and understanding stage and give more time to focus on the writing process;
4. Giving more practice in writing critiques in the students' disciplines.

IV.   Reflections and Recommendations

The objectives of the activity were adequately met. However, empowering students to be independent writers is not an easy process, as any teacher can attest. The objectives can be viewed in both the short and long term. In the short term, the students were able to cope with the five-part critique essay. The most difficult part was the Personal Response paragraph, in which they needed to support their arguments and provide logical evidence for them. Further support was provided in the next argumentative essay assignment, where arguments and counterarguments and fallacy-free logical evidence would be dealt with. In the long term, students develop their writing skills and writer's voice as they apply what they have learned from these sorts of structured critiquing activities to writing in their own disciplines.

The value of the activity was realized when a handful of students stopped in my office one day and asked for some sample critiques that they said are needed for practice for their Graduate Record Examination (GRE), in which a critique was obligatory. I smiled and handed them some samples. Not only is critique important on such standardized examinations, but it is also of value in one's education and career, in both of which contexts critical thinking skills are necessary and sought after.

Aside from the work, some humor was created in the class during the implementation of this activity, when one of the students distributed green tea bags to the students during one of the summary writing sessions. This led to a discussion of what each group thought was the best tea and students bringing in articles on tea to support their point, which I thought was a good starting point for the process of critique writing.

This activity has been beneficial over two semesters and will be improved upon by considering the following recommendations:

1. To begin introducing the critique two weeks after the beginning of the semester to allow more time for drafting the critique in groups, presentations, and discussions.
2. To base group and individual critique writing on more interesting, recent, and controversial reading selections taken from magazines or articles and/or from readings in students' courses, such as political science, social science, literature, business, and physical science, in order to promote engagement in real-life issues and reading/writing across the curriculum.

3. To encourage researching material online and in the library for relevant supporting sources to include as background in the Introduction and Personal Response paragraphs.
4. To include other supporting sources such as interviews with credible authorities and surveys.
5. To use other than reading selections to critique, such as films, plays, art, music, and policies related to academic and professional communities.
6. To apply the critique process to real-life decision-making situations in discussions and simulations.

The critique activity is adaptable and could be used in any class in the students' course of study, professional career, or other real-life situations. Students are most of the time engaged in giving their reactions to almost everything, such as something they want to buy, some entertainment they want to be involved in or see, an important decision to make about their education, or a choice of a life-long partner. The best results for written critiques are obtained by taking students through the teaching/learning journey in stages – through discussions, dialogue, group and individual work, researching, and presentations. In this way, the application of students' critical skills can be realized in other contexts. After all, writing is a thinking process which helps students shape their ideas and communicate them to a wide audience of peers and colleagues in a variety of contexts. Engaging in critique writing through a sequenced genre-based teaching/learning approach can help towards that end.

References

Bhatia, Vijay J. (1993) *Analyzing Genre: Language Use in Professional Settings*. London: Longman.
Behrens, Laurence and Rosen, Leonard (2005) *Writing and Reading Across the Curriculum*. New York: Pearson.

Devitt, Amy, Reiff, Mary Joe and Bawarshi, Anis (2004) *Scenes of Writing: Strategies for Composing with Genres*. London: Longman.

Eggins, Susan (2004) An *Introduction to Systemic Functional Linguistics*. London: Continuum.

Feeze, Susan (1998) *Text-based Syllabus Design*. Sydney: Macquarie University.

Halliday, Michael A. K. (1994) *An Introduction to Functional Grammar* (2nd edition). London: Edward Arnold.

Hasan, Ruqaiya (1985) The structure of text. In Michael A. K. Halliday and Ruqaiya Hasan (eds.) *Language, Context, and Text* 52–69. Geelong, Victoria: Deakin University Press.

Hyland, Ken (2006) *English for Academic Purposes: An Advanced Resource Book*. London: Routledge.

Hyland, Ken (2007) Genre pedagogy: language, literacy and L2 writing instruction. *Journal of Second Language Writing* 16: 148–164.

Hyland, Ken (2008) Genre and academic writing in the disciplines. *Language Teaching* 41(4): 543–562.

Johns, Ann (2001) An interdisciplinary, interinstitutional, learning communities program: Student involvement and student success. In Ilona Leki (ed.) (2001) *Academic Writing Programs* 61–72. Alexandria, Virginia: TESOL.

Johns, Ann (2008) Genre awareness for the novice academic student: An ongoing quest. *Language Teaching* 41(2): 237–252.

Jordan, Robert (1997) *English for Academic Purposes*. Cambridge: Cambridge University Press.

Kroll, Barbara (2001) (ed.) *Exploring the Dynamics of Second Language Writing*. New York: Cambridge University Press.

Martin, James R. (1992) *English Text: System and Structure*. Amsterdam: John Benjamins.

Muldoon, Phyllis (1991) Citizenship as shared inquiry: Literature study and the democratic mind. *English Journal.* 80(7): 61–68.

Paltridge, Brian (2001) *Genre in the Language Learning Classroom*. Ann-Arbor, Michigan: University of Michigan Press.

Russell, David (1997) Rethinking genre in school and society: An activity theory analysis. *Written Communication* 14: 504–554.

Shaaban, Kassim and Ghaith, Ghazi (1997) An integrated approach to Foreign language learning in Lebanon. *Language, Culture and Curriculum* 10(3): 200–207.

Swales, John M. (1990) *Genre Analysis: English in Academic and Research Settings*. Cambridge: Cambridge University Press.

Vygotsky, Lev S. (1962) *Thought and Language*. Cambridge, Massachusetts: MIT Press.

Vygotsky, Lev S. (1978) *Mind in Society: The Development of Higher Psychological Processes*. (eds. Michael Cole, Vera John-Steiner, Sylvia Scribner and Ellen Souberman.) Cambridge, Massachusetts: Harvard University Press.

Appendix A – Text 1

Stage 2: Modeling and Deconstructing a Text
Student Sample Individual Five-Part Critique

1.   Introduction

In his article "Opinions and Social Pressure" (*Writing and Reading across the Curriculum*, 2008, pp. 351–357), Solomon E. Asch experimentally asserts that group(social) pressure strongly influences and alters individual judgment, primarily because of the conformity to the majority's (peers') unanimity, and secondly due to "the sheer weight of authority['s views]" and social prestige. Since social relationships and societal bonds are the pillar/base of most societies internationally, then people must naturally be alerted of the effects of these elements on their own judgment and self; who better than an eminent social psychologist such as Solomon E. Asch, pioneer in social psychology studies? Being the Director of the Institute for Cognitive Studies at Rutgers University and author of Social Psychology (Asch, 1952) that identified man as a "socially-situated" and "independent" being, Asch is knowledgeable and thus a reference in assessing the portion of one's personal perception(s) mainly shaped under the effect of peer pressure. Also, having witnessed Hitler's notorious power and rule, not to mention the societal discrimination and chaos of the times, he accordingly unveiled the very first social instrument disrupting or even shaping new convictions in individuals, Propaganda. (STOUT, 1998) .This discovery

Good author's thesis 4/5

Effective and relevant background 5/5

motivated Asch to methodically delve into our specific topic under study. Accordingly, **I agree with the author that individual convictions and perceptions are highly vulnerable to external parasites of interference and that one is stripped from his/her own intellectual and emotional powers because of conformity's ascendancy over consensus.** [*Highlighted parts are the theses.*]

Clear focused thesis 4/5

No need to insert the paragraphs and line numbers
C = 4 0 4 0 4 1 5 t 5 = 22/25

2.   Summary

Asch demonstrates the significant effect of social pressure on individual perceptions and on one's interpretations, first blaming the conformity-to-mass phenomenon and second censuring social prestige/authority. [*Student summarizes the main points.*]

3.   Assessment

The author presents significant information to the reader; however he fails to define clearly and thoroughly his key terms, mistakenly taking for granted that the reader must be familiar with.

Good attempt at topic sentence

Good 11/12.5

a) <u>Significance of information:</u>

Solomon Asch, with his experiment originally carried out in the 1950s and well-replicated since, highlights a key social phenomenon known today as "conformity". Hence, the information he presents under this subject matter is highly valued and very significant, especially nowadays: "conformity" is a concept grabbing the attention of societal leaders, politicians, law – implementers, and other influential figures, whose sole aim is to work for the benefit of the community. By devising new concepts and laws to ensure a decent and fair life for everyone, the focal heads of society expect us, citizens, to follow these established doctrines and ultimately "conform" and comply with them, for the sake of personal and civil benefit/safety. This is where Asch's experiment steps in to broaden our mind and advance our knowledge on how the compliance of a large portion of citizens to common codes of conduct could 'oblige' or entail all others/rebels/non-conformists to conform and obey; ultimately achieving through this psychological, peer-interaction the wellness of society. [*A second example is given by the student.*]

─────────────────────────── Good 12/12.5

b) *Definition of key terms:*

Being an educated reader who has encountered the general issue of social pressure and individual conformity in other texts throughout my years of education, I could more or less understand what is categorized as "social influences", "social forces" in this article, and what the author means when he mentions the terms "engineering of consent" , "consensus" and "conformity". However, when writing an article addressed to a large audience, most probably youth (naturally because the subjects of his experiment were mostly "young men") and any other efficient member of a community – in Asch's case here – the author is expected to concisely delineate all those 'technical-psychological social' terms constituting the core of his discussion, experiment , and hence article. This is something Asch failed to fully accomplish; for instance, "social influences" could be mistakenly taken by a reader as entailing a bunch of bad social habits commonly dominating any society, such as smoking, alcoholism, or even drugs; whereas the writer's true intentions here are to focus on the strong influence of intellectual societal elements/figures (fellow citizens, co-workers, peers, members of the same group..) in re-shaping and modifying one's personal convictions under the effect of majority's unanimity. [*A second example is given by the student.*]

Support your ideas with two sources e.g. Smith (2006) states that ……

20/25

4.   Personal Response

I agree with the author that individual convictions and perceptions are highly vulnerable to external parasites of interference and that one is stripped from his/her own intellectual and emotional powers because of conformity's ascendancy over consensus. Countless mundane events/activities mirror human vulnerability to the majority's decision/rule, decisions, perceptions, and behavior. Most commonly, observing any of the society's aristocratic, prestigious women, we can instantly see the high degree of resemblance amongst the majority of these ladies, whether in terms of their pompous lifestyle, luxurious possessions, high prestige, fancy invitations/balls… As a result of the above-mentioned, most of this class of people will end up taking unanimous social, intellectual or business decisions whose high degree of similarity is reflected in public. However, when one really thinks about it, no one woman has the same thoughts on techniques of bringing up her children nor on the style of favored jewelry (fancy and flagrant versus simple and discrete), or on her preferred profession/occupation/lifestyle. So, how come that a glance at the everyday activities of that community shows such coinciding action? Here is where Asch's "conformity concept" interferes, first proving that people uncritically submit to external manipulation by PRESTIGE so as not to be left out by the other prestigious members; and second, demonstrating the "…[coming of] consensus under the dominance of conformity…". [*The second point is illustrated.*]

5.   Conclusion

In conclusion, the author's views coincide with my very own, for individual convictions and perceptions are primarily modified by external parasites, and one is stripped from his/her own intellectual and emotional powers because independency is distorted by the ascendancy of conformity over consensus. Asch corroborates that the core social instrument with a striking effect on individual judgment and perception is the 'majority's unanimity', along with social prestige. This "group pressure" is capable of fully shaping one's convictions all over again until they coincide with the group's, even if it meant stripping the inborn personal senses and perceptions. Deviating now away from the article's chief arguments, I believe that one of Asch's strengths was mainly his detailed descriptions and step-by-step explanation of the conducted experiment. Even though he missed out on directly defining key terms of his paper, Asch did explain and demonstrate what he meant INDIRECTLY (i.e implied) by assessing this physical evidence obtained from a significant, valid, applicable and true-today experiment. Ultimately, Asch thrived in alerting his audience on the magnitude and criticality of

9 out of 10 Conclusion sums up your arguments and gives an good efficient overview of the critique.

social pressure/influence in their life; as well, he succeeds in arousing their awareness on the issue of preserving some of their own, independent views and beliefs within this commonly-encountered vicious circle of social interaction and pressure versus the individuals.

Check APA format for internet source

<u>Works cited</u> *[The way the student wrote them. A few of the comments made by the teacher appear to the side of the critique.]*

Place the authors' name and the site and the date retrieved and place a citation in the personal opinion paragraph. Same goes for the other two references below.

1. http://www.brynmawr.edu/aschcenter/about/solomon.htm
2. *Solomon Asch Is Dead at 88; A Leading Social Psychologist* / By David Sutton / (Thurs. February 1998) http://www.nytimes.com/1996/02/29/us/solomon-asch-is-dead-at-88-a-leading-w social-psychologist.html
3. "<u>Social Psychology</u>" (Asch, 1952)
   [The above text is written by a student and is kept as it was originally written.]

Appendix B - Text 2

Stage 3: Students and Teacher Jointly Constructing the Introduction and Personal Response

1.   Introduction

a. *First sentence in the introduction is the author(s)' thesis and should be similar to the following:*

   The author (*put in author name(s) in; put in title of article/ book, the publisher and the journal*) **argues** (*reporting verb indicating author purpose*) **that 'disobedience is not always a vice and obedience is not always a virtue.'**
   [*This author(s)' thesis is repeated or restated at the beginning of the summary but without noting the full reference of the source.*]

b. *The second part of the introduction is to provide some background.*

c. *The student's thesis indicating agreement and/or disagreement with the author(s)' argument(s) then follows.*

2.   Personal Response Paragraph Writing Process

a. *Directions on writing the author(s)' thesis*

   YOU will decide on the argument of the author and place your own reasons for your agreement and/or disagreement to one or two of the author's argument(s).which is placed at the end of the introductory paragraph, the beginning of the personal response and concluding paragraphs.

b. *Some brainstorming ideas on author(s)' argument(s)*

   Disobedience is not always a vice.
   Disobedience shows involvement and commitment.
   Disobedience sometimes means that the person is using his humanitarian conscience.
   Authority may sometimes be wrong

Disobedience to one principle may be obedience to another.

Obedience will be the end of mankind

c. *Practicing writing the Personal Response Paragraph*

I agree with the author's argument that 'disobedience is not always a vice' (author's argument) because one may be obeying (your first reason) his/her humanitarian conscience and the authority may sometimes be wrong (your second reason). First, the author implies that disobeying authority is not always right. That is, in some cases the authority may be making one to submit. Take for example the German case during WWWI when the leaders indoctrinated the people to follow and obey the first Reich. (More details here). In this case, is it 'correct' to have people murder others just to obey the leaders. No. There are, sometimes, according to the author, when our humanitarian conscience overrides that of the authority and we disobey. For example, Antigone disobeyed the King and buried her brother as she believed that he needed a burial. She is damned by her people for this act, but this does not necessarily make her 'wrong'. Another example is Joan of Arc who disobeyed the Church and fought against the English and helped the French. She was burned at the stake (e.g. Smith, 2003, p. 3) and today she is a martyr (Jones, 2009, pp. 34–78).

Another reason for agreeing with the author that disobedience is not always right is the fact that sometimes the authority may be wrong. [*Students continue the paragraph in pair work.*]

Part 3
Writing for Specific Contexts

11 Academic Discourse Community Mini-Ethnography

Dan Melzer

I.   Background

The literacy project described in this chapter connects to recent work in Composition Studies that focuses on the study of language as social discourse (e.g. Bartholomae, 1986; Bizzell, 1992; Gee, 1996), the importance of genre and genre systems to understanding the way language works (e.g. Bawarshi, 2003; Miller, 1994; Russell, 1997; Swales, 1990), and the role of discourse communities in shaping readers and writers (e.g. Bazerman, 1988; Prior 1998). Underlying all of these approaches is a view of language that sees writers and texts as socially constructed. Writers are shaped by prior texts, by the genre they are writing in, and by the discourse community they are writing for. Swales (1990) argues that the defining features of a discourse community are that it has a common goal, a forum available to all participants, shared conventions and genres, specialized terminology, and a mix of expert and novice participants in the community. Swales, Bazerman, Bizzell and other social constructivists argue that the primary goals of composition courses are to both introduce students to academic discourse communities and help students critically reflect on the ways that academic discourse communities connect and conflict with students' personal discourse communities and self-sponsored literacies.

The assumption behind the project described in this chapter is that working with academic discourses is the primary purpose of composition courses, and that one helpful way for students to become more confident and rhetorically aware academic readers and writers is for them to investigate academic discourse in the role of ethnographers. By placing students in the position of investigators, analyzing academic conventions, looking closely at academic texts, and interviewing members of an academic discourse community, this project helps "demystify" academic discourse. Since students present their findings and consider the ways in which the academic discourse community they investigated is similar to and different from the academic discourse communities their peers investigated, the project emphasizes the idea that there is no singular academic discourse community, but multiple communities and often conflicting versions of academic discourse, as Patricia Bizzell and Joseph Harris have argued (e.g. Bizzell, 1992; Harris, 1989).

The mini-ethnography project asks students to both understand the conventions of the academic discourse community they investigate as well as problem-pose and think critically about the nature of academic texts – especially as they connect to or come into conflict with the students' own personal discourse communities. This project could be part of a sequence of assignments that make this critical literacy approach even more explicit. For example, the mini-ethnography project might follow a personal literacy history narrative in which students reflect on significant moments in their histories as readers and writers; or students might first analyze a text from their personal discourse community and compare it to an academic text they analyze; or students might interview a professor about literacy expectations in the professor's field (see appendix for example prompts in this sequence).

The primary goals of the academic discourse community mini-ethnography are to have students:

- Practice rhetorical analysis of academic conventions and genres;
- Critically reflect on the nature of academic discourse;
- Explore similarities and differences among a variety of academic discourse communities; and
- Practice academic research methods such as textual analysis, interviews and surveys, observation, and thick description.

II.   Description of Activity

This mini-ethnography project is designed for a first-year or second-year composition course. Since it is a demanding assignment that requires some scaffolding, it would best be assigned late in the semester, possibly as a culminating project. The project fits best with a course that focuses on introducing students to academic discourse communities, or a course with a theme of language and community, or a course that takes a "composition as writing studies" approach where the focus of the class is researching reading and writing processes. Assignments leading up to the mini-ethnography might include a personal literacy history narrative, an analysis of a personal/home discourse community, a rhetorical analysis of an academic text, a comparison of an academic text to a text the student reads outside of school, or an interview with a professor about literacy expectations in his or her field.

Following is an assignment description of the mini-ethnography from my course syllabus:

Mini-Ethnography Assignment

Choose an academic discourse community and use ethnographic methods (observation, interviews, surveys, analysis of documents) to investigate the reading, writing, and researching conventions of the community. The community could be broad (for example, a department or sub-discipline within a department) or narrow (for example, a class or a discussion group). The community should be focused on scholarly pursuits, since one goal of the ethnography is to help you succeed in the discourse communities of college class-rooms. In a 5–7 page report, write up the results of your research using the ethnographies we've been studying in class as a model.

Purpose:
In this ethnography project you'll need to draw on all of the skills you've been practicing: collecting data, analyzing texts closely for their rhetorical features, interviewing and observing individuals and groups, analyzing and synthesizing materials from your research, and reporting the results of your analysis to an audience. This project will also involve your most in-depth study of a discourse community, since you'll be analyzing data you've collected from a variety of research methods and sources. Since you're going to do extensive research, choose a discourse community you're interested in finding more about. You might choose a department that you're thinking of majoring in, a specific discipline you're interested in (for example, electrical engineering or cultural anthropology), a club or discussion group you might join (for example, the College Democrats or a Women's Studies discussion group), etc.

There are a variety of questions you could explore in your academic discourse ethnography:
* What purposes do texts serve in the community?
* What kinds of texts does the community value?
* What research methods are used by the community?
* What specialized terms do community members use?
* What are some common genres used in the community, and what are the conventions of those genres?
* What kinds of personas do writers in the community take on?
* How is power/authority distributed in the community?

Audience:
For this project, pretend you're a social scientist reporting the results of your research to an academic audience who is not familiar with

the genres and conventions of the discourse community you're investigating. You'll need to provide your audience with example documents from the discourse community (for example, assignments, passages from representative texts, excerpts from written/ digital/visual genres), evidence from observation and interviews, and your own in-depth analysis. Your audience will be looking for your insights into the way the discourse community communicates, and they will expect you to organize your thoughts and report your findings clearly. You will report the results of your research in a ten minute presentation to the class, so your audience for the presentation is your peers.

Genre:

As you'll soon see in our class readings, there are a variety of ways you can organize an ethnography, but the important thing to keep in mind is to find a way to organize your results so that your audience will be able to understand your analysis. In some ethnographies the researcher is just an observer of the community, in some s/he participates to a limited degree, and in some s/he's a full participant. You'll need to decide to what level you'll participate in the community, but it's OK if you just want to be an observer. Even if you just observe the discourse community, the expectations of the genre of the ethnography are that the researcher collects a lot of data from a variety of sources: documents, interviews, surveys, repeated observation, etc.

Evaluation Criteria:

The depth of your research will be an important part of the way readers will evaluate the quality of your results. Readers will expect your observations to be repeated and systematic, and to persuade them of the value of your findings, you'll need to use evidence from a variety of research methods. The way you report the results of your research will also be important. You should present plenty of evidence of the ways the discourse community communicates and an in-depth and organized analysis of that evidence. Your final draft should be clean and clear – your audience won't trust your research and analysis if you don't carefully edit in order to communicate clearly to your readers.

This is a complex project, and it requires exposing students to model ethnographies, giving them time to collect and analyze data, and building in feedback from peers and the instructor during the writing process. This typically requires 6–8 weeks. Following are some suggested activities for each week of the project.

Week 1: Analyzing Model Ethnographies

Discuss model ethnographies in class, considering the purpose, conventions, research methods, style, and audience for the genre of the ethnography. Some examples of ethnographies focusing on academic literacies include Marilyn Sternglass' *Time to Know Them* (Sternglass, 1997), Lee Ann Caroll's *Rehearsing New Roles* (Caroll, 2002), and Anne Herrington and Marcia Curtis' *Persons in Process* (Herrington and Curtis, 2000). A useful activity is to have students create a list of criteria for what makes for an effective ethnography after looking at the model – a tool they can use during peer response in Weeks 5 and 6 and which you can use to assess their ethnographies. If the concept of discourse communities has not already been introduced, it's important to discuss the concept in class early in the project.

Week 2: Invention

Brainstorm ideas for discourse communities on campus that students might investigate. Once students narrow their focus, ask them to begin thinking about who they might observe, who they might interview or survey, what textual artifacts they might analyze, etc. One option is to have students write a brief proposal and get feedback from you and from the class. Ideally, students should begin scheduling interviews by the end of Week 2, so they can complete their research by the end of week four.

Weeks 3 and 4: Researching

Help guide students through their research processes by discussing interview and survey strategies, practicing textual analysis, asking students to share progress reports on their research, and discussing research methods from model ethnographies.

Weeks 5 and 6: Drafting and Revising

Students write up the results of their research and participate in peer response activities and one-on-one conferences with you. If students created a list of criteria for what makes for a good ethnography in Week 1, they can use this list during peer response and you can refer to it during one-on-one conferences.

Weeks 7 and 8: Presentations

Students present the results of their research to the class in ten-minute presentations. Students might use PowerPoint if an LCD projector is available. Students might also prepare a handout or a poster (if there is not enough class time for each student to give a presentation, another option is to have a poster session day). It's helpful to make students accountable in some way for responding to their peers' presentations, either by participating in the evaluation of the presentations or by writing brief responses. In order to emphasize the variety of academic discourse communities on campus, and the different writing expectations and ways of thinking in different academic discourse communities, a final activity that involves comparing and contrasting the results of individual students' research is helpful.

III. Implementation

I originally assigned this project in a first-year composition course at Colorado State University, during a semester when the curriculum was revised to focus on the study of discourse communities. I assigned it again, in a first-year composition course with the theme of academic literacies, at Florida State University. The project has also been assigned at California State University, Sacramento, where we have recently revised our sophomore composition course from a theme course to a writing-in-the-disciplines course.

The ethnography project is complex and demanding, and it works best as part of a curriculum that is focused on writing studies, academic literacies, or the study of discourse communities. In my own course and in other courses I've observed, instructors define "discourse community" early in the course, and use it as a key concept for each assignment. Often instructors begin with a personal literacy history narrative, or a narrative focused on students' secondary school literacy experiences, or (in a sophomore composition course) a literacy narrative focused on students' experiences with academic literacies across the curriculum. Instructors typically build up to the mini-ethnography with briefer assignments such as interviews with a professor about literacy expectations in their field, rhetorical analyses of college writing assignments, analyses of writing guidelines from across disciplines, analyses of pieces of academic discourse from students' general education or core curriculum classes, etc. In my own course, I typically begin with a literacy narrative. I then ask students to rhetorically analyze writing assignments and assigned readings from their classes. Next, I ask them to interview a professor in a major they are interested in and ask questions focused on literacy expectations. The sequence of assignments ends with the mini-ethnography and class presentations on the ethnographies.

In addition to the scaffolding I've described above, one of the keys to successful implementation of the mini-ethnography is providing the students model ethnographies and having them carefully analyze them. Most students are unfamiliar with the genre of the ethnography, and it's important for them to understand both the conventions and the purposes of ethnographic research. They need a sense of *why* ethnography is valuable as a research method and *why* you are asking them to use this research method to investigate an academic discourse community, in addition to the "how" of actually writing up their reports. Asking students to create a list of criteria for assessing their ethnographies, after they've looked at some models, is a useful strategy for getting them to invest in the project.

One thing that needs to be addressed in the implementation of the project is the issue of what kinds of communities students might investigate. Is a campus online gamers' club an academic discourse community? Is a fraternity or sorority an academic discourse community? These questions have sparked interesting discussions about the difficulties of defining discourse communities in an academic context, though an ethnography on a gamers club or a sorority may not be as useful to the students in their future careers in college classrooms as an ethnography of an academic department or a club that is focused on academic pursuits. There are certainly plenty of gray areas (Is an ethnography of the College Democrats acceptable as an investigation of a scholarly community?), and it is probably best to help students on a case-by-case basis. A useful dividing line is whether the discourse community's primary focus is academic or social.

It's important for students to choose a community they are truly interested in investigating. The most successful ethnographies have been from students who are exploring a major they are interested in, observing a class they will be taking the following semester, or investigating an academic club/group they are thinking of joining.

A common problem with the implementation of the mini-ethnography is the logistics of interviewing. Students too often wait until the last minute, and then give the person they wish to interview very little lead time. It's important that students find a focus for their ethnography by the end of Week 2, and arrange interviews so that they can be completed by the end of Week 4. Since students typically have not been asked to conduct interviews before, some discussion of interview strategies is necessary. The same is true for students conducting surveys. It's helpful to have students look at example surveys/questionnaires and bring drafts of their surveys to class for feedback and piloting.

A final note about implementation concerns the tensions between academic discourse communities and students' personal discourse communities. At California State University, Sacramento, we have a mix of first-generation working-class students, children of migrant workers, international students, Generation 1.5 students, and others. These students' experiences embody what Mary Louise Pratt refers to as the "contact zone" (Pratt, 1991), where discourses meet and often clash, in the context of asymmetrical power relations. Even at less diverse institutions, students might experience a sense of loss as they are "initiated" to the discourse communities of the academy. For example, students who value affective and personal modes of expression might feel alienated by much of the discourse of the natural and social sciences. In any investigation of academic discourses, I encourage students to take a stance of critical self-reflection. I want students to reflect on both the connections and the conflicts between their home language communities and their self-sponsored literacies and the academic discourse communities they are encountering. I want students to understand the conventions of the discourse community they investigate and also to reflect on who has the power to speak, what is allowed and not allowed to be spoken of, and ways that genres and conventions might both help and suppress writers. One way to enact a *contact-zone pedagogy* is to have students reflect on and rhetorically analyze both academic discourses and their own personal discourses, and to have them compare and contrast their self-sponsored writing, such as Facebook posts or emails or blogs, and the writing they are assigned in their college classes.

IV.   Reflections and Recommendations

The discourse community mini-ethnography is valuable on many levels. It gives students a concrete experience of the concept of discourse community, which is a key concept for any type of literacy. It helps them realize that there is no single academic language, and that each course of study and each department is its own discourse community. It helps them critically reflect on academic literacies in ways they might not have a chance to in other courses. It gives them practice with research methods they are likely to use in other courses: textual analysis, interviewing, surveying, observing, and looking for patterns in human behavior. It helps them think about the concept of genre and genre conventions. It asks them to practice organizing extended research reports and supporting and synthesizing their ideas. It connects to their own experiences, requiring them to investigate a community that is of special interest to them. It also gives students practice with oral literacy (*oracy*) skills and listening skills if they present their findings to the class.

There are situations, however, when this project would be unsuccessful. Since it requires scaffolding, the mini-ethnography should not simply be added to a course that doesn't focus on academic literacy and discourse communities. The project cannot be squeezed into just three or four weeks, and it cannot be successful if significant class time isn't devoted to the writing and researching process in the form of brainstorming, freewriting, presenting proposals, piloting surveys, peer response workshops, one-on-one conferences, and other matters. Students find this project challenging, but ultimately rewarding, if they receive enough scaffolding and feedback.

Because it focuses on academic literacy in general and not a particular theme, this mini-ethnography project can be used in a variety of contexts:

- As a culminating project in a first-year writing course whose focus is writing studies, academic literacies, discourse communities, or language and literacy;
- As a way to help students make the transition to writing in their majors in a second-year or advanced composition course;

- As a project for a course in a major that introduces students to writing in the major (for example, if the focus of the ethnography is narrowed to the major);
- As a project in a first-year seminar course to introduce students to writing expectations in general education or core curriculum courses (for example, if the focus of the ethnography is narrowed to those courses);
- As a way to introduce international students to American academic discourse conventions.

References

Bartholomae, David (1986) Inventing the university. *Journal of Basic Writing* 5(1): 4–23.

Bawarshi, Anis (2003) *Genre and the Invention of the Writer: Reconsidering the Place of Invention in Composition*. Logan: Utah State University Press.

Bazerman, Charles (1988) *Shaping Written Knowledge: The Genre and Activity of the Experimental Article in Science*. Madison: University of Wisconsin Press.

Bizzell, Patricia (1992) *Academic Discourse and Critical Consciousness. Pittsburgh: University of Pittsburgh Press*

Caroll, Lee Ann (2002) *Rehearsing New Roles: How College Students Develop as Writers*. Carbondale, Illinois: Southern Illinois University Press.

Gee, James P. (1996) *Social Linguistics and Literacies: Ideology in Discourses*. London: Taylor and Francis.

Harris, Joseph (1989) The idea of community in the study of writing. *College Composition and Communication* 40: 11–22.

Herrington, Anne and Curtis, Marcia (2000). *Persons in Process: Four Stories of Writing and Personal Development in College*. Urbana, Illinois: National Council of Teachers of English.

Miller, Carolyn R. (1994) Genre as social action. In Freedman, Aviva and Medway, Peter (eds.) *Genre and the New Rhetoric* 23–42. London: Taylor and Francis.

Pratt, Mary Louise (1991) Arts of the contact zone. *Profession* 91: 33–40.

Prior, Paul (1998) *Writing/Disciplinarity: A Sociohistoric Account of Literate Activity in the Academy.* Mahwah, New Jersey: Lawrence Erlbaum.

Russell, David (1997) Rethinking genre in school and society: An activity theory analysis. *Written Communication* 14: 504–554.

Sternglass, Marilyn (1997) *Time to Know Them: A Longitudinal Study of Writing and Learning at the College Level.* Mahwah, New Jersey: Lawrence Erlbaum.

Swales, John M. (1990) *Genre Analysis: English in Academic and Research Settings.* Cambridge: Cambridge University Press.

Appendix

Prompts for Assignments Preceding the Academic Discourse Community Mini-Ethnography

Personal Literacy History Narrative

Write a 4-6 page literacy history narrative describing the most significant moments in your writing history. You can focus on a specific time frame (for example, middle school or high school or your first year of college), specific teachers, family members who had an influence on your writing, specific books that affected you, etc. You can talk about struggles with writing, successes, or both.

Purpose:
The purpose of this literacy history narrative is to get you to reflect on your writing experiences, think about how those experiences shaped you as a writer, and think about how you've evolved over time as a writer. By writing a narrative of your literacy experiences, hopefully you'll be able to get a better understanding of where you've been as writer and where you're going. This is also a chance to tell your teacher and peers a little bit about your previous experiences with writing so they can respond to your writing more effectively.

Audience:
A literacy history narrative usually has two audiences: the writer and the readers who would be especially interested in the writer's history. For example, two well-known literacy narratives are Malcolm X's "A Homemade Education" and Richard Wright's "The Library Card." Both of these literacy narratives are by African American writers who are trying to confront and comprehend the racism they faced in their past. In one sense, then, Malcolm X and Richard Wright are writing to reflect on their own experiences. Malcolm X and Richard Wright are also writing to African American readers who may have had similar experiences. And both writers also have a broader audience of general, educated readers who need to be made more aware of the inequalities Malcolm X and Richard Wright faced. In your literacy narrative, you're writing to

yourself – to explore your own experiences – and also to your classmates and teacher, so they can understand where you're coming from and what good and bad experiences have shaped you as a writer.

Genre:

The literacy history narrative is a storytelling genre. Usually when we tell stories we're trying to make sense of our experiences to ourselves and also trying to relate those experiences to others. In the literacy history narrative, you're telling stories of your experiences writing. You can use descriptive language and details to get your experiences across to your readers, and you may even want to write scenes with dialogue. Your literacy history narrative can have a theme that helps organize it – for example, your favorite books or struggles with writing. You don't need to sound "academic" in a literacy narrative. This is your story, and it should be in a voice that feels right for what you want to say.

Evaluation Criteria:

Focus on choosing significant experiences and really making these experiences vivid for your readers. Your readers should be able to move smoothly from one experience to the next as they read your narrative, and they should also gain an understanding of how your literacy experiences shaped you as a writer. Your voice and style as a writer should help capture your readers' interest and also help them understand your point of view.

Personal and Academic Writing Rhetorical Analyses

In 4-6 pages, conduct a rhetorical analysis of one of the readings you've been assigned in your classes this semester, a rhetorical analysis of a text you've read outside of school, and a comparison of the two texts. In your analyses, consider the purpose, audience, persona, context, and genre of each of the two texts.

Purpose:

The purpose of this writing project is to get you thinking about the conventions of academic writing and to begin to make comparisons between the writing you do in school and the writing you do out of school. Another goal of this writing project is for you to practice rhetorical analysis skills that you can apply to any of the readings you're assigned in college. Understanding how to rhetorically analyze something you've been assigned to read will make you a better college reader and a better college writer.

Audience:

Think of your audience for this writing project as both you and your classroom peers and teacher. You are analyzing and comparing these assignments to inform your peers in class, to perform your analysis for the teacher, and to critically self-reflect on your own reading.

Genre:

You'll probably be asked to write a number of papers in college where you analyze essays, books, films, paintings, etc. Teachers will ask you to write these kinds of analysis papers to get you to read closely and carefully and to think deeply about what you're reading. A rhetorical analysis asks you to focus on rhetorical features like purpose, audience, persona, genre, and context.

Evaluation Criteria:

The most important aspects of this writing project are the depth and quality of your analyses and the way you compare the example of academic writing you've chosen to the example of writing from your own reading outside of school. Your analysis should be well organized and written in a clear and concise style.

Interview with a College Professor

Interview a college professor about expectations for reading, writing, and researching in a major you're interested in finding out more about. Record and transcribe the interview, and then write a 2-3 page reflection on what you learned from the interview. Give a brief presentation to the class summarizing your findings.

Purpose:

The purpose of this interview project is for you to get information about writing in a discipline directly from a teacher in that discipline at your school. If you choose a major that you're interested in, you can get a better sense of the expectations for reading and writing of your future major. Even if you're not sure what you might major in, this interview will give you insight into junior and senior-level writing expectations. You might ask questions about the kinds of reading the professor assigns, their idea of what good writing is in the major, the kind of research methods used in the discipline, common genres students are asked to write in, etc.

Audience:

Your audience for this interview is both yourself and your classmates. Your primary goal is learn something about reading, writing, and researching expectations in a major that you're interested in, but you'll also be telling your peers about what you discovered in a brief presentation. Transcribing the interview will help both you and your teacher see exactly what questions you asked and what the professor said in response to your questions. Reflecting on what you transcribed and summarizing your findings in a presentation to the class will help you explore the most important things you learned in the interview.

Genre:

The interview is a common genre in college and beyond. Interviews are especially prevalent in the social sciences, since they are an important research method for qualitative studies. Interviews give social scientists a chance to ask focused questions and hear directly from the subjects they're studying. One convention of the genre of the interview is the interviewer's responsibility to accurately record and transcribe what the interviewee said. Since an interview is a direct transcription of someone's words, it's important not to just write down "the gist" of what someone said, but to make sure you have a person's exact words.

Evaluation Criteria:

Your peers and your teacher will be looking for you to design thoughtful, focused questions and to accurately transcribe what the professor has said and give a concise summary of your major findings in your presentation. You should also show in your reflection that you have carefully read over your transcription and thought about what you learned about reading, writing, and researching in the professor's discipline.

12 Using Writing Across the Curriculum Exercises to Teach Critical Thinking and Writing

Robert Smart, Suzanne Hudd, and Andrew Delohery

I.   Background

A Philosophy of Writing Across the Curriculum and Writing to Learn

In the writing workshops offered to Quinnipiac University faculty, the Writing Across Curriculum committee's pitch is that incorporating informal/ungraded writing which is keyed to specific thinking tasks in a course will not only improve students' thinking skills, but will also prepare them to do a better job in formal written assignments. In those first meetings with sometimes skeptical faculty, we articulate the thinking/writing connection behind our WAC pedagogy in a clear and practical way, as we have found that experiential approach more enticing than historical or theoretical introductions to Writing Across the Curriculum. "Practical" in this context refers to portability: For example, can the Biology teacher see in the array of exercises provided by the WAC committee something to promote clear thinking in the science classroom, at the same time as the Sociology teacher finds something to advance course objectives? At this broad buy-in level, the most portable tools are the informal writing assignments, "writing-to-learn" assignments, or (more familiarly) WTLs.

These are not new concepts. From its beginning in the 1970s, the WAC movement has been associated with informal writing as a tool to promote better thinking and writing, based mostly on the pioneering work of James Britton in the United Kingdom and Janet Emig in the United States. Every decade since the late 1970s, when Janet Emig published her groundbreaking study of informal writing, "Writing as a mode of learning" (Emig, 1977), has seen challenges to claims about the efficacy of writing to learn. This skepticism about writing-to-learn pedagogies has been countered by studies that show a powerful linkage between informal WTLs and student learning (Humes, 1983), especially for disciplines in which WTL work replaces more traditional student practices such as notetaking and highlighting (Newell and Winograd, 1989). One of the most successful texts advocating a WAC approach to improving writing that includes WTLs is John Bean's *Engaging Ideas* (Bean, 2001), which promotes the use of twenty-five informal, exploratory writing activities, each of which comes with an estimate of class time that the activity would require, along with groupings such as in-class writing (which require the least time), journals, reading journals or reading logs, creativity exercises and informal tasks for practicing thesis writing (which tend to be the most time-intensive exercises). In Bean's (2001: 118) estimation, the "payoff of exploratory writing is students' enhanced preparation for class, richer class discussions, and better final product writing." In our adoption of a WTL-based WAC program, we note three uses for ungraded low-stakes writing that is tied very directly to classroom learning outcomes:[1]

1. To promote sharper, more thoughtful class discussion;
2. To facilitate student understanding and retention of course material (by using exercises like end-of-class summaries and prioritized lists of lecture materials); and

3. To model critical thinking, especially when tied to longer, formal assignments, using informal writing to help less well-prepared students understand the specific kinds of thinking tasks that longer writing assignments assume.

As we reflect over the process that has emerged from our WAC workshops, we see the validity of Bean's claims for faculty-appropriate WTL pedagogy. Faculty prepare their students for class with directed prompts relevant to an upcoming writing assignment completed prior to class. Having considered the prompt before class, students are ready for a deeper level of engagement, manifested through another prompt in class. Working alone or in groups, students consider the second prompt, informed by their thinking about the first prompt. Ultimately, the result will be better formal writing, working on the assumption that doing the first two automatically yields a better written product. While Christopher Thaiss is correct in suggesting that the use of writing-to-learn within WAC "varies from school to school, teacher to teacher, class to class, assignment to assignment, even from thought to thought within a teacher's response to a group of papers or to a single paper" (Thaiss, 2001: 303), our emphasis at Quinnipiac University has been on focused use of WTLs, with frequent linkages to learning how to think like a major in a specific discipline when completing a formal assignment. This approach has yielded some powerful and profound work from faculty in various disciplines across the undergraduate schools. The WAC workshops themselves are framed around a critical thinking/writing model we have developed from research and experimentation to discover what would improve student thinking and writing most effectively and efficiently. This model, which we call *Concentric Thinking*, will be described before presenting an application of the model that emerged from one of our workshops.

Concentric Thinking

Evidence from cognitive psychologists and critical thinking specialists (especially in medical writing contexts[2]) suggests that the gateway task for any critical thinking exercise is *prioritization*, the ability to see the difference between the most important and the least important elements of a problem. Students who cannot separate the most important details of a problem from the less important details generally cannot do any critical thinking as commonly defined. Basic WTLs framed around prioritization have thus become the first strategy we offer in any introductory WAC workshop, essentially because we can better track the connection between the initial ungraded exercise and the final graded paper. Undirected freewriting may improve thinking and formal writing, but it might not be easy to show that an unguided five-minute writing task led directly or indirectly to a paper on, for instance, the influence of intersex births on gender reconstruction. In fact, carefully considered WTL prompts offer faculty a unique way to direct student thinking while at the same time providing an opportunity for constructive discovery. Additionally, we believe that offering undirected free-writing to a group of skeptical faculty would invite unnecessary resistance in a process that already has plenty of resistance points built into it.

To respond to demands that the thinking/learning/writing nexus be open to more useful measurements of success, we have developed a model of critical thinking that builds on a hierarchy of small, linked cognitive tasks that could be used quickly and effectively in a class to promote better thinking and learning, and which also can lead directly to the assignment prompts that we teach faculty to craft. The basic idea is that if you teach students to manipulate for themselves the cognitive tasks that we most desire from them, then crafting the assignment prompts around these same processes should accomplish three things:

1. It will make expectations of the students clear and specific;

2. It will make the prompts crafted for assignments more useful and accurate;
3. The analysis and arguments of the finished assignments will be more thoughtful and effective.

We called this critical thinking model "Concentric Thinking," and created a hierarchy around three linked tasks: prioritization, translation, and making analogies (PTA).

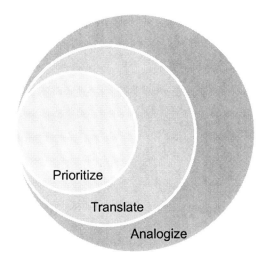

Figure 1: Concentric Thinking Model

Our model suggests that students must be able to *prioritize* material from their reading and discussions – including being able to explain the logic for the order of priority they have chosen – before they can *translate* difficult passages into their own words. Additionally, they must be able to both prioritize and translate in order to say that one issue, situation, or problem is like another, i.e. to draw analogies (*analogize*). For the WAC program at Quinnipiac University, this critical thinking model of Prioritize-Translate-Analogize (PTA) has become the bedrock for all of the writing workshops and consultations we have done across the university since 2001.[3]

II. Description of Activities

Teaching Concentric Thinking to Students Through Writing-to-Learn

Informal writing serves as the bedrock for the development of PTA skills during the course of the semester. The strategy we present here for integrating writing and thinking was implemented in an upper level Sociology class. Throughout the semester, students are required to complete writing-to-learn questions at the beginning of each class. This informal writing is designed to move the students through a series of critical thinking tasks:

1. To *prioritize* (e.g. pick the most important sentence in last night's reading and say why);
2. To *translate* (e.g. did competition or cooperation play a greater role in the reading last night, and say why);
3. To *analogize* (e.g. compare two readings, or describe a personal situation which then, in class, is contrasted with experiences in a reading).

As the students refine their thinking skills through these informal writing tasks in this Sociology class, they are required to apply these same skills in other assignments in the course: a formal paper that describes legislation pertaining to a social stratification issue; an opinion paper about a social issue; a final exam, which contrasts their opinion with "the facts" as they have been presented in the course materials; and a community experience that enables students to witness course concepts in the "real world" and that culminates in an oral presentation.

Student responses to the writing-to-learn questions are sometimes used to generate class discussion. In addition, the informal writing can provide students with an opportunity to clarify their thinking in relation to a reading that they completed overnight, to connect the current day's theme with work that was previously completed, or to encourage students to revisit their thinking on answers to prompts they previously provided. The students' written responses need not be discussed, however. They can also be used to encourage private reflection on personal issues that are applied to course concepts. For example, a prompt such as "Describe your greatest failure and why/how it happened" is intended to put students in touch with their own feelings of failure and enhance their sense of empathy for individuals on welfare. This prepares them to understand better a content for which many of them have no context and only stereotypical ideas.

The WTL assignments are compiled in a notebook that the students are required to bring with them to class throughout the semester. The notebook is collected once during the middle of the semester and instructor feedback is provided but the responses are not graded. Instead, the feedback offers suggestions for developing critical thinking skills (e.g., "Have you considered..." or "Are there other possible interpretations of...").

During one of the final class sessions, with all of their previous writing in hand, the students are required to evaluate their own writing and thinking as expressed in the WTL exercises using a series of guided prompts (see below). The responses to these questions, in conjunction with the informal journal writing they have completed all semester, facilitate a more complete evaluation of students' learning experiences in the class. The informal writing, along with the students' subjective assessments of what they have written provides documentation of the deeper thinking that the course readings and reflections are designed to foster. The grade for this informal written work is based on both the depth of the students' responses as well as the frequency with which they have responded. Thus, the students' collected writing serves as a measurement of course attendance, both cognitively and physically. It becomes the means for assessing class participation, as well as engagement with class materials.

Journal Exercise
To be Completed in Journals as a Final Writing Exercise

After journaling for nearly the entire semester about the issues and implications inherent in the readings we have done, I want you to take a few minutes to consolidate and revisit your work before you hand it in to me for a grade. This recursive exercise is called "interrogating the text," since you'll be asked to review something that you now know fairly well and then ask broader, connection questions of the writing. The result is that you'll understand the work you did more deeply. This will take about 30 minutes.

Step One: Look back at your responses to the questions I've been asking. Circle the strongest response. Write "Strong" next to it. In a sentence or two, BRIEFLY describe what makes this entry the strongest.

Step Two: Circle the response that was the hardest for you to answer? Write "Difficult" next to it. Again, in a sentence or two, say why you think it was the hardest question to answer.

Step Three: Circle the answer that you feel does the best job of demonstrating your values and beliefs in a general way – attitudes and beliefs that you have brought to your study of stratification this semester. Label this response "Attitudes" and briefly describe what these attitudes are and how they have affected your ability to understand what we have been studying.

Step Four: Look at the responses from the first couple of weeks in the semester and compare them to your most recent responses. Have your responses changed over the semester? Write a short paragraph that describes any changes you see in yourself, or in your ability to understand what we are learning about in this class? Is there something you understand or think about differently than you did at the beginning of this semester? What and why? If not, why don't you think so?

Step Five: Describe your reaction to doing these writings this past semester: (1) Has the writing you have done here affected your thinking about social class? (2) Has the writing affected your understanding of social class? (3) Has the writing affected your behavior in any way?

Teaching Concentric Thinking in a WAC Workshop: The Frame Paragraph

As with the Social Stratification class, when we teach concentric thinking in a WAC workshop, we require the participants to write first, in advance of any discussion of the model and its potential for teaching better thinking and writing skills. Typically, in a workshop designed to introduce this critical thinking/learning/writing model to faculty for the first time, we ask the participants to read a short text – a short story, a provocative article from the news, a piece of scientific analysis – and tell them to underline the most important line or phrase in the piece and then explain why they chose the one they did as the most important. The explanation is key here: it's in the written record of thinking that the recursive and reflective power of this process is exercised.

After a brief period of sharing responses, one important fact becomes clear in the workshop room: there is no "wrong" answer to the question(s). The major criterion for judging every response is its ability to reflect the writer's thinking process, and that in turn is governed by the specificity and length of the explanation for why a particular line or phrase seems to be the most important one. Since we tend to prioritize according to discipline or training background, this technique is especially applicable to writing-in-the-discipline (WID) contexts. Once the sharing is done, we usually introduce a second short text, something none of the participants has seen. This second piece is indirectly connected or relatable to the original reading, and we ask participants to comment on the first text using the second text as the lens. The fact that no one has seen these texts helps us "decenter" the participants so that their experience will follow that of a student coming new to the class and/or to the material.

One crucial part of this process – *thematic triangulation* (see below) – operates in the selection of texts, as a way to create op-portunities for linking texts thematically without dictating any single outcome. In practice, we almost never get identical choices and explanations; in fact, in the sharing sections of the workshop, the rich potential for triangulating the specific texts becomes clear, and participants walk away convinced (rightly) that there is no specific "correct" or "desired" answer to the triangulation questions. Again, the value of the exercise is derived from the explanations that faculty write about, not the particular choice of lines, words or phrases. The explanations capture and reveal on the page how faculty (and students) think.

After these two writing phases of the workshop are complete and participants have some confidence in their ability to link unrelated texts by constructing new knowledge, we push them into the "payoff strategy" for the two-hour workshop: *the frame paragraph.* Here is the direction that we give faculty:

> The frame paragraph is a composing tool first described by John C. Bean in Engaging Ideas (Bean, 2001: 115–116) at the end of a long list of short, ungraded writing assignments. This particular assignment is intended to focus and organize student "thinking about content," and so its logical place in the writing-to-learn process is in the gap between thinking on paper about content (WTLs) and crafting an argument that is grounded in understanding (constructed knowledge) about content. It is, we propose, the critical link between WTL and WID, writing in the disciplines.

Specifically, the frame paragraph – slightly revised for our purposes at Quinnipiac – moves constructed knowledge into something longer and more complicated, like a paper or research project. Here is Bean's extended description of the tool:

> Frame assignments are analogous to those old dance lessons for which the instructor pasted footsteps on the floor. A frame assignment provides a topic sentence and an organizational frame that students have to flesh out with appropriate generalizations and supporting data. Students have to dance their way through the paragraph, but the assignment shows them where to put their feet. Often the frame is provided by an opening topic sentence, along with the major transition words in the paragraph. Students report

that such assignments help them learn a lot about organizational strategies. More importantly, they see how structure can stimulate invention in that they must generate ideas and arguments to fill the open slots in the frame. (Bean, 2001: 126)

Our take on the frame paragraph anchors the exercise in thematic triangulation: faculty must read a third new text and then recalibrate their synthesis of the first two readings in light of this new reading. We tend to choose something contemplative, with a broad scope for this final reading – for example, a newspaper op-ed piece, or a provocative short meditation on the broader implications of the triangulation exercise. Our directions to faculty help them walk through the frame exercise:

In the opening writing exercise, you (the workshop audience) worked with two short pieces that would at first consideration seem to have nothing overtly to do with each other. Certainly, neither author(s) worked with any attributable knowledge of the other's work. An application of the second reading to the opening text created a connection – you exercised critical thinking and, cognitive scientists would suggest, you created knowledge.

We ask you to work (alone first, then with a partner) to craft an example of Bean's frame paragraph. Begin alone by reading a third short text. After you have read the piece through, underline what you consider to be the most important passage and explain in your journal notebook exactly why you believe this passage to be the most important.

Now pair up: you and your partner will craft a frame paragraph based on the triangulation between Reading #1, #2 and #3. <u>Begin by crafting an idea sentence</u> that links all three readings, and <u>then list the parts of the three texts</u> that you could use in support of the idea sentence. In a final sentence, reiterate the main idea of the passage you have written in different language than the opening sentence. Then write the whole thing in your journal notebook as a paragraph. What you now have is a hypothesis/outline for an entire paper.

Thus, in just shy of two hours, the participants have worked with three new texts, constructed a number of critical judgments about those texts that were anchored in the readings, and then framed a longer formal writing assignment that could easily be developed into a workable draft. This is the point of the WAC workshops, to provide faculty with tools that foster clearer thinking about new texts, as well as to offer a number of composing strategies based on those elements that would lead logically and meaningfully to longer written drafts. As some of the material in the conclusion of this essay suggests, these parts of the WAC story on our campus transcend schools and disciplines, and speak powerfully to both faculty and their students about how to learn in personal and powerful ways.

The faculty who leave these workshops are prepared with several skills that they can apply to the work they assign in their classes. First, and perhaps most importantly, they have experienced the student role: they have been put in the position of making sense of a reading that is new to them and then integrating that reading in the context of other related materials. This role reversal is part of the "decentering" process we mentioned earlier. In addition, they have been asked to reflect on the reading, and to record their reflections in writing both to enhance their awareness of the ways in which they are making sense of the material, as well as to provide a basis for exploring alternate interpretations of the material with others (in the case of the workshop, fellow faculty members). Participating in this exercise thus provides faculty with an appreciation for the trajectory of student understanding. It reminds them not to make false assumptions about the understanding of class content by putting them in the student role.

IV.   Implementation

In order to apply the concentric thinking approach presented here, the informal written work that students do must be situated within a broader understanding of the class goals. A first step is to assess the role of the course in relation to other aspects of the student's curriculum. The instructor will need to consider, for example, whether the class is part of the student's core curriculum, a required course in the major, or an elective course. In this context, the role of the informal writing can be better structured to produce the kinds of thinking skills that will foster appropriate learning experiences.

The Social Stratification course example we present here is the second required course for Sociology majors (after Introductory Sociology). An important course objective in Social Stratification is to teach students to observe the roles that both individual choices and social structural forces play in perpetuating inequalities of race, class, gender, and income groups. In addition to sensitizing students to the role of structure in individual lives, this course serves as the "gateway" course for disciplinary writing in Sociology. For many of the students, this is their first experience in the discipline writing a formal paper that requires the use of references to build an argument. With these goals in mind, the writing-to-learn prompts are developed to help students see the role of social forces in what they might otherwise assert to be individual choices (e.g. attending college), and to encourage them to react to readings and triangulate readings in a way that enables them to "play with" the skill of using their assigned readings to either support or refute their personal beliefs. In essence, these are the same skills students will use again as they build an argument in a formal reference paper. As you adapt this exercise to your own class, you will need to carefully consider each WTL at the skill level (e.g. what is the "thinking goal" that I seek to foster through the writing assigned in this prompt?).

Successful "graduates" of Social Stratification must understand social theories and terminologies that will help them to critique our system of social stratification (e.g. Tönnies' (1940) opposing principles of *Gemeinschaft* (a social system based on solidarity and communal values) and *Gesellschaft* (a social system based on impersonal bonds and specialized relationships). Thus, some of the writing-to-learn prompts are intended to foster an understanding of core concepts as covered during class and in the outside readings. These informal writings allow students to work through their thinking, and they enable the instructor to observe and guide student thinking in a very tangible way.

In sum, the abilities to prioritize, translate, and analogize are essentially "practiced" during the in-class written work and these informal writings also become the vehicle for engaging students in class discussions. When the informal writing that students do is structured with an appreciation for class goals, it can be used to foster thinking skills that underlie a student's ability to tackle the other formal graded assignments for the class. These earlier pieces of writing also enable the instructor to provide ongoing feedback, correct faulty logic and adjust students' thinking as they learn throughout the course. In essence, the WTLs enable the instructor to serve as a "thinking coach" throughout the course of the semester. As an added benefit, they can offer valuable opportunities for the instructor to restructure the class content so that it is suited to the needs and capabilities of the students while the class is ongoing.

IV.   Reflections and Recommendations

Concentric Thinking Across the Curriculum

Since we have begun working in these ways on campus, both students and faculty have reported favorably on the impact of the pedagogy on classroom discussions and written work. Two years ago, for instance, in the final report for our first grant from the Davis Educational Foundation, we surveyed more than 300 faculty about what they considered the key benefits of their WAC training and its application to their classes. Faculty from all of the schools and disciplines on campus, full-time and part-time, were part of the study. The percentage of faculty who either "strongly agree" or "agree" that students experience great benefits from their exposure to WAC is high across a number of different measures:

92.6% feel that the writing assignments improve students' thought
processes in a general way;

89.3% indicate that the written work helped them to better understand the ways students learn;

84.3% state that their students understand course topics better
because of the writing they assign;

78.5% believe their students got more out of the class because of
the writing they assigned.

In an open-ended question on our survey, faculty were asked to
describe the ways in which the work they assign in their classes
is different as compared to the ways in which they assigned work
prior to the WAC workshop, or to describe why they had chosen not
to make changes in their assignments if there had been none. Very
few faculty (n=3) report having made no changes, and in fact, the
vast majority report changes that go beyond the mere assignment of
written work. A large number of faculty, for example, indicate that
they have begun to use in-class time for writing-to-learn exercises.
Faculty also use WTL exercises for a variety of purposes and with
varying levels of frequency. On a more fundamental level, some
faculty report that their use of WTLs led to a fundamental change
in the way that they teach: "…[a] reversal of the way I construct
my syllabus. Previously, I considered evaluation at the end of my
syllabus. I will now consider evaluation first and construct my
WTLs and formal essays in a sequential learning process."

The faculty reported a wide range of goals and outcomes that
they associate with writing-to-learn. Some use WTL for the purpose
of "…encouraging the students to do more critical thinking rather
than just doing the minimal amount of work." Others state that their
WTL assignments are intended to "…make the students more active
in their learning," and "…to ensure the students are engaged." Some
respondents report the use of WTL strategies to "note important elements of the discussion," and as a "front-loading [strategy] to have
students come to class prepared to discuss a topic." Many faculty
refer to the development of non-graded, or "low stakes" written
assignments as one of the more important curricular changes they

have initiated as a result of their participation in the workshops. Interestingly, they also report that thoughtfully examining the use of writing in their course has enabled them to link the assignments that they give by "…bridging the gap between reading and writing" and the assignment of writing-to-learn reminds them not to "…take for granted that students are learning from their assignments."

What we have learned from these workshops and the collaborations among faculty is that the Concentric Thinking model has great potential for us, both as a means to interest faculty in rethinking their pedagogies and practices in order to encourage better thinking and better writing, and as a tool to restage syllabi and assignment prompts into more student-centered, process-framed formats. We think that this will yield a wide range of benefits for WAC and WID on campus far into the future, something that the Davis Foundation has affirmed in its continued support of our efforts to improve student thinking and writing at Quinnipiac University.

 Similarly, students' evaluations of their writing-to-learn experiences suggest that when writing is linked to course content and course goals, learning outcomes can be quite powerful. The most recent group of Social Stratification students shared a number of powerful insights about the effect of the written work on their personal growth, their understanding of course concepts, and in some cases, the ways in which the course materials have affected their way of being in the world. Students observe that they tend to think more and that they think differently. Their thinking priorities are shifted as a result of the WTL exercises. As one student notes, "…I think less about myself and more about society." A number of students speak of changes in their thought processes that are now characterized by "…mindfulness…of different classes of people" and an ability to "…ask myself 'why' as opposed to just 'what' I think."

This process of looking at deeper and broader aspects of an issue enables students to observe that their "…ability to understand what was taught in class absolutely improved," as they, for example, can begin to be able to "…take into consideration circumstances that could be beyond one's control." As a result of these changing priorities and more meaningful comprehension of the broader context in which social actions are situated, students are more fully able to translate the class materials: "I think about all sides of a situation now, not just the obvious." They are able to witness themselves in a process in which their thinking, initially characterized by one student as "merely scratch[ing] the surface," becomes thinking that is "more open-minded." As one student aptly summarized: "It seems that my understanding has grown, and my perspective has switched from a victim to an observer of stratification.... [My] beginning responses resembled reading comprehension responses. In the beginning, I spoke as a victim of stratification wanting to change it, now I know I can actively can."

This last quote alludes to what may be the greatest effect of the writing, what sociologists refer to as the "practice of the sociological imagination," or the ability to see the connection between one's personal experiences and trends in the larger society. In the Social Stratification course, this is the skill of creating analogies in practice: the ability to move back and forth between personal and social experiences, and to see a role for the self in a broader society. As one student aptly describes: "...[I am] encouraged to give back – philanthropically speaking, but also on a more intrapersonal level." In sum, the semester-long WTL exercise seems to offer students opportunities to change their thought process: "In the future, I will ask more questions before judging a situation to figure out why things are the way they are." Their informal written work encourages students to bring their studies of Social Stratification "...back to [their] own life," while it also enables them to "relate better, and understand the material better as well."

The feedback from students suggests that this work gives them a sense of both meaning and empowerment. It provides them with a deeper understanding of themselves, as well as of the complex interrelationships between self and society. As one student aptly summarizes:

…I never knew the detailed judgments of others existed in such a deep and somewhat structured way, never mind their lasting effects. My behavior as a result has also changed. I do more little things such as smiling and saying a simple hello rather than looking away. I teach others about what I have learned with hopes to open their eyes as well. I give more without the expectation that I deserve something in return. I have become a better person because of the reflections I made in my responses to the readings.

Thus, through informal writing, both student and instructor can observe and appreciate a new-found sense that one individual can exert an effect on invisible, but ever-present structural forces in society.

WTL and Student Performance

Based on the feedback received, we suggest that writing-to-learn exercises designed in a manner informed by concentric thinking can offer faculty a tool to promote improved student learning. Faculty and students report that student writing has improved with the implementation of WTL exercises as well as student perceptions of their writing. Faculty judge that student writing has improved, and students report that they themselves believe that they have become better writers. In our next assessment phase, we intend to look more closely at the actual written products of this approach to writing, but initially at least, we believe that progress has been made in the classroom; and both students and faculty sense that the products by which we judge student improvement and mastery of discipline material have improved in a WAC-enhanced classroom.

Notes

1. Since the late 1980s, the nature of writing-to-learn as a WAC pedagogical tool shifted from the less directed "freewriting" advocated by compositionists like Peter Elbow, toward more purposeful writing assignments tied to specific class objectives or formal assignments.

2. See, for example, Barbara A. Preusser, *Winningham and Preusser's Critical Thinking Cases in Nursing: Medical-Surgical, Pediatric, Maternity, and Psychiatric Case Studies* (Preusser, 2008); also, Jerome Groopman, *How Doctors Think* (Groopman, 2007).

3. In 2006, WAC-trained faculty at Quinnipiac University published specific results of these applications within their disciplines: Mary T. Segall and Robert A. Smart (eds.), *Direct From the Disciplines: Writing Across the Curriculum* (Segall and Smart, 2006).

References

Bean, John C. (2001) *Engaging Ideas: The Professor's Guide to Integrating Writing, Critical Thinking, and Active Learning in the Classroom.* San Francisco: Jossey-Bass Publishers.

Britton, James (1972) *Language and Learning.* London: Penguin Books.

Emig, Janet (1977) Writing as a mode of learning. *College Composition and Communication* 28: 122–128.

Groopman, Jerome (2008) *How Doctors Think.* New York: Houghton-Mifflin.

Humes, Anne (1983) Research on the composing process. *Review of Educational Research* 53(2): 201–216.

Newell, George and Winograd, Peter (1989) The effects of writing on learning from expository text. *Written Communication* 6: 196–217.

Preusser, Barbara (2008) *Winningham and Preusser's Critical Thinking Cases in Nursing: Medical-Surgical, Pediatric, Maternity, and Psychiatric Case Studies.* New York: Elsevier Health Sciences.

Segall, Mary T. and Smart, Robert A. (eds.) (2006) *Direct from the Disciplines: Writing Across the Curriculum.* Portsmouth, New Hampshire: Boynton-Cook, Heinemann.

Thaiss, Christopher (2001) *Theory in WAC: Where Have We Been, Where Are We Going?* Urbana, Illinois: National Council of Teachers of English.

Tönnies, Ferdinand (1940). Fundamental Concepts of Sociology (Gemeinschaft and Gesellschaft) (trans. Charles P. Loomis). New York: American Book Company (orig. pub. 1887).

13 Writing the "Professional": A Model for Teaching Project Management in a Writing Course

Sky Marsen

I.   Background

This chapter describes a narrative approach for guiding students in how to conceptualize a project and plan their writing in relation to this project. The model that this paper describes was developed for an undergraduate professional writing course, but is relevant for any type of writing for academic and specific purposes. In addition to classroom practice, this model has been tested in consultation projects with clients in business and industry.

In formulating my approach, I was motivated by two closely interrelated goals. First, I wanted to contribute to building a theoretical framework for writing that positioned it firmly as an academic discipline. Despite the increase in the number of writing courses offered in universities internationally, as well as the development of several new writing specializations, writing remains a marginal subject in many educational settings, where it lacks a defined identity and tends to be classified under "service" or "remedial" categories.

Although most activities in professional and academic contexts are associated with writing, and in many cases *defined* by writing, writing itself has in many cases been perceived as a secondary activity – at best as a direct communication channel through which knowledge is transmitted and at worst as a challenge to confront when transmitting this knowledge. Consequently, writing in such settings is often considered as a practical addition to academic or scientific work and takes the form of "how-to" instruction. This widespread perception tends to create a paradox in which writing is seen as a ubiquitous and necessary practice of knowledge creation but is not valued as an autonomous discipline.[1] At the same time, research on literacy and cognition has shown how writing structures the mind and forms thought processes that, in turn, shape and direct human activities and interactions: see for example, the work of Walter Ong (e.g. Ong, 1988), and Roy Harris (e.g. Harris, 2001). Clearly, there is a need for more channeling of such research into the design of writing courses in order to enhance their academic value.

Second, I wanted to address the issue of content in writing instruction. Students often ask me if they can take a business writing course if they know nothing about business, or if they can be science journalists without being scientists. This implies the important question: "Is being a good writer enough to write about any topic?" If we support the view that writing both forms and is formed by the information it presents, then we need to find strategies for writers to access the information content of documents they work with by conceptualizing and understanding the contexts in which this information was produced and the values of the discourse communities that produced it. As Lester Faigley, in his discussion of nonacademic writing, points out, we need "a theory that explains how we can participate daily in an all-encompassing social world and yet still see the structure of that world" (Faigley, 2003: 50).

My research on narrative theory provided me with a useful framework to meet both of these goals. Like other fashionable concepts that achieve academic prominence, the concept of narrative has accumulated different meanings, and more elaboration is needed to explain how this concept is relevant for the purposes of writing instruction. Narrative theorists have identified several ways in which story structure is instrumental in understanding and composing written texts. Interesting work has been carried out on documents written in particular situations, analyzing them in terms of the stories they create, that is, in terms of how they reflect narrators' professional roles, their level of subject knowledge, their rhetorical purposes, and the effects of adopting a particular point of view.

For instance, Emery Roe emphasizes the importance of understanding point of view when analyzing events and issues at play in policy development (Roe, 1992). He even goes so far as to recommend mandatory narrative training for policy makers, to make them aware of their assumptions, expectations and the number of points of view available to them in presenting their topic. Also, Boje and Rosile (2003) highlight effectively the importance of point of view in their analysis of media texts that documented the collapse of Enron. They propose that most of these texts construct the agents in the Enron story as tragic characters. In other words, they present the events that took place as examples of personal faults and failings, which leads to the public understanding of the events as being the result of misguided decisions on the part of irresponsible individuals. Boje and Rosile suggest that constructing these events as systemic flaws and contradictions would produce, instead, an epic narration that would be much more effective in indicating areas where social changes are needed.

Such findings, indicating the near-ubiquity of story structure in texts (even in those texts that are not considered narrative), have been complemented by cognitive science research which suggests that our perception and understanding of the natural and social world contain implicit narrative elements (e.g. Herman, 2001; Schank, 1990; Turner, 1996). This means that we create stories not only when we speak and write, but also when we perform our daily activities and in the ways we understand and make sense of our

surroundings. The stories we create in order to construct and negotiate our identities and goals are themselves strategies to advance
the stories that we perceive ourselves as acting in. For example, a
politician's speech is a set of rhetorical devices to attract votes, but
it also helps to construct the image which the politician wishes to
project and which directs his/her performance. The success of the
politician depends on a clear correspondence between the story
which s/he tells and the story in which s/he acts.

Extending this line of reasoning into the area of professional
communication, we can see that project management in organiza-
tions involves the creation of stories, as manifested in different
document-types, such as reports, proposals, and others; however,
the project management is also itself planned as a story with an
initial situation that gives context to the project, a goal to achieve,
conflicts to overcome, and helpers to assist along the way. Within
this overall story project, the documents that writers produce function as agents performing certain actions towards the accomplish-
ment of a goal.

This narrative framework provides much fruitful ground for
instructional design. Materials can be designed that highlight
how we both create stories and act in them, and such materials
can help writers to gain a stronger grasp of what they need to
do to maximize the effectiveness of their work. For example,
management consultant Barbara Minto has proposed that using
story structure when writing reports makes the document more
easily accessible and communicative, a view that challenges the
conventional classification of reports into a different genre from
stories and underlines the importance of creative techniques in
the writing of professional documents (Minto, 1998). Also, my
colleagues, Robert Biddle and James Noble, and I argued for the
relevance of narrative models in the communication practices of
software engineers with their clients (Marsen, Biddle, and Noble,
2003). We demonstrated that *use cases* (a method of writing the
requirements of a software application according to how it will be
applied by the end-user) have a narrative structure. We suggested

that recognizing this and explicitly employing a narrative model to write use cases would assist in improving communication between the software engineer and the client, and could make the product itself more functional.

In sum, narrative theory provides a number of useful concepts and strategies for teachers of writing, and can contribute to showing the significance of writing in academic and professional settings. The research briefly described above can be used to inform the design of writing curricula; however, it can also be used selectively as reading and background material in writing classes, in order to show students how they can conceptualize their rhetorical contexts and structure their discourse strategies accordingly.

What are the constituent elements of narrative? Here is a list of elements that can be used when devising new methods for the instruction of writing. A story is made up of:

- Actions towards reaching a goal, solving a problem or fulfilling a need
- Agents (both human and non-human)
- A set of opponents and helpers
- A narrator or point of view from where the action unfolds

Understanding that facts are always presented from a point of view can help one to recognize that a different point of view could produce different facts, and that others involved in the situation one is writing about may have different and conflicting points of view.

II. Description of Activity

I frame my professional writing course with two main concepts which form the "center of gravity" of the course and on which a number of activities are based: *the project* and *the brief* (Marsen, 2007). As most tasks in the professional workplace involve the completion of specific projects, encouraging students to think in terms of project planning and management helps them to practice the roles that they will have to perform as professionals. Using a narrative approach, a project can be defined as:

> The interrelational positioning of agents based on duties, skills, and expectations which are put together to perform a set of actions towards achieving a goal.

In this scheme, writing is a catalyst of action whose function is to perform a set of speech acts that advance the project (persuade, warn, instruct, etc.). In this way of conceptualizing it, writing is seen as part of a network of mutually reinforcing activities. For example, the question, "How do I write a report?" becomes rephrased as "What will my report do in the organizational context in which I am writing?"

Following a similar line of reasoning, the brief (or *terms of reference*) gives the "stage directions" for setting up and acting out the circumstances surrounding the professional writing task. It contains, explicitly or implicitly, the four aspects of all projects that involve writing for specific purposes:

- Setting the scene;
- Placing oneself as writer within this scene;
- Tracing and identifying specific elements and players in the scene; and
- Deciding on tasks that ensure the smooth functioning of these elements.

Taking the *brief* and the *project,* the activity involves planning out a course of action for the writing task or tasks. For this purpose, I have devised a model consisting of four interrelated categories, and I ask students to form groups, brainstorm ideas, and create a plan of action for their writing using these categories:

- *Event*: the concept, problem, goal, or need of a project;
- *Controlling Scene*: the players, audiences and stakeholders;

- *Role*: the project team members' expertise, duties, and level of authority; and
- *Treatment*: the actions taken to complete the project and reach the goal.

These categories are defined more fully below.

***Event*:** This encompasses the actual situation or question(s) that have created a problem needing a solution. It includes understanding the facts or occurrences that require a writing solution and what this solution should achieve. The Event consists of:

- A chronology of facts;
- The specific issues that should be addressed;
- The details of the topic;
- The raw materials, sources, and limitations that the writer is given to handle the task, such as funding, deadlines, access to resources, and equipment.

Assessing accurately the Event helps the writer create a role for him/herself within the project.

***Controlling Scene*:** This encompasses the scope of the project, the audience(s), and the different parties involved. It consists of:

- The big picture;
- The broad topic that the writer has to deal with;
- The context in which the problem has arisen and the roles that exist in this context;
- Who the writer is addressing, and what s/he is writing about directly or indirectly;
- The number of people affected by the context and the topic, and the extent to which they are affected. For example, decisions taken by government agencies (such as policy-making and legislation) tend to affect a greater sector of the public than decisions taken by small businesses. In the first case, the influence of the task can be said to be general. In the second case, it is local.

Note that the Controlling Scene is not just the audience. It includes everyone affected by the information presented in the document and is a category that is often neglected when writers focus only on their primary readers. For example, assume a project undertaken by a financial advisor for a client wanting advice on investment options. This project would include not only the advisor and the client, but also such parties as relevant banks and financial institutions (for share options, interest regulations, etc.), relevant government agencies that regulate capital flow, and other financial advisors (competitors from whom the client could get another opinion). In analyzing the Controlling Scene, the project manager would need to ask: "What is the story of investing for this client, and who are the characters that progress or hinder its development?" This way the advisor would be better equipped to position himself or herself as a helper, rather than an obstacle, in this story.

As regards teaching a writing course, analyzing the Controlling Scene of a project helps the students to understand the networks that are activated and to identify sources of information for the content of their writing tasks. It also helps them to identify the documents they would need to produce to complete the project (what I call the "treatment," described below).

Role: This indicates the writer's position within the Controlling Scene, his/her duties, freedoms and constraints, especially:

- The writer's position and status in relation to other participants in the Controlling Scene: Is the writer a junior employee? A technical specialist? The CEO? This will affect the register and style of the document as well as the information content.
- The writer's relation to the problem: Is the writer blamed for something and has to justify is/her actions? Is the writer an expert called in to solve a problem? This will affect the tone and organization of the document.

- The writer's relation to the audience: Are they clients? Peers? This will affect degree of formality as well as information content.

Understanding one's role in the project is vital in creating a communicatively effective persona. In other words, coming across as assertive, modest, respectful, extravagant, or whatever other quality is required for communicative effectiveness, depends on a careful assessment of the Controlling Scene and of the writer's Role.

Treatment: This involves the actions that should be carried out and the documents that should be produced to bring about an appropriate result. It includes:

- The tasks that will solve the problem, address the issue, or provide some form of resolution to the situation. This includes physical and interactive actions, such as organizing meetings and conducting interviews and focus groups.
- The type of documentation that should be produced. For example, a simple email message may be sufficient in some situations. In other cases, this may need to be accompanied by a letter or a memo, while a more serious situation would require the submission of a proposal leading to a full report.
- The media in which information should be presented according to audience needs. For example, would a PowerPoint presentation be enough to inform an audience of one's progress on a project? If submitting a document such as a report, should this contain tables, charts, graphs, etc.?

A project can be the composition of a single document or a lengthy investigation with many stages. The model described above can be used for both cases. For example, if we take the project to be the writing of a proposal, instead of just looking at what sections proposals conventionally have and what information to include in each section, following this model we would also look at the role that the proposal would play as a narrative agent, and we would plan the writing accordingly. So our plan would involve:

Event: What need does the proposed project satisfy? For whom is this a need? What assists and what hinders the successful outcome of the project?

Controlling Scene: Who is the funding agent? Who are the stake-holders? Who will benefit? What is their attitude? What do they already know about the project? Who are the competitors, and how should they be acknowledged? What other parties are involved, directly or indirectly, in the proposed project?

Role: What is the writer's credibility and experience? What re-sponsibilities does s/he accept? What relationship does the writer have with the reader(s)?

Treatment: Will the writer conduct primary or secondary research? Should the proposal be accompanied or followed by any other document?

Two important aims of this model are to make assumptions explicit and to represent tasks, both aims contributing to a better grasp by the students of what the project requires them to do and how they can best meet those requirements. The writing aspects of the project are, therefore, contextualized in a social perspective that encompasses participants, interactions, and possible conflicts.

The narrative model of project management is first described and discussed with examples of its use. In class discussions of this model, I draw attention to the problems that can arise when the Controlling Scene, Role, Event, and Treatment aspects of a project are not properly interpreted. The analysis of case studies works well here. A famous and well-documented example that can be used for this purpose is the Challenger space shuttle disaster of January 1986. It is now widely recognized that the explosion of the space shuttle was largely due to misunderstandings that occurred in the exchange of written information between NASA officials before the launch. Although some officials had detected a functioning error in the shuttle and knew what had to be done to fix it, they did not communicate their finding in an appropriate way to the responsible parties (Herndl, Fennell, and Miller, 1991). The social and pragmatic aspects of communication can easily be traced in this case study.[2]

Next, students are put into groups of 3–4, and a brief is given to each group to analyze using the model. Each group then presents its analysis to the class. A class discussion follows, which focuses on questions such as:

- What could go wrong with this project, and how could problems be anticipated?
- Is the Event clearly described in the brief, or are there implicit factors that also need to be taken into account?
- Whose point of view does the brief represent, and what other agents are part of the Controlling Scene whose interests may conflict with the dominant point of view?
- What documents will be produced as part of the Treatment, and what is the role of each in the project?

Here are three examples of briefs.

Example One

You are an Information Management researcher at the prestigious X University, and you specialize in security and copyright issues. The Motion Pictures Association (MPA) is concerned about the rise in illegal DVDs. MPA has commissioned you to investigate the problem and advise on possible solutions. Your investigation should consider how serious this problem really is, who the main types of copiers and buyers of illegal copies are, what tactics are used in illegally copying DVDs, which areas need to be closely inspected, what the current measures are, and how effective they are.

Example Two

You are an aviation expert. A major airline (name the airline so that students can find information about it), has commissioned you to assess its competitive position in the travel industry. The airline executives want you to investigate recent developments in aircraft construction, security measures in the light of recent terrorist threats, and client services, and to evaluate their airline's advantages and disadvantages in relation to those of competitors. Conduct an investigation that identifies pertinent issues and recommend a practical course of action for the airline to follow in order to remain competitive in the current travel market.

Example Three

You are a security expert. The Privacy Commissioner[3] has asked you to investigate current issues concerning privacy. With developments in surveillance technology, the spread of Internet published information, and digitally stored personal information, there is serious concern that individual rights to privacy are being eroded. The increasing presence of computer hackers and state-owned satellite systems means that individual privacy is being attacked from both private and public sectors. The Commissioner wants you to investigate the extent to which this fear is justified, to evaluate possible consequences and to suggest possible solutions.

III. Implementation

This model for planning writing projects has been used successfully in a professional writing course since 2005. The course runs over one semester (12 weeks), and consists of one 3-hour workshop per week in which students work individually and in groups, discussing issues relating to professional writing, analyzing texts, editing and proofreading copy, and planning projects that entail the composition of one or more documents. The workshops are made up of 16–18 students, male and female in approximately equal numbers. Students are mainly second-year (about 40%) and third-year (about

30%) undergraduates from Humanities (about 30%), Commerce (about 50%), and Science (about 20%) Faculties. There are also external students from the business community taking the course as professional development (20%), and a relatively small number of graduate students from Management and Science Faculties (10%). Ages range from early twenties to late forties, with the majority falling in the mid-twenties group.

The course is intended for native or near-native speakers of English (i.e. it does not provide specific instruction in English as a Second Language issues). However, it does attract a considerable number of students for whom English is an additional language (about 30%), possibly because it provides a forum to address language-related problems and obtain detailed feedback.

The course does not assume any knowledge of business practices or workplace documents, and, in fact, many students take the course expressly to learn about these subjects. It is an independent, elective course that does not form part of any major, so most students take it to complement their course of study and/or to acquire skills and strategies that they believe will assist them in their transition to the workplace and in their professional careers.

Because of its relative autonomy, the course attempts to define its identity by establishing its relevance to other academic subjects. To do this, the course is framed in terms of the concepts of *writing* (i.e. it addresses the question, "In what ways is writing a specific form of communication?") and of *professionalism* (i.e. it addresses the question, "What makes a professional attitude and how is this reflected in stylistic choices?"). The course has a required text (*Professional Writing,* Marsen, 2007), which contains explanations of principles and practical activities, and it is supplemented by readings which include extracts and selections from the texts referred to above.

The model of project management is introduced in Week 3 and acts as a framework for students to reflect on the key concepts of *writing* and *professional.* During the course, we return to the model of project management each time an assignment is planned in class. Students are required to analyze their assignment topics (which are presented in the form of briefs) using the model, and to include a one-page analysis of Event, Controlling Scene, Role, and Treatment with the final copy of their assignment. This analysis serves as evidence of how the students conceptualized the project in which their document performs a role before composing the document itself.

IV.   Reflections and Recommendations

The main aim of this activity is to show students the importance of contextual, or "big picture," factors for writing, and to provide them with a way to identify and respond to these factors. An additional aim is to support the academic rigor of a writing course, by incorporating theoretical and interdisciplinary elements in its design (in this case, elements from narrative theory).

The activity generally produces positive results. I have found that all students' writing improves, to varying degrees, in both clarity and audience dynamics. Many students also say that this approach has helped them in other courses, which suggests that the skills learned are transferrable and cumulative. The positive response of students is especially strong from those with professional experience, who generally maintain that they can adjust better to workplace environments when they conceptualize these in narrative form and that this attitude results in improvement in their writing. In particular, I have found that students:

- are encouraged to learn more about their writing contexts and come to understand the significance of this knowledge for successful communication;
- respond positively to the creative aspects of the activity, which in turn spurs their enthusiasm for writing.

The role of the students with workplace experience is instrumental in the discussion of briefs such as the three given above, as these students can provide first-hand testimony on the relevance of the model for real-world projects. Also, international students are valuable because they can describe the cultural elements in the successful planning of communication in projects (for example, such elements as forms of address, politeness, cross-cultural attitudes towards presenting "bad news," etc.).

As regards potential disadvantages, there is often a reluctance by some students to recognize that the model is conducive to effective writing, because of the widespread belief that writing is "words on a page" and is dependent on grammatical issues only. Introducing the model with examples from actual cases seems to help in dispelling this reluctance. This is especially evident if the examples have a dramatic effect, showing cases of miscommunication which have had disastrous results.

Finally, a benefit of the model is that it can be used in various educational settings, when the instructor wants a technique that would guide students to conceptualize abstract elements in a more tangible, and therefore more accessible, form.

Notes

1. This paradox has been described by a number of authors. For example, Keith Hjortshoj approaches it colorfully in terms of a parable that traces parallels between writing teachers and lower castes in India (Hjortshoj, 1995). Both provide valuable services that are not overtly appreciated by the wider society (or the academy in the case of writing teachers).
2. Interestingly, a similar situation occurred in the Columbia shuttle accident in 2003. Engineers, once again, suspected that the shuttle had been damaged during launch, but they did not communicate their suspicions with enough clarity and urgency to management, and so no action was taken. I provide a narrative analysis of the Columbia shuttle disaster in the website companion to my book *Professional Writing*. This can be accessed at: http://www.palgrave.com/studyskills/marsen/Home.aspx.
3. The privacy commissioner is an independent officer in the parliaments of Commonwealth countries (including the United Kingdom, Canada, New Zealand, and Australia) who is in charge of investigating allegations

of privacy infringements of individual citizens by government and corporations.

References

Boje, David M. and Rosile, Grace (2003) Life imitates art: Enron's epic and tragic narration. *Management Communication Quarterly* 17(1): 85–125.

Faigley, Lester (2003) Nonacademic writing: The social perspective. In Tim Peeples (ed.) *Professional Writing and Rhetoric: Readings from the Field* 47–59. New York: Longman.

Harris, Roy (2001) *Rethinking Writing*. London: Continuum.

Herman, David (2001) Narrative theory and the cognitive sciences. *Narrative Inquiry* 11: 1–34.

Herndl, Carl G., Fennell, Barbara A. and Miller, Carolyn R. (1991) Understanding failures in organizational discourse: The accident at Three Mile Island and the shuttle Challenger disaster. In Charles Bazerman and James Paradis (eds.) *Textual Dynamics of the Professions* 279–305. Madison, Wisconsin: University of Wisconsin Press.

Hjortshoj, Keith (1995) The marginality of left-hand castes (A parable for writing teachers). *College Composition and Communication* 46(4): 491–505.

Marsen, Sky (2007) *Professional Writing: The Complete Guide for Business, Industry and IT* (2nd edition). Basingstoke: Palgrave.

Marsen, Sky, Biddle, Robert and Noble, James (2003) Use case analysis with narrative semiotics, *Proceedings of the Australasian Conference on Information Systems* 58–69. Available at http://aisel.aisnet.org/acis2003/86/.

Minto, Barbara (1998) Think your way to clear writing. *Journal of Management Consulting* 10(2): 45–53.

Ong, Walter (1988) *Orality and Literacy: The Technologizing of the Word.* London: Routledge.

Roe, Emery M. (1992) Applied narrative analysis: The tangency of literary criticism, social science and policy analysis. *New Literary History* 23: 555–581.

Schank, Roger C. (1990) *Tell Me a Story: Narrative and Intelligence.* Evanston, Illinois: Northwestern University Press.

Turner, Mark (1996) *The Literary Mind.* Oxford: Oxford University Press.

14 Writing for an Authentic Audience

Kate Kessler

I.   Background

When I began teaching writing in the 1980s, instructional emphasis was on product: teaching students to produce an error-free document. During the next ten years, instructional emphasis shifted to process: teaching students to be conscious of how writing developed through stages, including invention, arrangement, style considerations, and revision.

This evolution from an emphasis on product to an emphasis on process was accompanied by an evolution in audience awareness. Writing teachers themselves became aware that to prepare students for writing they would use beyond the classroom, students needed to compose for audiences beyond the teacher. We began to craft assignments with specific audiences in mind. The evolution from writing only for the teacher to writing for an authentic audience nudged product writing and process writing into a new instructional emphasis. Writing for an authentic audience blended concern for both an error-free document (product writing) with a consciousness of how writing develops (process writing). This new instructional emphasis came to be called *"post-process" writing*.

"Post process" is one of those buzz words in composition pedagogy. Essentially, post-process writing is writing that has evolved beyond preoccupation for process into rhetorically sensitive writing that also demonstrates concern for product. Post-process writing, according to William Covino, is writing that "…is not restricted to self-expression…or the formulaic obedience to rules, but instead keeps in view the skills and contingencies that attend a variety of situations and circumstances" (Covino, 2001: 36). In other words, post-process writing works for both the writer and the reader, and is ideal when writing for an authentic audience.

First-year composition moves into an extra dimension when students write for an audience beyond the instructor. When they write for authentic audiences, the writing instructor serves as mentor, rather than as primary audience and evaluator. In first-year composition classes at James Madison University, my students write about real issues and deliver their written work to real audiences. They also receive real responses. Writing for an authentic audience and receiving an authentic response is worth much more than just a grade and so motivates the students to try harder and to enjoy writing more.

The aim of writing for an authentic audience is to help students become aware of the power of their pens. When they leave the classroom, how effectively they write to others, whether a memo on the job or a persuasive letter to the town council, depends on both the quality of their composition and their ability to address the concerns of a particular audience. Because of the inherent promise of a real audience, writing for an authentic audience can motivate students to link writing for process and self-expression with a sense of responsibility for writing conventions.

II.   Description of Activity

A good way to begin teaching writing for an authentic audience is to invoke what John Trimbur terms "the call to write." In his text, *The Call to Write*, Trimbur (1999) describes a call to write as the impulse we feel when we have something to say and writing is the best medium for saying it. I ask students to begin by thinking of something they want to say to someone in a letter. To participate in civic as well as academic life, students must learn to write public discourse, and the familiar genre of a letter is a good context for practice. There are many types of professional letters students will have to write in their lives: legal letters, medical letters, and letters of complaint, request, and thanks.

My students spend one or two class periods brainstorming topics for writing. While working in this first stage of the process, I encourage them to explore their calls to write. They brainstorm, freewrite, map, and list ideas. I write along with my students because there are things that I really want to say too, and modeling is a good way to show students that writing for delivery matters to adults in the "real world." We call this stage *invention*.

As our brainstorming activity moves into rough drafting, we decide which idea we want to present first. What is our main concern? That concern becomes our thesis and the rest of our writing depends on it. We then begin to decide how we want to present the points that work to support our thesis. Which point should come first? Which second? We call this stage *arrangement*.

My students and I fill pages easily. Some students are ready to lick the envelope right away. They are unfamiliar with the third stage of process writing, which involves consciously deciding what emotional stance to take and which level of formality will have the best effect on their audience. Rather than pop the letters into the mail, we sit back and consider how we want to "sound" to this particular audience. Although the concept of writing for an audience is not new for most students, few have considered that they have the power to effect change through writing because few have ever written for an audience other than the teacher. Students are excited by this new thought: When they write something, and physically deliver it, will they actually receive a response? This new thought causes them to stop and reflect how the third stage of the process, their word choice, their sentence structure, and their tone will affect the person they are writing to. We call this stage of writing *style*.

Both arrangement and style involve editing and revision. Revision can feel tedious to students at first, but then I ask a crucial question: "What do you want from this person or group that you are writing to?" How you write to them makes all the difference in what kind of response you will receive. Writing for an authentic audience is writing that will be delivered; it is not just a "rhetorical" activity.

I come to class prepared to share several of my own letters that were delivered to authentic audiences and have received responses. One is to the mayor of Baltimore protesting a $70.00 ticket from a traffic officer. After sharing the letter I wrote to the mayor, I show the students the letter Mr. O'Malley wrote back to me. Granted, I had to pay the ticket, but the Mayor of Baltimore wrote back to me! Another letter to "Mattress Warehouse" had even more favorable results: a free mattress delivered to my house. A corrupt cable company, an incompetent check labeling company, and a myopic prosecuting attorney have all been the recipients of my powerful pen. All have written back, and each time I have gotten satisfaction: an apology, a refund, and a retrial. The point is not lost on my students: writing for delivery can elicit response with real results. But to get the results they want, their writing must be carefully crafted and rhetorically sensitive.

Rhetorical sensitivities such as audience, purpose, occasion, register, and style are not often consciously considered when writing. Strategies for teaching rhetorically sensitive writing need a safe and supportive environment in which to practice them. The writing workshop can provide that environment.

While brainstorming in her writing workshop, a student named Bethany shared her concern that dorm housekeepers were taken for granted. "They work so hard, and we make such a mess." Her peers encouraged her to write a letter of appreciation because this was her true call to write. At first, writing a thank you letter seemed too elementary for a college writing assignment. But in addition to the call to write, the letter genre also offered rhetorically sensitive writing practice for an appropriate audience and a specific purpose. Bethany decided to write her housekeepers a letter so that they would know that their efforts were appreciated. "Really, how else would they know?" Bethany asked. Bethany further decided that the best way to thank her dorm housekeepers was to write to them indirectly through their most senior supervisor. That way, her thanks would not only touch them, but also let their boss know what a great job they were doing. Research on the administrative structure of the university led her to the Vice President for Administration and Finance.

Although Bethany didn't know her audience well, her purpose was clear. She decided that a moderately formal register would be most appropriate and began by assuming a polite and friendly style: "I am writing this letter to express my appreciation of the wonderful housekeeping staff at Eagle Hall. They are exceptional members of the James Madison University community, and should be commended for their efforts in making our campus a better place." Bethany described in detail how meticulous and conscientious the housekeeping staff was. She then added, "Everyone goes above and beyond their job description. What truly makes them special is the way they treat everyone around them. The staff not only greets everyone who walks by, they also open doors, hold elevators, and are happy to throw a smile anyone's way." Bethany then singled out one housekeeper for special praise:

> I would like to recognize one housekeeper in particular. I see Dave Rothwell on a daily basis. He is truly a southern gentleman and handles himself very professionally. Before he even thinks of walking into our communal living space he knocks and does

his special whistle so we know he's coming. He sings while he's working so we know he really enjoys his job, which makes every girl on our floor want to make his job easier. Dave also looks out for us. Several times my door squeaked so badly that it actually woke me up when my roommate came in late at night. When I mentioned it to Dave he whipped out his WD 40 and took care of the problem on the spot.

At the beginning of the year he brought us potpourri oil and for Halloween he gave us a bucket of candy. For Christmas we got candy canes and a lovely card. Dave goes the extra mile and we appreciate it!

Bethany concluded that

The staff at Eagle Hall is more than a group of people doing their jobs. They are a team that goes far beyond what is required. I wish more people appreciated housekeepers' efforts; they certainly are loved by everyone on our hall. They make our dorm a home.

Because Bethany chose the housekeeping staff's most senior supervisor as her audience, the staff received recognition and praise up and down the chain of command, beginning with this reply from the Senior Vice President:

Dear Bethany:

Thank you so much for the wonderful letter about the house-keeping staff in Eagle Hall. I will make sure that Dave and the others know how much you appreciate their efforts in making your residence hall a better place to live.

I often receive notes about individuals who excel in their jobs but I do not think I have ever received such a thoughtful and profes-sionally done letter from a student. Thank you for taking the time to send your letter. It made my day and when I share it with my leadership team in Facilities Management I am sure it will have the same impact on them.

Sincerely,
Charles W. King

Dr. King forwarded Bethany's letter and this letter of his own to custodian Dave Rothwell:

> Dave, I wanted you to have a copy of this wonderful letter. It is a testament to the exceptional job you do in Eagle Hall. I have often received notes concerning employees who provide excellent service but this is one of the best letters I have ever received. You should be very proud. Thanks for all you do in Eagle Hall.
>
> Keep up the good work.

Dave and the other housekeepers and custodians must have been pleased with both letters because Bethany soon shared this email with me:

> Dear Professor Kessler:
>
> About five minutes ago, the entire housekeeping staff knocked on my door and thanked me for writing that letter. In return they are treating me to Chinese for lunch. I must say that I feel amazing right now. I was able to make an impact on such a great group of individual. Thank you for making that assignment. It was nice to make a difference rather than be assigned a paper that would have just been thrown in my desk drawer. Have a fabulous break; mine has already started off on a good note! ☺
>
> Bethany Riley

It was the true call to write that led Bethany to care enough to create a rhetorically sensitive letter that she was proud to deliver. Product had become as important as process.

Our letter assignment began with simple directions:

> Your first task will be to identify a call to write within this genre: What moves you to share information with another human being or group? Your second task will be to identify an appropriate audience: who needs to hear what you have to say? Your third task will be to identify the form and function of your letter. After you do these three things, you will have a topic, an audience, and an idea of how you want to write your letter.

Students collaboratively created an evaluation checklist. For this first assignment, they combined elements of product and process writing that showed concern for rhetorical sensitivity. They negotiated that the checklist for this assignment would require:

- An opening paragraph that clearly establishes the purpose for writing (thesis);
- Effective use of a deliberate rhetorical stance (who you are in relation to your topic);
- Credible evidence that supports the thesis;
- Choice of an appropriate audience (that is, the person with the power to effect the change you seek);
- Appropriate register, tone, and word choice for the audience and purpose;
- Standard writing conventions for the audience (grammar, punctuation, and mechanics).

Of course, different calls to write required different checklists. Students learned to tailor checklists to assignments. For example, while a letter sent to an individual required an opening paragraph that clearly established the purpose for writing, a short story submitted for publication in a school magazine required a rhetorical hook such as an engaging opening sentence.

While letters may be considered by some to be "academically lightweight," students moved on to more complex calls to write quickly. These more complex calls progressed to more challenging writing assignments. One of our complex calls to write involved arguing for civic and service improvements. Students were very interested in civics and service, ranging from expanded Big Brother Big Sister services to extended campus dining hall hours. To demonstrate how powerful writing to an authentic audience can be, the second assignment evolved into learning how to write a proposal.

A proposal argues that something in existence should be changed, that something in existence should be eliminated, or that something is lacking and should be called into existence. The register, tone, and research requirements of proposals requires more formality than letters. The same is true of the presentation of a proposal. Audiences being called upon to do something are impressed by cotton-bond paper, business formatting, and eloquently integrated, credible evidence that such a proposal has been implemented before. Audiences, especially in the political and civics world, want to know that what is being asked of them can be done; they also want to know what is in it for them.

Our proposal assignment began with a definition: the proposal is a form of writing that puts forth a plan of action and seeks to persuade an audience that the plan should be implemented. The assignment then proceeded through the following series of instructions to students:

> Begin by clearly stating that a problem exists: something lacking needs to be added, something exists that needs to be eliminated, or something amiss needs to be remedied. While you're describing the problem, give your audience enough details that they can "feel your pain." Examples are always good ways to engage your audience and prepare them to hear what you have to say.
>
> Next, show that you've done your research. You'll need to demonstrate convincingly that evidence supports your assertion that a problem exists. Make yourself ethical: what's your involvement here? Why do you care? It's appropriate to reveal your rhetorical stance to your audience; that is, why do you want them to become involved and why should they do what you say they should do?
>
> Your sources must be impeccable. You won't have a bibliography page for your proposal because a bulky bibliography is inappropriate for this type of writing (it might seem off-putting to your audience) but you will have parenthetical (in-text) citations of a page or paragraph number if you have direct quotes or a paraphrase from print or an interview.
>
> After you have primed your audience with examples and evidence, make your proposal. A proposal will probably contain the words "should," "ought," or "must," at least implicitly. Write your proposal as a simple sentence so it stands out clearly. Put your thesis at the end of their first paragraph or even in a paragraph by itself.

The last part of a proposal should contain details that make your audience believe that they can realistically make this thing happen. Make details concrete: how, <u>exactly,</u> can the audience/receiver of the proposal make the change? This is an important step and one that most students forget to do. It's not enough to simply point out a problem, then drop the ball. A proposal is more likely to be implemented when it suggests concrete steps toward a solution. If a problem similar to the one in a proposal has existed and been remedied in the past, offer it as proof that solutions exist and can be implemented. Be sure throughout to impress on the audience the benefits to them in their position.

When the first draft is complete, read the proposal through your audience's eyes. Will he or she believe it is necessary? Will he or she believe it can be done? If not, you have some revision to do.

Research who your audience will be for your request. Such research is an integral part of writing for an authentic audience. The guiding question should be: who has the power? Who has the power to effect the change you seek? What are their views on the topic? What does this person stand to gain or lose by adopting the proposal? You'll need to find a specific full name, title, company name, and address.

As with the first writing for an authentic audience assignment, students negotiate the evaluation rubric for the proposal. A typical evaluation rubric might look like the following:

3 Points: The thesis is presented clearly and persuasively
4 Points: The audience is appropriate and has been researched
5 Points: Evidence is credible and effective
3 Points: Evidence is integrated skillfully
3 Points: Arrangement is effective
3 Points: Sentences are related and transitions are used
4 Points: The conclusion is a powerful call to action

First-year composition student Alli chose a topic close to her heart, the welfare of animals. Not just any animals: Alli chose animals not already protected under the Animal Welfare Act. Her research led her to Cindy Smith, Administrator of the U.S.

Department of Agriculture's Animal and Plant Health Inspection Service, who lives in Woodstock, Maryland. After careful research, Alli addressed Mrs. Smith directly. Following are excerpts from Alli's proposal:

Dear Mrs. Smith:

Most people do not know that factory farms are large warehouses where animals are confined in small cages or stalls until they are sent to slaughter houses. Because factory farm animals are excluded from the well-known Animal Welfare Act, I'm writing to request your help in creating a law to protect these protect animals.

I was surprised to learn that farm animals are excluded from the Animal Welfare Act. People like me had no idea of the suffering that farm animals are put through. According to the U.S. Department of Agriculture's National Agricultural Statistics Service, each year about ten percent or 900 million farm animals raised for food never even reach the slaughterhouse. This ten percent die from disease or inadequate care. Pigs and cows are forced to live in cramped pens not nearly spacious enough for living conditions. Chickens are packed in chicken houses so crowded that there is not one inch between them.

Mrs. Smith, as administrator of the USDA's Animal and Plant Health Inspection Service, I believe you have the power to help make factory farms more humane. Specifically, I am writing to request that you use your position to work to extend the Animal Welfare Act to include protection of factory farm animals. Please help create this necessary legislation.

Section thirteen of the Animal Welfare Act exists to protect animals "for handling, housing, feeding, watering, sanitation, ventilation, shelter from extremes of weather and temperatures, adequate veterinary care, and separation by species where the Secretary finds necessary for humane handling, care, or treatment of animals." The Animal Welfare Act, however, only applies to animals by handled by dealers, research facilities, and exhibitors. It does not apply to animals used to feed our nation. While there are twenty-eight sections of the Animal Welfare Act, none protect factory farm animals.

You and your agency could help create and pass laws to help factory farms become more humane without compromising business interests. The voice of the USDA's Animal and Plant Health Inspection Service is a strong one and would go a long way toward creating legislation to improve factory farms.

I would be happy to hear back from you.

Sincerely,
Alli

I would love to report that Alli received a heartening letter in response to her proposal. In truth, she received no response at all. The lack of response is part of the learning process of writing for an authentic audience. Mrs. Smith was certainly the person with the power to effect the change that Alli sought. We will probably never know why Mrs. Smith did not respond. Perhaps she already knew everything that Alli had written, or perhaps she didn't care. Perhaps she had already tried to improve the situation. The good news is that Alli was not deterred by the lack of a response; she turned her attention to her congressperson and is crafting a letter to him, requesting specific legislative oversight of factory farms.

III. Implementation

An interesting phenomenon occurred when students wrote for authentic audiences: when their writing became true calls to write and less like assignments, students created sophisticated and challenging evaluation checklists.

Students shared drafts in writing workshops during each stage of composition, beginning with invention, through discussing effective arrangement, and finally considering the most appropriate style for a particular audience. Students compared final drafts to checklists during late-stage revision and editing workshops. When they were satisfied that everyone's writing was as perfect as possible for its audience and purpose, we walked the letters to the campus post office together for a celebratory mass mailing.

I made sure the first letters got mailed because students confessed that if delivery were left to them, they would not mail these early calls to write. Delivering writing was a new activity for them. Writing for an authentic audience had to be reinforced with response from that audience before it became an activity they welcomed. Response gave them a feeling of power, and it became a happy tradition at the end of each class for students to share responses they had received.

Writing for an authentic audience, then, is not independent of a written message; it is an integral part of the message. There is a huge difference between imagining an audience for a classroom exercise and imagining an authentic audience for actual delivery. Rhetorical sensitivity has meaning when writers know that their work will actually be delivered, read, and responded to.

IV.   Reflections and Recommendations

How do writing teachers help students compose with academic vigor while also helping them engage with the world? How do we help our students realize that language, and writing in particular, has the power to create change? One of my students offered this feedback on writing his proposal assignment:

> I had never had the opportunity to write an actual Proposal before. I was a bit overwhelmed when I found out that these proposals were going to be sent to someone to be read and taken seriously. This made me work much harder; knowing I was going to have someone actually read my letter, and then respond. I think the most rewarding part of writing was putting a lot of effort into it and then getting a response back from my intended audience.

Another noted:

> Until now most writing I ever did was for a writing assignment in school. I thought writing was just something I had to do for English class when the teacher told us we had to write a research paper

that I only wrote because I would be graded on it. Now I realize that I can use writing when I have a point that should be heard. The papers we wrote were addressed to real people and we wrote about something that was actually important to us. From this class I realize that writing will be with me all the time no matter what profession I choose, whether I want to be a lawyer, a businessman, or even a doctor.

One student in particular provided me with the motivation to continue teaching writing for an authentic audience:

> My writing class was a total success. I learned things about myself and my writing capabilities and what it takes to fulfill the call to write. I learned a lot about reading, writing, and myself, and that's all you can ask from a writing class.
>
> Out of all my classes, the one that was the most useful was my writing class. By useful I mean that it aided me the most for my future. It introduced writing as a real life situation, not just a teacher assignment. Being able to identify writing as a necessity not a punishment is hard thing to be taught, but my writing class did it. The class helped me learn that if I have something I feel strongly about, it would be a shame not to let my voice be heard. The most important thing about the class is that it showed me that my writing is a tool that should be used to reach out to the world.

As reflective teachers, our evolution in teaching writing will continue. As we evolve our craft, let us look for ways to combine the good things of product, process, and post-process writing instruction. I have found that a return to writing for an authentic audience may be a useful way to put these good things into practice.

References

Covino, William A. (2001). Rhetorical pedagogy. In Gary Tate, Amy Rupiper, and Kurt Schick (eds.) *A Guide to Composition Pedagogies* 36–53. New York: Oxford University Press.

Trimbur, John (1999) *The Call to Write*. New York: Longman.

Part 4
Interactive and Self Assessment of Writing

15 The Write Path: Guiding Writers to Self-Reliance

Lisa Nazarenko and Gillian Schwarz

I. Background

The idea presented here has been developed over many semesters of teaching language classes to English as a Foreign Language (EFL) students at the University of Vienna, Austria. The initial impetus for this activity came from our observations that while our students appeared competent when speaking, as soon as they put pen to paper their competence evaporated and they produced texts (for a variety of tasks) in which the main barriers to understanding were not the surface errors of grammar and vocabulary, but lay more deeply embedded in the overall structure and organization of the text. Students, however, were so focused on producing an "error-free" text on the surface level that they tended to disregard any feedback that dealt with organizational problems and found it difficult to understand why the text did not then receive a good grade.

Another observation we made was that students were often completely unaware of the typical features of the different text types they were writing, so that the work they produced did not conform to what a reader might expect of a text written in a certain genre. In order to help our students develop strategies for approaching writing assignments which could be transferred to a variety of tasks, we turned to the ideas about genre analysis discussed by Swales (1990) in *Genre Analysis* to develop an approach combining aspects of genre analysis with the method of instruction we were using (largely based on the process approach to writing as outlined by White and Arndt, 1991).

We also introduced the idea of reflection. We were convinced that if students reflected on what they were doing and tried to analyze where they had writing problems and where they were confident in their writing, it would help them develop strategies to *help themselves* become better writers and so move away from a reliance on their teachers.

The main aims of the activity can be summarized as follows:

- To help students learn how to identify the generic features of a specific text type;
- To give students a set of skills for approaching this writing task;
- To introduce students to the idea of reflecting on their own writing practice;
- To empower students to analyze and improve their own writing process and products and thereby increase their confidence and independence as writers.

II.   Description of Activity

The description of our method uses an opinion (or argument) essay as an example. This writing task is done by second-semester students in a six-semester program. They work on this text type throughout the 3-month semester, typically writing three to four essays, and have 40 minutes to write one opinion essay during a common final test taken by all students at the end of the second semester. This activity is intended to be the first of these essays and aims to give students an overview of how they should approach the task and what they should pay attention to in order to produce a successful opinion essay that will achieve a good grade.

Step 1: Analysis of Essay Question and Model Text

Before the first class, we create a handout for the students (see below) with information about the opinion essays they will be required to produce and the guidelines they will be assessed on. We also select or write a model text which students will use to work through a selection of activities in order to analyze typical features of the genre they are eventually to produce. If we write the text ourselves, we make sure we have an organization plan for the text; if we select a text from a publication, we work backwards to produce an appropriate plan that could have been used to write the text.

Handout 1: Guidelines for Assessment

Guidelines for Assessment

This writing task requires you to ***answer a question convincingly*** by presenting evidence (reasons) for your point of view. The answer is in the form of an academic essay of 250–300 words. Take the time to read the question carefully, to make your answer as suitable as possible.

Remember that for every idea you put into your essay, you must prove or explain to your reader why it is so.

To write a good essay:

I.   Content, Arguments, and Evidence
- Make your viewpoint clear and related to the topic (the specific issue).
- Present a reasoned argument, supported with evidence and examples.
- Use evidence that is relevant and of interest to your audience.
- Do not digress from the topic.

II. Organization
- Structure your text into introduction, body, and conclusion.
- Present the topic / viewpoint in the introduction.
- Organize your paragraphs clearly, and use topic sentences.
- Use a variety of appropriate linking devices between paragraphs.
- Indicate logical relations between sentences and the overall method of development (e. g. result, cause and effect, comparison, etc.) by the appropriate use of vocabulary, conjunctions and discourse markers.

III. Vocabulary
- Use a wide range of vocabulary appropriate to the task.
- Avoid repetition by using paraphrase and synonyms.
- Use register ranging from neutral to formal.

IV. Grammatical Patterns and Sentence Structure
- Write correctly.
- Use a range of language patterns and structures.
- Keep the grammatical structure more formal (e.g. complex sentences).
- Be careful about spelling and punctuation.

V.   Length: Keep within the required word limit.

During the first class session we look at a sample question (based on our model text) and discuss with the students what the key ideas to be addressed are.

> **Sample Question**: Some people think that new forms of communication have been a benefit for society, while others think that instant communication is causing a breakdown of social relations. Do you think that instant communication is more of an advantage or disadvantage?

Students then brainstorm ideas alone, before working in pairs or small groups to pool their ideas. In a class feedback session, we collect everyone's ideas on the board, separated into *pro* and *con*. At this point, we suggest any ideas used in our model text which have not been elicited from students and add them to the list on the board.

Next, we undertake a think-aloud exercise and reproduce our sample organization plan on the board, talking students through the choices made in order to produce the plan. For example:

> "My point of view is that instant communication is a benefit for society and so in my introduction I am going to briefly explain what I mean by instant communication and then state my point of view. As I want to persuade my readers that instant communication is a benefit, I'm going to focus on the advantages in my first paragraph, so let's see what I think the strongest arguments for my point of view are in the list of points we brainstormed...."

The end result is a sample organization plan on the board for students to see.

Handout 2: Sample Organization Plan

Organization Plan

Introduction
- Types: cell phones, e-mail, Internet
- Viewpoint is Pro

Body

Paragraph 1: Advantages
- Communication itself is "human"
- Helps people learn
- Share knowledge
- All benefit from results of shared knowledge

Paragraph 2: Rebuttal of disadvantage
- People still socialize
- Instant communication is an addition, not substitution
- More contact possible with those far away

Conclusion
- More of an advantage than disadvantage

When students have seen the process of constructing an organization plan from their brainstorming, they read the model text (see below) to see how the plan can be transformed into a full text, and in groups/pairs/individually they do the following tasks:

1. Identify the sentence in the introduction that makes the writer's point of view clear.
2. What is the main idea of each paragraph? Highlight the topic sentence in each.
3. Indicate the support and/or examples that are given in each paragraph to support the main idea expressed in the topic sentence.

4. Highlight or underline the vocabulary that indicates:
   - linking of ideas;
   - transition from one idea to another.
5. What vocabulary items could be substituted for those you found in (4)?
6. Summarize the author's point of view (i.e. the answer to the question) in 1–2 sentences.

Performing this sequence of tasks helps students to see a connection between the guidelines for assessment they were given for the text and a model text. A class discussion afterwards focuses on how well the model text follows the guidelines given.

Handout 3: Sample Model Text

By the beginning of the 21st century, many new methods of instant communication have become available, including cell phones, electronic mail, and the internet. The rapid increase in the number of these methods as well as the wider accessibility to each has, like all forms of human advancement, both positive and negative aspects. However, all things considered, the advantages far outweigh the disadvantages.

Most importantly, humans have a need to communicate, and have always developed new and more effective ways to do so. Communication of knowledge and ideas helps people to learn more and to benefit from the achievements of others; for example, by taking advantage of advances in medicine, agriculture, and technology. This in turn raises the standard of living for all, even those who did not have access to the original information. Being able to do this faster and in more ways, therefore, eventually benefits all humankind.

Although many believe that more of such communication reduces face-to-face interactions, thereby adversely affecting social relations, there is really no effect on the social life that humans have always had, namely time with family, friends, and neighbors. One is not likely to stop seeing those people one sends e-mail to or calls on a cell phone. On the contrary, one increases social contact these ways with people one is not able to meet; for example, friends and colleagues in other cities. In addition, social contacts can be initiated and maintained with people all over the world, which would be impossible without such communication methods.

Since humans have always strived to know more and have always developed faster methods to communicate this knowledge, it is unrealistic to see instant communication as a problem. Considering the far-reaching advantages, it should instead be seen as an advantage for humankind.

Step 2: Preparation of Organization Plan and Introduction to Reflection

When students are ready to write their first essay, we prepare a writing workshop and introduce the idea of reflection. We explain why we feel that this can help them and show them (e.g. on the overhead projector, PowerPoint) our guidelines for reflection, which provide ideas for the kind of details they might like to make note of on their Reflection Sheet (see *Handout 4*). The main goal of this workshop is for the students to develop a clearly written organization plan for their answer that we will approve before they go on to write the first draft.

Guidelines for Reflection

What is the purpose of reflection?

   I. <u>Become aware of your strengths and weaknesses</u>
- What do you feel confident about in your writing? Why?
- What are you not so confident about? Why?
- What is fairly easy for you? Why?
- What are you having difficulty with? Why?

  II. <u>What may be causing your problems</u>
- Too tired, upset or not feeling well
- Not sure what to do / what the task is
- Lack of interest / No feeling for the topic
- "Can't think" / No ideas
- Lack of language ability
  1. Trouble expressing self in English
  2. Too much internal translation
  3. Low level of English skills
- Feeling time pressure
- Don't really understand topic / question
- Feel disorganized / Don't know where to start

III. <u>Solutions to the problems</u>
- Why is this happening?
- What change(s) could help?
- How can you ***help yourself*** to become a better writer?

Students are then given the essay question and a time limit (10–15 minutes) in which to individually brainstorm the topic for *pro/con* ideas and roughly organize them into an organization plan, which includes a topic sentence for each paragraph and support/exemplification for this. This is followed by a point in the workshop when students stop working and fill in their Reflection Sheet (below), in this case the section on *Prewriting.* This involves checking a choice from 1 to 5, where 1 is the highest and 5 the lowest rating, to reflect how well they managed each particular stage and adding any other comments they feel relevant.

Handout 4: Reflection Sheet

Reflection Sheet: _____   **Name:** _____

How do you feel? □tired □hungry □upset □distracted □okay □great □other:

Prewriting	1	2	3	4	5	Comments
Understand topic						
Brainstorm ideas						
Support for ideas						
Organization plan						
Topic sentences						
Potential vocabulary						
Timing						
Other						

Peer Discussion/Feedback: usefulness: ideas generated, changes made, etc.

Reflection on First Draft: strengths/weaknesses; easy/difficult; etc. – Why?

First draft	1	2	3	4	5	Comments
Organization						
Ideas/support						
Introduction						
Conclusion						
Vocabulary						
Grammar/ sentence structure						
Timing						

Reflection on Final Draft: are you satisfied/unsatisfied so far? Why?

Overall Comments: with Final (revised) Draft – anything learned? Changed? Why?

Students then form small groups to share ideas and get feedback from each other on their own rough organization plan. During this time (which generally takes up the rest of the session), they can amend and improve their work, the only stipulation being that they should have a finished organization plan for their essay to hand in by the end of the session. Five minutes before the end of the session, we stop students so that they can fill in the next part of the Reflection Sheet: *Peer Discussion/Feedback*.

We collect students' organization plans and give brief written feedback on structure (not grammar or vocabulary) – for example, inconsistencies, pointing out questions raised but not answered, lack of support – and indicating whether individual students can start writing their first draft, or whether they should revise the plan as indicated in the feedback.

Step 3: First Draft

Step 3 either can take place in the next class session or can be given as homework. Students' organization plans are returned and they either start writing their first draft, or revise the plan and then start writing. Students should be reminded that they need to fill in the relevant section of the Reflection Sheet: *First Draft* after they have completed the first draft.

Step 4: Feedback

When students have a neatly prepared copy of the first draft, we start the feedback process. In class, students exchange essays in pairs to get preliminary feedback on their work. This stage can take various forms. Initially, students need detailed guidance to make this task worthwhile, or else they just tend to say that everything they read is "fine." This guidance can take the form of a list of features to look for and check off as illustrated below:

Handout 5: Sample Peer Feedback Sheet

PEER FEEDBACK for (writer): _____

By (peer reviewer): _____ **Text:** _____
First look at the overall organization of the text.
Is it well-organized?

yes ½ no Organization: did the writer
☐   ☐   ☐   structure the text into introduction, body, and conclusion?
☐   ☐   ☐   organize the paragraphs so that each has a clear focus?
Any further comments about organization?

Alternatively, a list of tasks similar to those done on the model text can be given, e.g.:

✓ Identify the sentence in the introduction that makes your colleague's point of view clear.

✓ What is the main idea of each paragraph? Highlight the topic sentence in each.

Students then hand their essay to us, along with the Peer Feedback Sheet, so that we can see the kind of comments students have given each other.

When we read the essays, we fill in a Feedback Sheet (*Handout 6*) that mirrors the features identified in the Assessment Guidelines (*Handout 1*). For example, students have been told to put their viewpoint in the introduction, so the feedback checks whether they have done this (Did you…?).

Handout 6: Feedback Sheet from Instructor

Feedback Sheet: *Opinion Essay*   Name: _____

yes ½ no

1. Content, Arguments, and Evidence: Did you

☐ ☐ ☐ focus on the topic (the specific issue)?

☐ ☐ ☐ present a reasoned argument?

☐ ☐ ☐ support your argument with evidence and examples?

☐ ☐ ☐ provide evidence that is relevant and of interest to your audience?

☐ ☐ ☐ not digress from the topic?

2. Organization: Did you

☐ ☐ ☐ structure your text into introduction, body, and conclusion?

☐ ☐ ☐ present the topic / viewpoint in the introduction?

☐ ☐ ☐ organize your paragraphs clearly, using topic sentences?

☐ ☐ ☐ use a variety of appropriate linking devices between paragraphs?

☐ ☐ ☐ use appropriate vocabulary and linking words to indicate logical relations between ideas (e.g. result, cause and effect, comparison, etc.)?

3. Vocabulary: Did you

☐ ☐ ☐ use a wide range of vocabulary appropriate to the task?

☐ ☐ ☐ avoid repetition by using paraphrase and synonyms?

☐ ☐ ☐ use register ranging from neutral to formal?

4. Grammatical Patterns and Sentence Structure: did you

☐ ☐ ☐ write correctly: grammar / awkwardness / unclear?

☐ ☐ ☐ use a range of patterns and structures?

☐ ☐ ☐ keep the grammatical structure more formal (e.g. complex sentences)?

☐ ☐ ☐ use correct: spelling / punctuation?

5. Length: Did you

☐   ☐ write: too short / too long?

Further comments:

Depending on the time available, we either fill in only the Feedback Sheet, or add written comments to the text as well. Language errors (tenses, incorrect vocabulary items, spelling, punctuation, etc.) are noted with proofreading marks.

Step 5: The Final Draft

Students receive their corrected essays and refer to the proofreading marks and Feedback Sheet (*Handout 6*) in order to produce a final draft. Before handing in both versions of the essay and all Feedback Sheets, students fill in the last two sections of the Reflection Sheet: *Reflection on Final Draft* and *Overall Comments* (*Handout 4*), which is also handed in. We take into account both drafts in giving them a grade – either a numerical mark or written feedback – so students see that all stages of the process are important, and all contribute to a well-written final product. If the earlier stages of the essay had not been done well, but the student has revised the text very well, this will be reflected in the grade. Likewise, a student who wrote a fairly good first draft, but didn't bother to revise it very well, will also have this reflected in the overall grade.

Step 6: Consultations

Whenever possible during the semester – generally after students have worked through at least two texts – we arrange time for short consultations with each student. They are instructed to come prepared with specific points of reflection so we can discuss which aspects of the writing process that they feel more or less confident about, and why. This encourages students to develop insight into their development as writers and reinforces the importance of reflection. It is also intended to send the message that we feel students are able, and indeed required, to work actively to improve their skills themselves and that we are working as a team rather than in a hierarchical situation in which the teacher is the authority students must rely on to understand and improve their writing.

Sample Questions for Students to Consider

Consultations

As we have only a short time to talk about your writing this semester, it will be a more effective use of time if you think *beforehand* of any issues you want to bring up.

   As a starter, read through the following questions and jot down answers to them, and add anything else you want to talk about:
- What do you enjoy most when writing?
- Where do you feel you have made the most progress this semester?
- What have you found yourself to be best at?
- What can you do to build on these strengths?
- Where have you found the most problems?
- What do you feel you can do to help yourself overcome these problems?
- Anything else?

III. Implementation

This activity has been carried out over four semesters (2006–2008) with eight classes of first-year, second-semester students (192 students). Approximately three-quarters of the students are Austrian nationals, with the remaining quarter coming from non-Austrian (largely Eastern European) backgrounds. Over the four semesters, some modifications have been made as we incorporated feedback on the approach from students and our own observations. In the first semester, we were very prescriptive in the time allowed for each section of the workshop, but we have subsequently relaxed this to allow students as much time as it appears the particular group needs.

   At various points during the prewriting process, students are given time to work in small groups. In these collaborative sessions, students are encouraged to both give and receive feedback on their ideas and organization plan. In giving feedback, they show their colleagues how their ideas came across, and whether they are clear enough. The object is not to judge others' writing as "good" or "bad," nor to point out mistakes in grammar. These can be worked on later in the post-writing stage. The primary objective is to respond as a reader to others' written ideas, so that they see their compositions from a different viewpoint. Our approach is intended to teach students to look at their own writing from the perspective of a reader. Although students sometimes need supervision to ensure that they stay focused on the purpose of this discussion, peer feedback is a part of the writing workshop that students generally respond positively to. They appreciate seeing what their colleagues are doing, and often feel that if others have ideas similar to their own, this in some way confirms that they are on the right track, which has a motivating effect.

It often takes the students the entire semester to develop the reflective skills necessary to work with the Reflection Sheet and to see its benefits. Our students are not used to reflecting on their work, so they do not consider why some aspects of their writing process are effective while others are not. We present the Reflection Sheet as a way for them to think about this and to show them that they can improve their writing skills if they develop an ability to understand their own writing and thinking processes, which is a revelation for most of them.

The Feedback Sheet is a significant factor in enabling students to identify their strengths and weaknesses and has been much revised from our earliest versions of the activity. It was clear that for students to really improve their writing from essay to essay, they needed detailed feedback on their work, yet this was very time-consuming. The Feedback Sheet allows us to give detailed feedback to students regardless of the amount of time available to us: a simple check or more detailed comments. This type of feedback allows students to see an overview of the assessment of their writing, and focuses on the positive aspects of their work – not just what is "wrong." They can see at a glance in which areas they are stronger or weaker. For example, they might have done well in the "Organization" section, but not as well in "Vocabulary." Students appreciate the completeness and clarity of this type of feedback.

Over the course of the semester, both we and the students can see improvements in different aspects of their writing. After filling in the Reflection Sheet for several assignments and receiving Feedback Sheets detailing their performance, individual students may begin to see patterns and so become aware, for example, that they always have problems with vocabulary, whereas organization causes them little trouble. This means that they are able to focus on specific problem areas when trying to improve their performance, and so see improvement as a manageable task rather than being overwhelmed by it.

IV.   Reflections and Recommendations

The basic plan outlined here with the example of writing an opinion essay has been effective for a range of groups and texts. All of our writing workshops have these basic components:

- Clearly spelled-out out guidelines for the text;
- Models texts to read and analyze;
- "Hands-on" interaction with students within the classroom when they first start writing the text themselves;
- Controlled prewriting stages;
- Student reflection;
- Peer consultation and feedback;
- Focused feedback that mirrors the assessment guidelines;
- Revision and rewriting of the text;
- Repeated work with the same text type.

One of the greatest advantages of our approach is that it is extremely flexible and so is adaptable to whatever timeframe is available. The steps can be broken down and done in shorter classes, or combined to be used in longer classes. For example, there might only be time to do part of Step 1, up to the presentation of the sample organization plan, in one class, and then students start work on the exercises with the model text in the next class; or it could be that the whole of Step 1 is dealt with in one class. The important things are that the steps be followed in order, and at certain points in the process the instructor needs to take in student work to give feedback. This flexibility extends to the method of working, and so the suggestions given at each stage for how the students work (individually, in pairs, or in groups) can easily be varied to suit different situations.

We used the same approach for first, third, and fourth semester students at the University of Vienna, as well as first to sixth semester engineering students in an English for Specific Purposes program at the University of Applied Sciences Technikum Wien. Text types have included graph descriptions, text analyses, book and film reviews, process descriptions, technical proposals, business letters, and technical abstracts. We also feel that our workshop approach would work well with other age groups and education levels (secondary school students and adult learners), and could be used with native speakers of English in writing programs from secondary school to university level. In different level groups, and with different text types, or as students improve, the instructor can change the balance of what is done in and out of the class, and how much time is spent on material related to different stages of the writing process. It is also possible to make some use as needed of EFL or bilingual students' mother tongue for some purposes. In lower level and technical groups at our university, for example, we conduct the reflection process in the students' first language.

In teaching writing, as in other areas of life, it is easier to prevent a problem than to fix it. We find that guiding the students to organize their ideas before beginning to write, as well as assisting them to reflect on their work, pays off significantly in the postwriting stages.

References

Swales, John M. (1990) *Genre Analysis*. Cambridge: Cambridge University Press.

White, Ron and Arndt, Valerie (1991) *Process Writing*. London and New York: Longman.

16 Conference-based Writing Assessment and Grading

Robert T. Koch Jr.

I.   Background

The process of collecting, grading, and returning compositions is almost universally regarded as a trying one, both for the teacher doing the work and the student receiving the grade. Like Belanoff (1991, 1993), many writing teachers simply dislike grading. We collect documents, pore over them first to determine and then to justify a grade, write marginalia and end comments designed to both help the student improve and stand up to the grade appeals process, then return the document. For this effort, students reward us by racing to the back page, ignoring our comments (sometimes temporarily, other times permanently), complaining about the grade and our handwriting, and filing complaints against us with the Department Chair. While this may sound like a worst-case scenario, undoubtedly, many writing teachers, myself included, have been beaten by this process and frustrated by its results.

One possible response to this problem is the use of conference-based assessment and grading, in which the paper being assessed is compared to a set of characteristics, first by the student, then by the instructor. The two parties engage in an intellectual discussion of the characteristics, and a grade based on the observable qualities of the paper, as covered in the discussion, is assigned. This activity requires students to develop their use of *logos* in intellectual discussion, and, more importantly, helps them understand the thought processes and criteria that result in good writing. Simultaneously, the instructor's comments are given a more detailed context, not only as responses to a paper, but as part of critical discussion and within the framework of the student's overall arc of writing development. When this activity is further integrated with reflection and revision, the end result is usually a student who is more keenly aware of his or her own strengths and weaknesses, who can articulate those writing qualities, and who possesses a more mature writing process that will, in turn, enable and encourage development beyond the classroom.

This activity draws from writing assessment, reflective practice, and grading scholarship. First, it is a practical response to Brian Huot's call to implement instructive evaluation in the composition classroom (Huot, 2002). Instructive evaluation is a pedagogical effort to actively involve students in the entire act of writing, from establishing criteria and developing decision-making skills, through revision and reflective analysis of the written product's qualities. In order to do this, instructors must subscribe to the belief "that being able to assess writing is an important part of being able to write well" (Huot, 2002: 165), the consequence of this belief being the integration of pedagogy and assessment. This activity, which keys classroom activities on decision-making and writing quality to an assessment rubric and actively engages students in a discussion of their own processes and observations about a piece of writing, emerges in large part from Huot's work.

Although the concept of instructive evaluation is foundational to this practice, it does not resolve the conflict between assessment and grading, two terms that have been conflated over time. To summarize Huot's (2002) description of the two, assessment involves analysis of the characteristics of a given text at a given moment in the writer's process, while grading is the rendering of a largely subjective judgment of a student's specific skills at a specific instant in time, a judgment that will be carried forward into the social and political arenas of the student's career and life. As a result, the kind of evaluative statements which instructors attempt to make in order to enhance students' abilities are lost if they are accompanied by a judgment that, more often than not (at least to students) seems arbitrary. Ultimately, this conflation of terms leads to the kind of situation described in the opening of this chapter. Years ago, Donald Murray reminded the discipline that "a grade finishes a paper" (Murray, 1972: 14) and that instructors of writing should therefore not grade drafts. What should also be remembered is that the development of the writer is still more important than the development of the paper, although like assessment and grading, it seems more often that the writer cannot see the distinction, in this case, between his or her own learning and the text s/he produces. Like grading and assessment, teachers, like students, have pedagogically conflated the development of the writer with the development of his or her text.

In the absence of a clear resolution to the grading problem, a variety of grading practices such as portfolio grading, contract grading, and pass/fail grading have been implemented, all of which come with drawbacks that do not necessarily resolve the conflict (Shiffman, 1997). Whereas portfolios only delay judgment, or spread judgment to a committee, contract grading raises questions about inconsistent standards, even as it achieves Shiffman's search for a more feminist classroom. Meanwhile, pass/fail grading is administratively – and more to the point – culturally unacceptable, although some schools willingly give NC, or "No Credit," to students who fail first-year composition. The practice described here doesn't attempt to delay, undermine, or circumvent grades and grading. Instead, it attaches qualities of good writing in various categories to each letter grade, and holds students accountable for giving themselves an honest assessment before the text is presented to the instructor.

The power of instructive evaluation as a tool for uniting decision-making processes, revision, and evaluation can be increased if it is performed as a sustained reflective activity. Yancey's (1998) constructive reflection and reflection-in-presentation become valuable concepts for the instructor who implements this activity. Depending on how the assessment conference is situated within the course, it may promote both learning goals, each fulfilling a different purpose for the writer. As an act of reflection-in-presentation, the assessment conference gives the student an opportunity to reflect upon, with evidence from the text and guideline or rubric for assessment, the decision-making and evaluation processes s/he engaged in while producing the text. Because the presentation is a conversation, the instructor has the opportunity to help the student analyze and understand more about critical writing decisions. If the assessment conference is situated as one in a sequence of sessions, over the course of the semester, and especially if students are given a one to two week revision period at the end of the term, it also serves as part of a constructive reflection sequence in which students and professor can identify trends of strengths, weaknesses, and improvements that have been made across assignments during the semester. Awareness of such trends will enable students to prioritize revision according to areas of need, and should encourage them to move beyond the grade as a personal judgment and into the realm of grade as an indicator of current skills along an increasingly visible learning curve.

Given the strain and conflict that normally accompany grading situations and the scholarship of the field in the areas of assessment, grading, and reflection, the goals of this activity are as follows:

- Develop student understanding of the qualities of good writing as it occurs in an academic context;
- Increase each student's ability to evaluate his or her own writing given the criteria discussed in the course;

- Raise each student's awareness of trends in strengths and weaknesses that characterize her or his own writing; and
- Engage the student in strategizing to maintain strong characteristics and strengthen weak ones.

II.   Description of Activity

Conference-based assessment and grading, as it is described here, may be used in any writing course or other course that employs written assignments. It should be conducted during the final week of any multi-week essay assignment, and may be used with multiple assignments over the course of a semester, so that emergent trends may be discussed. A few assumptions are necessary for this activity to be successful:

1. Students are given a rubric or other explicit assessment guidelines. This rubric will be used not only for assessment, but for shaping and guiding class discussions and conferences. In effect, the rubric must serve as a teaching tool. Additionally, the rubric brings a structure to conferences and facilitates students' understanding of writing issues.
2. The conference is not focused on grammar. This activity allows instructors to engage students in meaningful conversation about their writing development. A focus on correcting every grammatical error instead of identifying trends will slow the conference down and undermine the usefulness of the activity.
3. The instructor will see student work before the Assessment Conference. Familiarity with students' writing, and with their processes and concerns over the course of the assignment, will enable a smoother and more successful conference.
4. The conference is not viewed just as an act of grading, but as an opportunity to individually analyze students'

decision-making processes through examination of writing characteristics and trends.

The time commitment for this activity depends on the length of the paper. A 2-page assignment may only require a 15-minute conference. Larger research papers may require 30 minutes. For a class of 25 students:

15-minute conferences will take approximately 6 hours, 15 minutes.
20-minute conferences will take approximately 8 hours, 20 minutes.
30-minute conference will take approximately 12 hours, 30 minutes.

The amount of time needed will depend on the instructor's ability to read quickly and effectively.

Step 1 (The Date the Assignment is Given): Document Distribution

At the start of the semester, two documents are distributed: a grading rubric and a grading conference explanation sheet. The grading rubric can take any of a number of forms, depending on what the instructor needs or wishes to do. Individually or departmentally designed rubrics of any type – rating scales, descriptive rubrics, or holistic rubrics – may be used, although Suskie's (2004) explanation of descriptive rubrics makes them seem most appropriate for conference activities. Rubric choice and design is very important; it will serve as a guidepost for writing terminology, classroom discussion, and the assessment and grading conferences themselves. In a course like first-year composition, it may be effective to design a descriptive rubric based upon McAndrew and Reigstadt's (2001) higher and lower order concerns, since this material is arguably the "content" of the discipline. The higher order concerns are audience, purpose, thesis, organization, and development; the lower order concerns are grammar, mechanics, punctuation, and spelling. These concerns provide a good set of terms and definitions that can serve as a starting point for discussing writing decisions, while also providing a foundation for assessment criteria.

The second document, the grading conference explanation sheet, should establish the guidelines for conference meetings, providing expectations, requirements, and rules for conferences. Clear policies should help students understand instructor expectations on several issues, including how to present reasoned arguments with textual evidence, how effort may be accounted for in the grade, and how overly emotional responses will be handled. Strong guidelines generally result in positive interactions with most students. The guidelines may also specify whether or not grades should be marked on a copy of the rubric, or whether or not the student should provide some reflective justification for the grade, one that preferably refers to pages and paragraphs that demonstrate requisite essay characteristics.

Step 2 (The Assignment Duration): Contextualized Instruction

During the course of the semester, classroom discussions, mini-lessons, and peer group work can be related back to key phrases and terms in the rubric. For example, discussions of organization may begin with understanding that a good academic essay is one that uses the argument itself to drive both form and content. The conversation may turn to overall structure and patterns of organization, but will ultimately end with an activity in which students must understand what they have done to develop their work: the form, the content, or the argument. Over the course of the term, students gain repeated exposure not just to the rubric as a document for grading and assessment activities, but more importantly, to the terminology of writing. This exposure teaches students the language they will need in order to understand and accurately reflect upon their writing processes, decision-making, and texts. The rubric thus ceases to serve exclusively as an instrument of assessment or grading and becomes a foundation for understanding writing decisions and course content, providing knowledge that is necessary during both the writing process and evaluation.

Step 3 (The Week Prior to Conferences): Conference Sign-Up and Self-Assessment

The week before an assignment is due, students sign up for conference times to discuss their work. As noted above, the times and lengths of conferences may vary according to individual instructors' needs. It is often a good idea, as with regular writing conferences, to remind students to put this information down in their cell phone calendars or date books. Assessment conference dates may also be listed in the syllabus. Note that this conference does not replace conferences held during essay development.

Step 4 (Final Week of the Assignment): Conference

The conference itself usually involves three steps:

1. A preliminary read of the finished text;
2. Evaluation of the text, with discussion; and
3. Discussion of strengths, weaknesses, and growth within and across assignments.

The preliminary read is necessary to do an assessment of what is in the text. Most writing teachers realize that within a few minutes of reading, the quality of the paper is known; all that remains is justification. Upon completing the preliminary read, the instructor may request the student's reflective comments based on the rubric, if they were required as part of conference preparation. The instructor then evaluates the paper, engaging the student in discussions of the criteria as demonstrated in the text, and discusses the student's grade selections. At points where the student has done an effective job of assessing his or her own work, this should be noted; where opinions differ, the student can be asked to read the criteria and then consider these in light of an example from his or her own text. Through this process, students begin to understand not only how to critically evaluate, but why they receive the marks they do.

Finally, when the criteria on the rubric have been discussed and the final grade tabulated based on the stated criteria, the instructor discusses with the student what their discussion, analysis, and assessment mean for the next assignment. Where should the student pay more attention? What does the student do right? If this is a second or third assignment, it may be useful to have students bring copies of all of their essays and rubrics, so that the grades and evaluations can be compared and contrasted. Were prior issues addressed? Did new problems appear? What should the writer do next? This moment of constructive reflection is a prime opportunity to help a student lay out a plan for the next assignment, for any assigned revisions, for the next course, or for writing in the future.

III. Implementation

As a reflective writing teacher, I have implemented several variants of this activity nearly every semester for five years, to great success. The description and appendices provided below explain how I implemented this activity in two courses, Basic Writing and First-Year Composition I, during Fall 2008 semester. My basic writing course was composed of students who scored 15 or below on the SAT Verbal examination, and was composed mainly of international and ethnic minority students, many of them non-traditional. My first-year composition class was the first course of a two-semester sequence; this course focused on expository writing. Demographically, it consisted primarily of women between the ages of 18–20.

My rubric (Appendix A) is a descriptive one built around higher and lower order concerns, with the addition of introductions and conclusions. It includes spaces where students can grade themselves, and where I can do the same. This rubric, as well as the practice described here, will continue to evolve because my teaching materials remain under a constant state of reflection and revision. This rubric is not perfect, and while it works well for me, many colleagues might adjust it in a number of ways. What is important is that the rubric is used to provide a common language and a set of guidelines so that students can understand how to think about their writing and assess their work.

In addition to conference guidelines, I explain in class what is expected of students during these conferences. I require them to bring me their essays, a reflective letter discussing what they learned from the assignment, and a single-page grade justification referring to specific pages and paragraphs in their texts. I also require them to bring the course rubric, described above, which we have used throughout the term. Beyond the required materials, I remind students of the guidelines described in the prior section. I encourage them to behave as adults discussing adult issues in a setting that privileges *logos* over *ethos* and *pathos*. I remind them that hard work alone is not sufficient to achieve a good grade, but that they can improve by paying attention to the criteria and learning to incorporate them into their writing.

The rubric is a regular part of our class, appearing during discussions of all our higher order concerns of our class, as well as during peer review, so students are very comfortable with it, and with the terminology used, by the time the first set of assessment conferences begins. When students arrive in my office for the first conference, I begin with their reflective letters, looking at what they have identified as strengths, weaknesses, and areas for improvement. This gives me an idea of what to expect when I read their essays. I have graded their reflective letters too, as part of a departmental essay requirement, although this practice turned out to be detrimental to the process, making students unnecessarily nervous about their quality and content, even though I had designated the letters as a writing-to-learn activity. These reflective letters often properly identified the weaknesses of the assigned essay.

Next, I give their essays a preliminary read, looking for obvious cues that reveal larger issues, such as a lack of a clear thesis, poorly integrated or absent evidence, short paragraphs that reveal a lack of academic development, or exceedingly long paragraphs that reveal issues in organization. We discuss these problem areas, and I will often write down the purposes of each paragraph in the margin so that students see what they missed when we discussed organization in class. As we address the higher order concerns, I ask students to direct me to the places in the paper where I should look to see evidence justifying their chosen grade. If the student has not provided evidence, or if I see contrary evidence, I point these out to the student, and we discuss what these differing pieces of evidence, or their absence, mean for the reader as well as for the grade. I do not try to address every instance of a given problem in the paper, although I do address overall organization, since that involves the whole work. However, a properly worded rubric can indicate what needs to be in the paper in order to justify a grade. For example, my rubric says that one out-of-place paragraph results in a "C" grade for organization; more than one is a "D." As a result of this wording, a student who cannot justify the placement of a single paragraph's location in the paper knows what the grade will be. A student who has multiple misplaced paragraphs knows the grade as well. In the end, we work together to do what I would normally do alone: we find strengths or weaknesses that justify the grade.

While addressing higher order concerns, lower order issues of grammar, mechanics, punctuation, and spelling often emerge. If they don't, I take sample readings from various parts of the paper, usually a paragraph every other page, in order to talk more about these matters, as well as about style, audience, and purpose. When I see high-priority grammar errors, such as a comma splice or a subject-verb agreement issue, I begin looking for a trend (three) of those problems, and I stop when I find the trend. As with the other criteria, the wording of the rubric guides the grade. A single trend results in a grade of "C"; more than one is a "D." As I stated earlier in my assumptions, conference grading is not an advisable activity for those teachers who identify every error in a paper. These conferences are far more effective when used to help students understand linear thought, the logical progression of an idea through a system of well-developed and purposeful stages, to arrive at some conclusion, and concepts relating to high order concerns, that require complex critical thinking and decision-making to shape the message of any text, whether linear, hyper-linear (such as a website), or non-linear. These topics should be the primary emphasis of conference discussions, with grammar commentary limited to identifying error trends, and perhaps discussing how to fix them or where to find them advice or solutions in a handbook.

In subsequent essay conferences, I ask my students to bring their prior graded rubrics so that we can chart their progress on specific writing criteria, an act of constructive reflection. For example, if a student receives an "A" grade for organization on the first essay and a "C" on the second, we can discuss the nature of this change, whether brought about by the nature or the relative difficulty of the genres or topics of the two essays, or whether it was a function of employing a less familiar organizational pattern. The latter is often the case, especially when students who write good narratives must then try to organize more complex thoughts outside of a narrative structure. This gives students an idea of what to work on, where they are strong; in some cases, it can change their minds about whether or not they perceive themselves to be good or poor writers.

IV. Reflections and Recommendations

Thus far I have emphasized my own beliefs about the value of this activity. A better evaluation and reflection on this practice can be offered through the voices of my students. At the end of the Fall 2008 semester, I received approval to collect student responses to this activity, using a university Institutional Review Board-approved methodology that incorporated blind questionnaires collected by students during the final exam period. Five of twelve Basic Writing students and nineteen of twenty First-Year Composition I students completed the questionnaire. Below are some of their responses regarding the various components of this practice.

Regarding the course rubric:

- "No strong opinion either way. It worked."
- "It was organized, well thought out, and useful throughout the whole semester."
- "The rubric was very valuable in this class. It causes you to think about the parts of the paper rather than just the paper as a whole."
- "I thought the rubric was very fair. It gave me a structure to go by as I wrote."
- "I would like to have the rubric in future English courses."
- "The course rubric was wonderful; [it] allowed me to basically know my grade on the essay before it was evaluated."

Nearly all of the rubric comments discussed the fairness of the document, or how it made the grade understandable.

Regarding the reflective letter:

- "The reflective essays were very helpful; [they] made me think about my processes for writing"
- "The reflective essay makes you learn from what you did in your paper."
- "It was easy to write a paper on how I was developing in the class and it also made me aware of the areas I needed to work on."
- "The reflective essay possibly helped all students to better understand their strengths and weaknesses in writing."
- "It helped me think more clearly about my paper."

- "The reflective essay was a great learning tool, making you look back on how or why you did what you did, mak[ing] you think about that the next go around."
- "It allowed me to step back and assess the work."

Many of the students who opposed the reflective essay discussed it in terms of a poor grade, described it as an additional burden, or simply did not specify reasons for their opposition.

The students approved of the grade justification because it provided them with a sense of fair play and involvement, and allowed them to compare their thoughts with my own. They wrote:

- "If I thought I deserved an A but you were going to give me a B I had an opportunity to show you why I deserved an A."
- "I really liked being able to discuss each individual grade. It helps us to be more fairly judged."
- "This allowed us to critique our work and justify our grades in certain areas."
- "Encouraged critical thinking about writing."
- "Allowed me to set my own standard for what I thought my grade should be and got me involved in the paper. I prefer it."
- "Good because you can see how you graded it and see if the teacher feels the same way."
- "It gave me guidelines to go by and made whatever grade I received fair."
- "Forces students to think about their work, and to think about what grade they deserve."
- "I had to take an honest approach to grading my own paper. This made me learn where my strengths and weaknesses were, thus teaching me more."

Those who opposed the grade justification did so more on the grounds of having go to the trouble to write it out. Some students felt that I should have looked at it rather than have them read it aloud. Although a few complained that I did not use it, these may well be students who simply didn't provide a realistic assessment of their own work or of the course.

The conference itself received strong support from many students, who appreciated the opportunity to discuss their work, defend it, and just have one-on-one time. They wrote:

- "We got to discuss our papers and argue points. And I liked that we got our grades that day."
- "Helps student-teacher understanding. Personal learning enriched."
- "The conference was the greatest help. Forced to grade then stand up for your paper inspires better writing."
- "I liked it because it really showed me areas I needed to work on."
- "I love it. It gives us the opportunity to sit down with you and really share our paper and to share with you what we were thinking. It provides fair grading and a better sense of completion."
- "I think all teachers need to do this with papers so students know how you grade."
- "You actually get input on your grade and see why your teacher did what he did."
- "During the conferences I was told what I was doing wrong in my essay and how to make it better."
- "The assessment conference is very valuable. It helps the student learn what to look for, and where their weaknesses are."

The few students who opposed the conference felt that it was intimidating or that their faults were put on display, or they admitted that they had trouble taking criticism.

These comments reveal several points about how writing teachers or other teachers who assign writing can integrate assessment and make grading a more palatable activity for everyone involved. First, students want to know that their voices are heard and that they are treated fairly, even if they don't get what they want. Students also want to be held accountable to a higher standard. They may complain about the work and the writing process in the public domain of the classroom, but when asked to rise to the challenge, they often do. Finally, students want to learn, and they want to improve in their writing. I am by no means an easy grader, but above comments suggest that the grade is only part of what matters to students. The practice of conference-based assessment and grading may thus be a possible strategy through which instructors can attach the grade to learning and assessment in a way that is meaningful to students.

As stated above, my practices and assignments are always subject to reflection and revision. For a person implementing this strategy for the first time, I make the following recommendations:

1. Provide an end-of-semester open revision period, during which students may revise pieces graded earlier in the term. This open revision period will give the constructive reflection process during the semester some impact on grades at the end, while allowing students to demonstrate what they have learned through the process.
2. Keep tweaking the rubric. While I have had success with my descriptive form, I am considering a holistic using form, although I am concerned about how much more arguable everything becomes if specific criteria are not given. I am still not settled on the best way to handle grammar.
3. A reflective letter, such as that described by Yancey (1998) and others may be useful; but if the purpose of the letter is to help students reflect, and to have them demonstrate their reflections to you, be wary of trying to use it to fulfill a grade requirement. It may be best not to grade the student's work at all, or to grade it only on the depth of their analysis.
4. In planning conference times, remember to schedule regular breaks. These will be useful not only for recharging, but

also for making up for lost time if conferences run longer than expected.

5. Finally, keep a box of tissues on hand. This is an entirely new experience for students, and as noted above, not every student handles the initial event well.

Although some students exhibit nervousness in the first conference, and a few even break into tears, by the end of the semester, most students seem to enjoy coming to show and defend their work. They take pride in pointing out how they have been able to strengthen a former weakness or in describing how they made their decisions as writers. In these situations, the grade, while still important, can be backgrounded by the learning, if the instructor makes a point of emphasizing the learning and growth of the writer. There is a chance here to separate writer from text, to encourage the growth of the writer, and to minimize the impact of the grade on the student's sense of self-worth and maximize its impact on students' learning by reattaching it to the text.

References

Belanoff, Pat (1991) The myths of assessment. *Journal of Basic Writing* 10(1): 54–66.

Belanoff, Pat (1993) What is a grade? In Wendy Bishop (ed.) *The Subject is Writing: Essays by Teachers and Students* 179–188. Portsmouth, New Hampshire: Boynton/Cook-Heinemann.

Huot, Brian (2002) Toward a new discourse of assessment. *College English* 65(2): 163–180.

McAndrew, Donald A. and Reigstad, Thomas J. (2001) *Tutoring Writing: A Practical Guide for Conferences*. Portsmouth, New Hampshire: Boynton/Cook-Heinemann.

Murray, Donald M. (1972, November) Teach writing as a process not product. *The Leaflet*: 11–14.

Shiffman, Betty G. (1997) Grading student writing: The dilemma from a feminist perspective. In Larry Allison, Lizbeth Bryant and Maureen Hourigan (eds.) *Grading in the Post-Process Classroom* 58–72. Portsmouth, New Hampshire: Boynton/Cook-Heinemann.

Suskie, Linda (2004) *Assessing Student Learning: A Common Sense Guide.* Bolton, Massachusetts: Anker Publishing.

Yancey, Kathleen B. (1998) *Reflection in the Writing Classroom.* Logan, Utah: Utah State University Press.

Appendix A: English Grading Rubric, 2008

Name: _____ **Essay:** _____ **Grade:** _____

After examining your thesis-driven essay in light of each criteria and its descriptor, enter the score for each criteria that most accurately describes your essay.

		Student	Teacher
Audience & Purpose (10%)			
A+ 99 / A 95 / A- 91	Consistently purposeful style & tone (word choice, arrangement, & POV) imply clear audience & purpose	_____	_____
B+ 89 / B 85 / B- 81	Purposeful style & tone (word choice, arrangement, & POV) imply audience(s) and/or purpose	_____	_____
C+ 79 / C 75 / C- 71	Lapses in style & tone (word choice, arrangement, & POV); multiple audiences or purposes	_____	_____
D+ 69 / D 65 / D- 61	Hints at style & tone (word choice, arrangement, & POV); self-emphasis	_____	_____
F 50	Random style & tone (word choice, arrangement, & POV); no discernable audience	_____	_____
Thesis (10%)			
A+ 99 / A 95 / A- 91	Thesis makes a clear, arguable assertion that reveals critical and purposeful content organization	_____	_____
B+ 89 / B 85 / B- 81	Thesis makes a clear or arguable assertion, but may lack critical or purposeful content organization	_____	_____
C+ 79 / C 75 / C- 71	Thesis offers unnecessarily form-driven organization and lacks critical or purposeful content organization	_____	_____
D+ 69 / D 65 / D- 61	Thesis is unclear; it cannot stand alone as a complete and independent thought	_____	_____
F Absent 0	No Thesis	_____	_____

Paragraph Organization (10%)

A+ 99 / A 95 / A- 91	Organization is content & assertion driven while properly attending to applicable modes	___ ___ ___
B+ 89 / B 85 / B- 81	Organization is content or assertion driven while largely attending to applicable modes	___
C+ 79 / C 75 / C- 71	Organization is unnecessarily form-driven, forces transitional words, or has an isolated unclear paragraph	
D+ 69 / D 65 / D- 61	Organization is loose, with no clear driving force or multiple unclear paragraphs	___ ___
F 50	No sense or arbitrary sense of organization; no definitive paragraphs	___ ___

Support / Evidence (10%)

A+ 99 / A 95 / A- 91	Invaluable evidence, properly integrated and documented from a credible source when required	___
B+ 89 / B 85 / B- 81	Strong evidence, properly integrated and documented from a credible source when required	
C+ 79 / C 75 / C- 71	Appropriate evidence, properly integrated and documented from a credible source when required	
D+ 69 / D 65 / D- 61	Hypothetical, inappropriate, or inaccurate evidence; non-credible source; poor integration or documentation	___ ___
F 50	No evidence; evidence improperly integrated and documented	___ ___

Development of Connections (10%)

A+ 99 / A 95 / A- 91	Discussion of support thoroughly interconnects with other paragraphs and thesis	___ ___
B+ 89 / B 85 / B- 81	Discussion of support often interconnects with other paragraphs and thesis	
C+ 79 / C 75 / C- 71	Discussion of support shows relevance to adjacent paragraphs or to thesis	
D+ 69 / D 65 / D- 61	Minimal discussion of support; Interconnections between paragraphs and thesis unclear at times	___ ___
F 50	No intentional effort to relate supporting evidence or paragraph to thesis	___ ___

Introduction & Conclusion (10%)

A+ 99 / A 95 / A- 91 Thoroughly developed introduction and conclusion interrelated and show idea maturation from start to finish

B+ 89 / B 85 / B- 81 Developed introduction and conclusion interrelated, but may not show idea maturation from start to finish

C+ 79 / C 75 / C- 71 Unexciting Introduction and conclusion offer no clear interrelation

D+ 69 / D 65 / D- 61 Minimally developed Introduction and/or Conclusion with no clear uniting rhetorical strategy as a hook

F 50 Either Introduction or Conclusion or both are absent

Grammar & Spelling (20%)

A+ 99 / A 95 / A- 91 Few to no errors in grammar or spelling

B+ 89 / B 85 / B- 81 Isolated to occasional errors in grammar or spelling

C 75 One trend (3 or more of the same error) in the essay

D 65 Two or more trends (3 or more of the same error) in the essay

F 50 Little to no attention paid to grammar or spelling

Mechanics & Punctuation (20%)

A+ 99 / A 95 / A- 91 Few to no errors in mechanics or punctuation

B+ 89 / B 85 / B- 81 Isolated to occasional errors in mechanics or punctuation

C 75 One trend (3 or more of the same error) in the essay, or Punctuation / Formatting errors in Works Cited

D 65 Two or more trends (3 or more of the same error) in the essay, or Content errors / Missing Information in Works Cited

F 50 Little to no attention paid to mechanics or punctuation or No Works Cited

Appendix B: Assessment Conferences

The assessment conference is an essential and important part of this course because it requires you to demonstrate that you can assess good writing when you create it. This is an important skill in text production because it allows you to properly and honestly assess your strengths and weaknesses against the expectations of professional academic writers. Once you know these strengths and weaknesses, you can read appropriate handbook sections to get a better grasp of the issue, and you can revise and edit your essay more appropriately.

Conference Preparation

To prepare for the conference, do the following:

1. Complete your essay.
2. Write a reflective essay discussing your strengths, weaknesses, and writing process for this essay
3. Identify the grade you would give your essay (using +/- if you wish) for each of the criteria on the rubric (Audience, Purpose & Thesis, Organization, etc.). Then, write a justification why you would give each grade using specific support from the text. In conference, I will compare your comments and grades to the text itself.

In Conference

I will read your essays, grades, and justification, comparing your reading of the essay to my own. Where we disagree on a grade, we will discuss the reasons why the two assessments differ. During the conference, I will mark the rubric and other texts as appropriate.

Please note that this is a major opportunity to conduct yourself professionally and in an academically appropriate way. I expect you to clearly justify your stance, using evidence in the text, as opposed to telling me how hard you worked. **If you become aggressive, dismissive, or take a confrontational or sarcastic tone, you will be immediately dismissed. The grade you have upon dismissal will be your grade for the assignment.** It is important for you to develop the ability to converse clearly and rationally as part of your academic literacy.

Part 5
Working With Technology in the Writing Class

17 Scavenger Hunt: A Model for Digital Composing Processes

Sally Chandler and Mark Sutton

I. Background

In order to succeed at school and at work, today's students must be effective writers in both print and digital spaces. Because composing in digital spaces is not simply composing in print with technology added, instructors must provide a range of experiences specifically designed to help students develop digital writing processes (Lankshear and Knobel, 2007; WIDE, 2005). While instructors frequently say, "My students know more about the Internet than I do," many students need direction in acquiring effective practices for digital composing (Hargittai, 2002, 2008; Rampell, 2008). In addition, adult learners returning to school, students from high schools without effective digital writing programs, and individuals who do not have experience composing digital texts for academic purposes need support in the seamless use of technology for writing. Courses in which students meet face-to-face but use a course management system, such as Blackboard or WebCT, can provide these kinds of experiences. The Scavenger Hunt was designed both to introduce students to course management software and – more importantly – to model and teach processes for digital composing.

The Scavenger Hunt was originally designed as an interactive, critically reflective assignment to introduce college writing students to WebCT. From the outset, the assignment was both popular with students and effective in providing them with a directed, interactive model for the reading and composing processes used in academic writing. Specifically, it:

- directs students' attention to connections between the WebCT site's structure and the kind of information it provides;
- walks students through participating in threaded discussions and chat spaces;
- provides an initial supported experience with formatting and submitting electronic texts; and
- engages students in reflecting on the various experiences within composing processes.

In other words, we use the Scavenger Hunt to provide initial, facilitated digital experiences with reading critically, gathering information, offering and receiving feedback, drafting, and reflecting on one's own and other people's writing.

In keeping with the "good learning principles" which James Gee has identified in video games (Gee, 2003), the Scavenger Hunt structures interactive exploration and allows for help at the point of need. Often, instructors' first response to students who have "experience gaps" with technology is how-to workshops or handouts. Research indicates, however, that what learners really need are directed, supported experiences that help them learn how to learn (Burnett, Chandler, and Lopez, 2007; Chandler, Burnett, and Lopez, 2007; Duffelmeyer, 2003; Oblinger and Oblinger, 2005). Within digital spaces, research shows that this learning will be most effective when: (1) instructors are aware of students' technical abilities; (2) assignments build on and connect to practices in sequence rather than through isolated experiences; (3) technology and writing components are developed incrementally throughout the semester; (4) assignments are fun; (5) assignments include reflective, critical components; and (6) assignments help students learn to use and create learning networks (Selfe, 2005: 156–164). Information, communication networks, and learning practices brought to the students' and the instructor's attention through completing the Scavenger Hunt set up a solid ground for using digital writing to learn and compose for the rest of the semester.

Although the Scavenger Hunt is designed to engage students across all levels of proficiency, it is particularly important for students who are either new to digital writing in general or to academic writing in digital environments in particular. For these students, the Hunt provides an initial supported experience of learning to learn in digital spaces. It walks them through a process for assessing and negotiating expectations embedded in digital spaces; it suggests strategies for effective problem-solving and directs them to help in the form of information embedded in the Scavenger Hunt itself, as well as in the course website and associated links. Even more importantly, it engages these students in thinking about how and where needed information is most likely to be found. For students who are comfortable with technology but uncomfortable or unfamiliar with academic conventions, the Hunt provides an opportunity to build on strengths by providing a model for course expectations. By walking students through the processes for reflective rhetorical analysis, it provides a pattern according to which they can consciously explore their expectations for using a wide range of digital spaces.

The particular learning objectives of the Scavenger Hunt are:

- to introduce students to a course management site through guided interactions with it;
- to connect to digital writing practices which students bring to the classroom and provide sequentially more challenging, supported experiences with digital spaces for newcomers;

- to provide students with comfortable, facilitated experiences working together through communicating online;
- to model practices for critical, reflective rhetorical analysis of digital spaces, texts, and communications; and
- to engage students in the interactive creation and submission of different types of digital communications.

II.   Description of Activity

The Scavenger Hunt is patterned on the children's party game by the same name. In the children's game, teams are given a list of household items and told to collect them from within a particular environment. The digital Scavenger Hunt follows a similar format in that students are required to find and collect information from the course management site. Unlike its material-world counterpart, the Scavenger Hunt requires participants to find, interpret, and compose written responses to texts presented through a particular website; this process structures critical, rhetorical-analytic practices that are a central focus in most writing courses. The Hunt itself is an electronic document with a conversational list of requests asking students to interact with the course website and associated links. Students work on-screen, toggling between the Hunt and the site as they enter their answers. As students work through the assignment, the Hunt engages them in three interrelated but slightly different kinds of experiences: finding and retrieving information; interacting with classmates and the instructor through the course website to find, interpret, and convey information; and reflecting on the processes they are using to solve problems presented by the Hunt. These three experiences are generally presented sequentially. Tasks in which students look for information are clustered at the beginning, tasks providing students with experience using the site's communication options are presented in the middle, and requests for students to compose short reflections about what they have learned occur in the last section of the Hunt. This organization is not rigid, and all three kinds of experiences can be scattered throughout the activity.

The first cluster of experiences emphasizes critical analysis and information retrieval, familiarizing students with the site's structure. It begins by directing them to specific icons and dropdown lists and prompts them to analyze the kinds of information those features provide. For example, students are walked through different approaches for retrieving the course calendar and syllabus. Subsequent requests are less specific and become more complex: students are requested to find information about plagiarism, to locate readings and assignment sheets, and to reflect on how the readings or the learning modules are organized and on why they are organized as they are. To complete later tasks, students download, save, and print files, and then they answer questions about file content. While skills to accomplish such rudimentary tasks are essential for success in most composition courses, they cannot be assumed. This cluster of activities provides students who are newcomers to digital spaces with experience accomplishing the fundamental actions that they will need to navigate a site. The first activity sequence then prompts them to reflect on what they are doing, asks them if they are having trouble, offers hints, directs them to help, and provides a variety of models for finding information and additional interactive help.

The second cluster of experiences focuses specifically on walking students through social networking practices, both in terms of face-to-face conversations and through on-site communication. Prompts in this part of the Hunt encourage students who have had difficulties with earlier activities to ask the person sitting next to them for help. Over the last four years, various versions of the Hunt have also required students to send each other and/or the instructor emails, to use chat spaces to request information that may have stumped them, to post to a discussion board, and to "google" information on the Internet. This cluster of activities helps build the kind of classroom community which research identifies as pivotal in successful student writing (Selfe, 2005), and it ensures that technology newcomers will become part of this community. It helps students make connections to one another and encourages them to think of their course site and the Internet as interactive social spaces where they can find information by contacting other people as well as databases.

The final cluster of experiences establishes critical, reflective practice as integral to work on all assignments for the course. While reflective activities are interspersed throughout the Hunt, the final section draws attention to critical reflection as central to writing practice. The Hunt's last task is to compose a paragraph describing the day's class, with specific reference to the Scavenger Hunt, and attach it to an email to the instructor. Students write about what worked and what did not work for them in the Hunt (and why), and describe how they feel about using technology for academic writing. This last prompt has moved increasingly toward helping students reflect on how digital technology affects their writing process by asking them to think about how academic writing may require them to use technology differently from the ways they use it outside of an educational environment.

III.   Implementation

We began using the Scavenger Hunt in a Spring 2004 first-year composition course, and we have used it in a range of beginning writing courses, including basic writing and a summer writing workshop for pre-college students who need additional writing support before starting the regular school term. We think that one of the Hunt's strengths derives from assigning it as a whole-class, interactive activity, so we have always assigned it on a day when students are in a computer lab. Because the discussion that precedes the activity can provide students with basic connections both to classmates and to information, we generally have students introduce themselves and then spend some time talking about course objectives and procedures before we move on to the Hunt. We have found that the assignment works best when student introductions include informal discussion of experiences with technology. This conversation familiarizes students with classmates' expertise and helps identify student roles in communities of support.

We begin the assignment itself by explaining what a course management system is and by talking students through logging onto the site. Most of the time, we then introduce the site's primary navigation tools – icons, the course menu, breadcrumbs (a list representing the path users have traveled through a site) – before directing students to download the Scavenger Hunt file. After all of the students have opened the assignment as a Word document, we talk a little about format, touching on rhetorical functions of document design. After this brief discussion, we ask how students plan to enter their responses to the first cluster of tasks. Students generally say they will enter text in bold or colored font in order to emphasize their answers – which is exactly what we had in mind. At this point, many students have read ahead and a few are lost. Before having them begin the Scavenger Hunt, we discuss, as a group, what strategies they might adopt for completing the assignment. This conversation suggests that less experienced students partner with more experienced students. Students often volunteer to form a support team for individuals who need help, and students who feel overwhelmed self-identify and ask for help. The discussion usually results in some seat switching and further introductions. After emphasizing the importance of networking, we point out that "divide-and-conquer" approaches (i.e. splitting up the assignment and swapping answers) are not acceptable. We make clear that each individual needs to do his or her own typing (helpers can only talk and/or send messages) and that all students need to turn in their own assignment through their own email account on the course system.

At this point, students work on the assignment in loosely structured interactive groups. As they work, we circulate around the room to check progress, but we do not offer any answers when students get stuck. Rather, when students ask for help, we respond with leading questions or direct them to a hint embedded in the site. In this way, students are directed back to what they already know, given some direction as to where to find the needed information, and encouraged and supported as they learn how to learn. As in writing center practice, when students simply do not have sufficient domain knowledge – which in this case translates to insufficient experience with technology – we direct them to specific information embedded in the site and walk them through its application if necessary (Shamoon and Burns, 2008).

Students usually need little assistance from us; if they become confused, a peer often supports them. As mentioned in the description of the assignment, the final task is to compose a reflective paragraph on the experience of working through the assignment. When students are finished, they submit their work as an attachment via the course site's email program. Answers to the Scavenger Hunt are also communicated through an attachment available in students' e-mailboxes during the next class. This attachment is a key listing the location of requested information. Answers direct students to the appropriate page, discussion, link, or element containing the anticipated answer. Because some questions are open-ended or require reflection, not all questions have "right" answers. Class discussion of this method for "correcting" assignments helps consolidate learning practices presented in the Scavenger Hunt.

IV.   Reflections and Recommendations

Although this particular assignment is not part of a series focused on content (e.g. learning course management sites), it embodies practices for digital reading and composing as they will be practiced throughout the semester. Assignments for the remainder of the course reiterate, deepen, and extend critical site analysis; gathering information through networking; designing texts appropriate for the assignment; and revising through peer feedback. For example, throughout the course we use in-class brainstorming and peer review sessions that build on collaborative communication practices set up in the Hunt. For an analytic project presented at the middle of the semester and for a research/argument assignment at the end of the semester, students brainstorm topics and participate in invention strategies using the discussion board. They exchange drafts electronically for peer review sessions, and they sometimes comment on them electronically. Reflective elements of the Hunt help students decide how they should approach all aspects of their writing process. The Scavenger Hunt, then, introduces the processes, communication practices, networking strategies, and critical-reflective strategies that first-year students will continue to develop throughout the semester and through future experiences using technology.

Consistent with social constructivist pedagogical theory (Bruffee, 1984; Haynes, 1996), the process of working through the Scavenger Hunt serves to dispel notions of writing as solitary and as taking place largely "inside the writer's head." Through providing an experiential basis for thinking about writing as intimately tied to social processes, it makes a more convincing argument for peer-assisted, interactive composing than a theoretical reading assignment. The Hunt emphasizes interactions among students, between the students and the instructor, and between students and the Internet as places where inspiration occurs, knowledge is created, and writing unfolds. Each student may be responsible for answering the questions on their own Hunt, but most students cannot answer them without getting information from others. Because of their experience with the Hunt, students begin to see peers, the Internet, and reflection as part of the writing process. We believe this perception translates into more effective writing workshops and group assignments.

While stereotypes suggest that today's students are extremely tech-savvy, even tech-savvy students have gaps in their experience, especially in terms of academic expectations for using software (Rampell, 2008). As a result, our revisions of the Scavenger Hunt have focused on supporting the particular gaps in experiences with technology which our students bring to the classroom. For example, we always have some students who have never downloaded a file, who do not know how to exchange files across platforms, who have trouble attaching files, and who have never saved files to a USB drive. Because the particular gaps are always changing, we are constantly updating the Hunt activities. In doing so, we address patterns in gaps from previous years through embedding links and support in the subsequent year's Hunt.

Ideally, the Scavenger Hunt should be conducted in spaces where students have access to a learning network of peers – both online and face-to-face. In cases where time or computer access is limited, we have introduced the activity by walking through the initial tasks face-to-face in the classroom, and then assigned completion of the Hunt for homework. While this approach works better with classes of more technically advanced students, these students seem to do just as well as those who complete it in the classroom. When students work on their own, problems with design (such as unclear directions or tasks without enough preparatory information) can become more problematic than when they arise in the classroom. Nonetheless, our experience suggests that the activity could be equally effective for distance education in cases when students are sufficiently technically advanced to make use of chat and discussion boards, which allow them to tap into expertise and support from classmates online.

Planning for a Scavenger Hunt will reflect the design of the site which students need to learn and the learning objectives for the assignment. The activity should introduce students to the site's components by providing directed experiences. For example, if the site functions primarily as a library of readings and handouts, the Hunt might prompt students to notice how the files are organized and engage them in locating, downloading, annotating, and exchanging files with classmates. Regardless of the site's content, for the assignment to provide effective socialization in digital composing, the Hunt must include prompts for digital communication as well as prompts that engage students in critical, rhetorical, and reflective analysis. The word-processed document representing the Hunt should be located on the page with other assignments and course documents. This provides the teacher with an introductory example for downloading files and can serve as a walk-through example for the students of rhetorical analysis of form. We generally use our introductory talk about the Hunt itself to introduce students to the vocabulary needed for analyzing the site and the associated texts.

After planning the activities, instructors need to consider the places in the activity where students might get stuck. Hints can then be embedded on pages or put in emails or on discussion boards. In addition to helping students when they have trouble progressing in the Hunt, these hints help socialize students in the use of digital spaces. Students need to learn to "read" digital spaces before they can interact with them effectively. Unlike material spaces, digital spaces can be designed with embedded clues about how they should be read. Teachers can plan to include meta-hints – hints to help students learn how to identify and use embedded hints, as well as regular hints with direct information about how to use academic sites.

The Scavenger Hunt is one example of an assignment designed both to teach students how to use a particular piece of software and to socialize them in digital literacy practices suitable for academic communications. We have found that students enjoy the assignment and that it fosters a mindset which helps them become effective digital writers.

References

Bruffee, Kenneth (1984) Collaborative learning and the "conversation of mankind." *College English* 48: 773–790.

Burnett, Joshua, Chandler, Sally and Lopez, Jacklyn (2007) A report from the digital contact zone. In Danielle DeVoss and Heidi McKee (eds.) *Digital Writing Research: Technologies, Methodologies, and Ethical Issues* 319–336. Cresskill, New Jersey: Hampton Press.

Chandler, Sally, Burnett, Joshua and Lopez, Jaclyn (2007) On the bright side of the screen: Material-world interactions surrounding the socialization of "outsiders" to digital spaces. *Computers and Composition* 24: 346–364. Retrieved on 13 February 2009 from http://dx.doi.org/10.1016/j. compcom.2007.05.007.

Duffelmeyer, Barb B. (2003) Learning to learn: New TA preparation in computer pedagogy. *Computers and Composition* 20: 295–311.

Gee, James P. (2003) *What Video Games Have to Teach Us about Learning and Literacy.* New York: Palgrave.

Hargittai, Eszter (2002) Beyond logs and surveys: In-depth measures of people's online skills. *Journal of the American Society for Information Science and Technology* 53: 1239–1244.

Hargittai, Eszter (2008) The role of expertise in navigating links of influence. In Joseph Turow and Lokman Tsui (eds.) *The Hyperlinked Society* 1–22. Ann Arbor, Michigan: University of Michigan Press.

Haynes, Cynthia (1996) Social construction. In Paul Heilker and Peter Vandenberg (eds.) *Keywords in Composition Studies* 221–224. Portsmouth, New Hampshire: Heinemann.

Lankshear, Colin and Knobel, Michele (2003) *New Literacies: Changing Knowledge and Classroom Learning.* Milton Keynes, United Kingdom: Open University Press.

Oblinger, Diana G. and Oblinger, James L. (eds.) (2005) *Educating the Net Generation.* Retrieved on 22 April 2009 from http://www.educause.edu/ EducatingtheNetGeneration/5989.

Rampell, Catherine (2 May 2008) Linked in with: Eszter Hargittai. *The Chronicle of Higher Education* May 2: A13.

Selfe, Richard J. (2005). *Sustainable Computer Environments: Cultures of Support in English Studies and Language Arts.* Cresskill, New Jersey: Hampton Press.

Shamoon, Linda K. and Burns, Deborah H. (2008) A critique of pure tutoring. In Robert W. Barnett and Jacob S. Blumer (eds.) *The Longman Guide to Writing Center Theory and Practice* 225–242. New York: Longman.

Writing in Digital Environments (WIDE) Research Center Collective (2005) Why teach digital writing? *Kairos 10. Retrieved on* 30 April 2009 from http://english.ttu.edu/kairos/10.1/binder2.html?coverweb/wide/index. html.

18 Virtual Mediation: Audio-Enhanced Feedback for Student Writing

Carter Winkle

I.   Background

To err is human; is error correction divine? This chapter describes a method of enhancing coded feedback with embedded digital audio files to make available "virtual mediation" during students' revision processes. Providing composition students with meaningful and comprehensible feedback on their writing is considered essential to the development of their academic writing skills. The audio-enhanced feedback method described is grounded within second-language (L2) research as this domain of education is the area of my own specialization, research, and teaching. I suggest, however, that the L2 research and theoretical constructs underlying the prescribed feedback method are relevant to rhetoric and composition and to education more generally.

Second language research literature presents contradictory evidence as to the efficacy of error correction in L2 writing, notably the conflicting exchanges between Truscott (1996, 1999) and Ferris (1999). Truscott's (1996) "The case against grammar correction in L2 writing classes" suggested that grammar correction in L2 writing should be abandoned altogether because contemporary research had failed to provide sufficient evidence as to its efficacy. Through his selective interpretation and presentation of existing research literature, Truscott also charged that grammar correction is counterproductive and oftentimes harmful to language learners. Ferris (1999) strongly disagreed with Truscott and suggested that he had harshly and hastily come to conclusions regarding corrective feedback efficacy before consensus had been established within the L2 research community. While Ferris agreed with Truscott that "no single form of correction can be effective for all three [syntactic, morphological, and lexical]" types of grammatical errors (Truscott, 1996, p. 343), she cited her own research (Ferris, 1995a, 1995b, 1997; Ferris and Hedgcock, 1998) which found that learners benefited from indirect error correction, that is, feedback which identifies the error placement and type, but does not explicitly or directly correct the error. Further, Ferris remarked on error types which she considers to be "treatable:" subject-verb agreement, comma splices, and run-on sentence errors. Because these types of errors are rule-driven, Ferris reported that learners are more successful in repairing them. The conflicting research findings of passionate scholars on both sides of the issue led Guénette (2007) to consider whether inconsistencies in research designs and methodology, as well as the effect of unidentified variables of the studies, may have been influential factors in determining significance. Guénette concluded that the differences in research design, such as proficiency level, task type, correction method, student motivation, and procedures, are arguably the explanation for the diversity of significant findings. This supports Ferris' assertion that Truscott's hasty and biased representation of existing research made unfair comparisons between and among causative studies as regards error correction with L2 writers.

While the jury remains out as to the efficacy of teacher feedback to writing, teachers remain engaged with students in classrooms and must manage and respond to students' expectations regarding feedback and the roles and responsibilities of teachers. Further, the academic institutions in which teachers work generally call for and expect them to provide meaningful feedback to students' writing as a means of promoting development. Teachers are thus left wondering just how best to provide feedback to students.

Writing teachers each have a preferred method of providing feedback on students' writing (Nurmakhamedov, 2009). Some handwrite or insert electronic comments in the margins of students' papers; but depending on the detail and complexity of the feedback, an essay revision task can quickly become the additional burden of a reading assignment. Others employ the use of error coding using abbreviations or acronyms for typical mistakes or errors. In a study by Zacharias (2007) of student perceptions, participants stated that acronymic codes were useful in identifying location and type of grammatical problem, but did little to aid in the revision process itself. Some participants in Zacharias' study remarked that receiving oral feedback as a clarification of written feedback would be productive. Johanson (1999) describes tape-recorded feedback as an alternative to hand-written comments on students' written work, but he warns that audio feedback should not be a replacement for teacher-student conferences.

Certainly, students benefit from teacher-student conferences in order to better interpret the teacher's feedback given on their writing. Today, however, a greater number of writing courses are being offered as web-enhanced hybrid courses, and some are beginning to be taught entirely at distance. Whether in traditional or online courses, for many learners visiting instructors during offices hours for face-to-face interaction is logistically difficult or even impossible. In my own community college context, nearly all of my students have full-time jobs in addition to their studies. Many are married adults with familial responsibilities. Prior to my use of audio-enhanced feedback, it was seldom practical for me to provide individualized mediation for my students outside of the classroom.

Praxis relates to the cyclical intersection between theory and practice, and teachers' view of the world impacts the pedagogical decisions we make in our classrooms. *Sociocultural theory* (SCT) is the frame through which I view learning and development. In addition to its notions relating to the social origination and construction of knowledge (Lantolf and Poehner, 2004, 2007), Vygotskian or sociocultural theory contends "that teaching should not wait for development to happen but should drive development" (Lantolf and Poehner, 2007, p. 31). Further, cognitive development and higher order thinking occurs not as a *result* of social or instructional mediation, but *as the mediation is itself taking place* within its cultural context.

A foundational concept of SCT is that the human mind is *mediated*; our relationships with ourselves and others are mediated through the use of symbolic tools or signs. The nature of these relationships is thus changed as a result of mediation. Humans do not have a direct relationship with the world; their relationship is *mediated* by culture, society, tools, and cultural artifacts (Lantolf and Poehner, 2004, 2007). Another key Vygotskian construct is that of the *zone of proximal development* (ZPD; Vygotsky, 1978). The ZPD is often described as being the virtual space between what a learner is capable of doing unassisted and that which she or he can do with mediational scaffolding from a more knowledgeable peer, though the necessity for a peer to be "more knowledgeable" has also been challenged (Lantolf and Poehner, 2004). Based on an understanding of a learner's ZPD, Lantolf and Poehner (2007) suggest that the minimal level of mediational guidance be provided to the learner in order to complete the activity or task. Thus, assistance to the learner should initially be implicit and only become more explicit if the learner fails to take the desired action. Conflicting tension occurs when the learner is engaged in an activity beyond his or her independent ability. An individual's "responsiveness to assistance is an indispensible feature for understanding cognitive ability because it provides an insight into the person's *future* development" (Lantolf and Poehner, 2004, pp. 50–51). For writing students, teachers may be able to intervene and provide mediation that is sensitive to each learners' ZPD when this tension occurs in the context of the classroom or writing lab; but who is available to provide mediation when the learner is alone at home or elsewhere during their revision processes?

SCT has three classifications of a construct known as *regulation: object-regulation, other-regulation,* or *self-regulation.* Object-regulation refers to an individual being reliant upon a tool or cultural artifact in his or her environment. Textbooks and written teacher feedback are excellent examples of objects on which a learner may be reliant. Other-regulation is quite simply reliance upon another individual or individuals for mediational support. This might be realized through teachers or peers. Finally, self-regulation occurs when an individual is able to draw upon internalized or *appropriated* knowledge from within. Regulation is fluid, and individuals have continuous access to all three forms of regulation (Lantolf and Poehner, 2004, 2007). A person can be self-regulated one minute, for example, giving a speech on a very familiar topic, and then object-regulated the next: the speechmaker has lost his or her train of thought and looks down at the notes on the lectern. The same speechmaker may then become other-regulated when he or she looks to a colleague in the front row for help, receiving mediational support by way of a whisper or gesture.

Dynamic assessment (DA) is the final construct to be discussed in the context of this theoretical introduction to the audio-enhanced feedback methodology. DAs are forms of alternative assessment following the socio-cultural principles of Vygotsky. Mediational assistance of various forms is provided to learners *as they are engaged* in activities that are slightly ahead of what they are capable of doing independently, while they are working within their ZPD. DAs blur the line between teaching and assessment; they are the same activity (Lantolf and Poehner, 2004, 2007). The assessment is a process of development rather than a tool for measuring acquired learning. A key difference between DAs and more traditional formative assessments is the generally more interactive nature of DAs, as learners are mediated within their ZPDs during the assessment itself (Rea-Dickens and Gardner, 2000). Because the construct of DA is still emerging in its meaning within the research community, new methods for administering DAs are continually being developed. Rather than viewing DAs as a construct bound by specific or set procedures, it may be helpful to consider DAs more as a philosophy for conducting assessments which are formative, lead toward transformation for those engaged in the activity, and provide insights into learners' potential performance levels. There are, however, two approaches to DA under which most will fall: *interventionist* and *interactionist* DAs. Generally, interventionist DA provides for a more standardized assistance to the learner or learners, in some cases using specific graduated prompts from the implicit to the explicit; interactionist DA is more responsive to the precise needs of an individual learner or group of learners (Lantolf and Poehner, 2004, 2007) at the time that the assessment is being conducted.

The audio-enhanced feedback methodology presented in this chapter provides opportunities for individualized interactional mediation within learners' ZPDs while they are engaged in revision activities which may be beyond their unassisted ability; hence, it is a new form of protracted dynamic assessment.

II.   Description of Activity

This feedback methodology is appropriate for any writing activity that requires students to produce at least one revision. While I have primarily used the audio-enhanced feedback with adult English language learners, I have also had success providing feedback to native-speaking, mainstream pre-service K-6 teachers in a university teacher-education program context. Because time is a constraint when using this method of feedback (as addressed later in this chapter), it will likely not be possible to provide audio-enhanced feedback for every course assignment. For the first time it is tried, I would suggest using it in the context of an early-semester diagnostic writing assignment or mid-semester progress check.

If you do not already have a digital audio recorder, you will first need to download two types of software to your computer. The software is completely free and can be accessed from the following links:

Audacity (freeware audio recorder/editor)
http://audacity.sourceforge.net/about/

LAME MP3 Encoder
http://audacity.sourceforge.net/help/faq?s=install&item=lame-mp3

Audacity is free software which records and mixes audio. The LAME encoder is addendum software that one will need to download separately from Audacity. It allows the user to export Audacity files into an MP3 format. My understanding is that the developers of Audacity had to isolate this software code from the Audacity recorder software code in order to comply with copyright concerns. Be sure you *save this file in the same location where your Audacity program files re*side. See the Audacity website for more information.

While I own my own digital audio recorder, I prefer to use the Audacity software since it forces me to locate and name files while I work, and I can access both the students' documents and the re-cording software at the same time on my computer screen. Using Audacity is fairly intuitive and is reminiscent of the old cassette tape recorders that some of us will remember. If you are unclear as to the function of a particular button, tool, or icon, just hover your mouse over the image, and the function name or description will appear in the lower left-hand corner of the Audacity window. You will want to play around a bit with the recorder to become familiar with the various features you will need to access in order to record and save your audio feedback.

The basic procedures are the following:

1. Have students create writing assignments in Microsoft Word.
2. Have students upload their assignments to your course website (Blackboard, Angel, Moodle, etc.); if you do not have a course website, have students e-mail the file to you.
   - Recommendation: *Save* student document files to your computer as MS Word 1997–2003 in case your students do not have the most recent version.
   - Recommendation: Establish a folder- and file-naming strategy to aid in your administration. For example, a student's feedback file could be named, "carlos.vargas.fdbk.wpd."
3. Using MS Word's *comment* feature and a coded feedback system (e.g., SVA = subject-verb agreement, CS = comma splice, etc.; see sample in Appendix), code the errors/mistakes in your students' work.
   - In the 2007 version of Word, you will find the *comment* feature under the *Review Tab*.
   - Using your mouse, select the location of the error/mistake, click *New Comment*, and type in the appropriate acronym or code.
   - Just to be safe, go ahead and save your document, but do not close it.
4. Open the Audacity software.
5. Resize both your Microsoft Word and Audacity windows so that you can access the student's writing while you record.
6. Record individualized feedback to the student, addressing him or her by name. While you record, make specific reference to the numbered comments in the student's document. For example: Imagine that you have used your cursor to select the student's text containing two independent clauses improperly linked with a comma in the student's

document. You have clicked *New Comment* and coded the error as "CS" (for comma splice). Each comment in Microsoft Word is numbered, so as you are recording the feedback, you can direct the student to the location of the error, reinforce their interpretation of the code, and provide mediational assistance that is specific to the needs of the individual student. E.g. *"Julia, take a look at comment number 4. You have a comma splice here. Remember that last week we examined the three common ways to repair a comma splice.... "* Based on your experiential knowledge or understanding of the learner, provide mediation within your students ZDP. Generally, I tend to be rather implicit in the feedback I provide, but if have a fairly good understanding of the students' strengths and weaknesses, I will provide or withhold explicit feedback in accordance with this understanding. In other words, I may have a sense that Julia would benefit from a mini-teaching episode on comma splices or independent clauses, while Jorge, whom I know understands these concept and merely made a mistake, may only receive a *"...you can see you have a comma splice here. You know what to do!"* Another strategy I employ is to direct students to resources from our textbook, the Internet, or other resources. Obviously, because writing is not only concerned with grammar, it is important to include feedback about genre, form, content, voice, structure, and of course, positive feedback!

- Use the *pause* button (not the *stop* button) during the recording process.
- Use the *stop* button only after you have finished recording all of your audio feedback for the student.
- Note: If you accidentally use the *stop* button, know that the next time you click the *record* button Audacity will create and start recording on a new track. This will leave you with two audio tracks that when played will overlap one another. If this happens (and it will!), you can use

the *Time Shift Tool* (↔) in Audacity to slide the second track toward the right and line it up with the end of the first track. Confused? Play around with Audacity for a while, and it will soon become clearer.

- Keep your audio feedback to around five minutes or less. The longer the recording, the larger the file becomes. Count on about 1,000 KB for each minute of recording. I have uploaded files as large as 10,000 KB, but it does slow down the upload process, and if you intend to deliver the feedback via email, some internet service providers impose limits as to the size of attachments; this could be problematic for your students.

7. You are finished recording. Now what? Audacity creates audio files in a proprietary format. You will need to convert the file to MP3 format so that it can easily be embedded in your student's document.

- Under the *File* menu, select *Export as MP3…*
- A *"Save MP3 File as"* dialog box will appear prompting you to name the file. Important: Be sure that you have selected an appropriate folder location where you can organize and easily retrieve your saved files. I typically save the MP3 file with the student's name and locate it in the same folder where the student's papers reside.
- Once you click *save*, a second dialog box will appear. Click OK.

8. Now, return to the student's document in Microsoft Word. Position your cursor in the location where you would like the audio file to appear. I typically embed the file under the student's name.

9. Click the *Insert* tab and find the *Object* icon within the *Text* section to the right of the menu ribbon. The icon looks like a picture of a tiny cactus and sun. Click the icon.

- A dialog box will appear. Click on the *Create from File* tab.

- Browse to find the appropriate audio file and then click *Insert* and then *OK*.
- An icon with a small musical eighth note should appear. You did it! Want to be sure? Try double clicking the icon to confirm. Your default media player should open the file and begin playing.

10. Save the MS Word document and close it.
11. You should now be ready to re-upload the student's audio-embedded document file to your course website under the student's account, or you can use email to return the document to the student.
12. Back in Audacity, close the Audio Track without saving. Each audio track in Audacity will have a small x in the upper left-hand corner. Click on the x to close the track without exiting Audacity altogether. Note: You already have the audio feedback saved as an MP3 file, so there is no need to keep this file.
    - Important Note: Be sure that you have closed the prior student's Audio Track *before* recording audio for another student. If you keep both tracks active in Audacity, the MP3 file you create for the second student will be an overlapping mess from both virtual conferences.

III. Implementation

I have been using audio-enhanced feedback with intermediate to advanced English language learners for the past several years. Specifically, I teach in an adult English for Academic Purposes (EAP) program within Miami Dade College. The EAP program is a six-level English language learning program designed to provide non-native English speakers with opportunities to develop their language and academic proficiencies to a level satisfactory for college admission.

The writing courses I teach typically meet one day each week for sixteen weeks, two and a half hours per session. The courses are designated as web-enhanced, so many course activities take place synchronously or asynchronously via an online courseware environment called Angel. Nearly all major writing assignments are uploaded to this platform, and teacher feedback to drafts is returned in this same manner.

The first semester I decided to use audio-enhanced feedback, I bit off more than I could chew. I had determined that I would provide audio feedback for every major assignment. This meant that for the reaction essay, the compare-contrast essay, the cause-effect essay, and the argumentative essay, I would provide audio feedback for both draft and revised versions of 30 students' work. No need to get out your calculator, I have done the math for you: two-hundred and forty audio recordings during a sixteen-week period. My students loved it; I had no personal life whatsoever.

I then got the idea of using audio-enhanced feedback as an early-in-the-semester diagnostic activity. The mediation I provided was arguably not targeted within the ZDP of each individual student since, by such an early point in the semester, I did not yet have a sense of their current abilities. Still, it was a good way for me to connect, albeit virtually, with new students and identify for both myself and the learner the kinds of skills we would need to focus on during the semester.

I have since continued to use audio-enhanced feedback as a diagnostic early in the semester, but I now additionally use it for both draft and revised submissions of one mid-semester essay assignment. In addition to providing audio-enhanced feedback to English language learners, I have begun using the feedback methodology with mainstream pre-service elementary school teachers. One of the teacher-education courses I teach is entirely online; therefore, having the ability to provide audio-enhanced feedback within this context seemed a natural fit.

IV.   Reflections and Recommendations

Does it work? I have yet to explore efficacy issues related to audio-enhanced feedback, nor am I aware of such a study having been carried out. In 2008, I did small-sample, informal qualitative inquiry which attempted to describe how L2 writers responded to audio-enhanced teacher feedback as virtual mediation during their revision processes (Winkle, 2008a; 2008b). The intent was not to determine efficacy of audio-enhanced feedback, but rather to engage with several students in order to gain insights into their opinions as regards the method or any judgments pertaining to perceived efficacy. Guiding questions for the exploration included: "Do learners describe audio-enhanced feedback as being effective in (a) communicating the nature of the error; (b) reinforcing the appropriate interpretation of acronymic feedback; and (c) providing sufficient and actionable feedback, such that they could successfully regulate their revision processes?"

Focus group data revealed that all three participants preferred to receive feedback on all errors that could be identified by the instructor. Ernesto (all names are pseudonyms) acknowledged that seeing a high frequency of errors on a piece of writing can be frustrating, but he believes that if students are not given an opportunity to correct each type of mistake, they will not learn. Marco complained that written feedback received from some instructors only identifies the existence and location of a problem, but does little to help the learner actually repair the error. Ernesto concurred and noted that students seldom have time to visit their teachers during office hours in order to consult with them to determine how best to repair their errors. He felt the audio-enhanced feedback replaced the need to meet with the teacher for clarifications.

Regarding the relationship between the coding and the audio feedback, Ernesto remarked that well-delivered audio feedback makes the acronyms unnecessary for him. He appreciated hearing examples of how to repair similar problems, even if the example provided did not exactly repair the error within his own paper.

Ernesto explained too that he read the acronyms and made repairs to his writing as he was listening to the feedback. Marina said she listened to the audio twice while she examined the acronymic feedback and reviewed her own writing. She then made the repairs to her paragraph. Marina also noted that the audio feedback helped her to understand the acronym-coded feedback without having to access the resource of the printed key to the acronym system. She felt this saved her time and allowed her to concentrate on her writing rather than the memorization of a written resource. She also said that she enjoyed having the instructor's voice in her head while she worked.

Having our own voices in the heads of our students may not be what most of us had in mind. Yet, by providing audio-enhanced feedback to students during the moments that they need us most – during their revision processes – we may be contributing to their development within their respective ZDPs.

Further notes and recommendations that I think are important are these:

Students may require training. Depending on your teaching context, you may have students who are tech-savvy, who are novices to technology, or more likely, some combination of the two. Further, some students may have limited access to reliable technology, so you will want to assure that computing resources are available in your teaching and learning context.

Be organized. Develop a systematic means of organizing both your student's documents and the audio files you create.

Practice makes...better. Audacity may seem cumbersome at first, but once you get the hang of it, it will seem like second nature. If you find it easier to use another type of digital audio recorder, do so.

I hate the sound of my voice. Your students probably love the sound of your voice, so try your best to get beyond trying to record "perfect" feedback. Yes, you will stumble. Yes, you might even mispronounce a word. No, you will not be able to get your husband, wife, or partner to stop asking you questions while you are recording. Life is life. If you try to make the perfect recording for each of your students, you will find that providing audio-enhanced feedback takes three times as long as your traditional method. Just record it, embed it, and return it to the student.

Link to additional resources. In addition to acronym codes in your Microsoft Comments, consider embedding hyperlinks to resources on the internet or available on your university's Angel or Blackboard website.

Use Audacity to create mini podcasts. The methodology described above is framed as a form of interactionist dynamic assessment. One could, however, create more standardized or interventionist podcasts providing mediation on an array of typical errors. A teacher could prerecord, for example, his or her familiar spiel on repairing comma splices. Such audio files could be embedded in student documents or uploaded to the course website as additional resources to which students can be directed.

Audio record face-to-face conferences. When students do actually visit me for office hours, I offer them the option of having our conference about their writing recorded. It provides students the opportunity to focus on the interaction itself and not be too concerned with taking notes which may be incomprehensible once the student heads off for the library.

Consider an audio "dialog journal". There is no reason why students should not be creating their own audio recordings as well. Students could embed audio files describing the kinds of troubles they are having with their writing processes, to which teachers can respond with appropriate mediation.

Alternative audio recording means. Microsoft Word 2002 and 2003 have a facility for recording audio comments at the moment the comment is created. At press, Word 2007 continues to have problems with this utility when operating in a Vista operating system environment. One drawback to using Microsoft Word voice comments is that they produce larger document files than when MP3 audio files are embedded. Free screen-capturing video software such as Jing (n.d.) and CamStudio Open Source (n.d.) are also viable alternatives. My preference, however, has been to have students engage with the feedback from within the word-processing environment rather than external to it.

A final point. New technology is appearing almost daily: experiment and see what works best for you and your students.

References

Audacity, the Free, Cross-Platform Sound Editor (n.d.) Retrieved 10 March 2009 from http://audacity.sourceforge.net/

CamStudio Open Source: Free Streaming Video Software (n.d.) Retrieved 8 May 2009 from http://camstudio.org/.

Ferris, Dana R. (1995a) Can advanced ESL students be taught to correct their most serious and frequent errors? *CATESOL Journal* 8: 41–62.

Ferris, Dana R. (1995b) Teaching ESL composition students to become independent self-editors. *TESOL Journal* 5: 18–22.

Ferris, Dana R. (1997) The influence of teacher commentary on student revision. *TESOL Quarterly* 32: 315–339.

Ferris, Dana R. (1999) The case for grammar correction in L2 writing classes: a response to Truscott (1996). *Journal of Second Language Writing* 8: 1–11.

Ferris, Dana R. and Hedgcock, John (1998) *Teaching ESL Composition: Purpose, Process, & Practice.* Mahwah, New Jersey: Erlbaum.

Guénette, Danielle (2007) Is feedback pedagogically correct? Research design issues in studies of feedback on writing. *Journal of Second Language Writing* 16: 40–53.

Jing (n.d.) Retrieved 8 May 8 2009 from http://jingproject.com/.

Johanson, Robert (1999) Rethinking the red ink: Audio-feedback in the ESL writing classroom. *Texas Papers in Foreign Language Education* 4: 31–38.

Lantolf, James P. and Poehner, Matthew E. (2004) Dynamic assessment of L2 development: Bringing the past into the future. *Journal of Applied Linguistics* 1: 49–72.

Lantolf, James P. and Poehner, Matthew E. (2007) *Dynamic Assessment in the Foreign Language Classroom: A Teacher's Guide.* University Park, Pennsylvania: CALPER Publications.

Nurmakhamedov, Ulugbek (2009) Teacher feedback on writing: Considering the options. *Writing & Pedagogy* 1(1): 115–126.

Rea-Dickins, Pauline and Gardner, Sheena (2000) Snares and silver bullets: Disentangling the construct of formative assessment. *Language Testing* 17(2): 215–243.

Truscott, John (1996) The case against grammar correction in L2 writing classes. *Language Learning* 46: 327–369.

Truscott, John (1999) The case for "The case against grammar correction in L2 writing classes": A response to Ferris. *Journal of Second Language Writing* 8: 111–112.

Vygotsky, Lev S. (1978) *Mind in Society: The Development of Higher Psychological Processes* (eds. Michael Cole, Vera John-Steiner, Sylvia Scribner and Ellen Souberman). Cambridge, Massachusetts: Harvard University Press.

Winkle, C. (2008a). Audio-enhanced feedback for emergent students' writing. Paper presented at the TESOL Convention and Exhibition. New York. 4 April 2008.

Winkle, C. (2008b). Audio-enhanced feedback for emergent students' writing: How English language learners respond to virtual mediation. Paper presented at the Second Language Writing Symposium. West Lafayette, Indiana. 5 June 2008.

Zacharias, Nugraheny T. (2007) Teacher and student attitudes toward teacher feedback. *RELC Journal* 38: 38–52.

Appendix

Sample Acronym Correction System

Grammar		**Example**
SVA	Subject-Verb Agreement	* The three men **walks** to the store.
S/P	Singular/Plural Usage	* The three **mans** walk to the store.
ART	Article Usage	* He gives his son **a** apple every Monday.
VT	Verb Tense	* He **gives** his son an apple yesterday.
VF	Verb Form	* **Gives** apples is a nice thing to do.
WF	Word Form	* She is a very **friend** woman.
PRO	Pronoun Use	* **He** is a very friendly woman.

Word Choice		**Example**
PREP	Preposition Usage	* I like to picnic **in** the beach.
WW	Wrong Word/Phrase	* I like to picnic on the **peach**.

Sentence Structure		**Example**
FRAG	Fragment	* **When they went to the theatre.**
RUN	Run-On Sentence	* **He has a blue car it is expensive.**
CS	Comma Splice	* **He has a blue car, it is expensive.**
WO	Word Order	* My brother has a **car blue**.

Organization: Paragraph/Essay

TS	Topic Sentence Issue or Concern
THESIS	Thesis Statement Issue or Concern
SUP	Support Issue or Concern (sufficient and relevant)

Mechanical and Miscellaneous

SP	Spelling
CAP	Capitalization
PUN	Punctuation
DEL	Recommend the deletion of a word, phrase/clause, or sentence
WC?	Word Choice MAY need to be considered; writer's intent is unclear
UC	Intended meaning of a sentence or phrase is unclear to the reader
MISS	Missing word

19 Academic Writing in the Foreign Language Classroom: Wikis and Chats at Work

Ana Oskoz and Idoia Elola

I. Background

Academic writing is a difficult skill to master, even for native speakers; yet, advanced-level students in foreign language programs are expected to tackle a range of academic work demonstrating not only their second-language proficiency but also a clear understanding of the academic writing conventions relating to diverse genres. Achieving the language accuracy, depth of content and organizational skills required for such academic writing can become an overwhelmingly daunting and solitary task for many students. The need to ease foreign language students into academic writing requires a shift in writing pedagogy. The use of an approach such as collaborative writing, when two or more people work together to produce one document, may be seen as an appropriate shift that facilitates the process of mastering academic writing skills; it also serves to highlight the social aspect of writing, which can help prepare students to enter the work force. Making use of a collaborative approach, this chapter documents a collaborative assignment in an advanced Spanish writing class in which students worked in pairs on an argumentative essay using wikis and chats as their communication tool.

Collaborative writing, which has been examined in both first-language and second language contexts, encourages reflective thinking; focuses on grammatical accuracy, lexis, and discourse, and promotes a pooling of language-based knowledge (DiCamilla and Anton, 1997; Ede and Lunsford, 1990; Hirvela, 1999; Storch, 2002; Swain and Lapkin, 1998). By including inherently social tools (such as wikis and chats) in the collaborative writing process, students are provided with an environment that encourages reflection and discussion, allowing them to focus on the multiple components of the academic writing task. Influenced by social constructionists' views of the development of knowledge and discourse practices, writing theorists now understand writing as a socially embedded activity (Hirvela, 1999). From this perspective, writing is not an individual act, but rather a social one. Indeed, even in those instances in which the composing process is performed alone, writers are aware of their intended audience, which in turn results in a social act. The social dimension of the writing process can be further emphasized by the use of wikis (web pages that are available for anyone to edit, allowing students to create, transform, or erase their work) and oral or written chats (online meeting places where they can communicate with each other in real time).

The use of online tools to support collaborative writing incorporates two major aspects of social learning, on the understanding that content "is socially constructed through grounded interactions, especially with others, around problems or actions" (Brown and Adler, 2008: 18). First, social learning does not focus "so much on *what* we are learning, but on *how* we are learning," and on the learning activities and human interactions that accompany the content (Brown and Adler, 2008:18). By integrating wikis and chats into the writing process, students learn both about the subject matter – content, structure, and accuracy – and also become better writers in a social context. Second, social learning implies "not only learning about the subject matter, but also learning to be a full participant in the field" (Brown and Adler, 2008: 19). This implies that successful use of communication tools prepares students for future real world and work contexts in which they will need to collaborate on projects (Moore, Fowler, and Watson, 2007). Students are thus exposed to community participation in an integrated way as part of their whole learning process. They expand their linguistic knowledge while at the same time they practice their social writing skills. Student writing then becomes the result of an ongoing, dynamic discussion in which students have debated issues with their classmates.

II.   Description of Activity

Students have two weeks to complete each writing assignment in the wiki, which includes two major drafts to be submitted to the instructor (Table 1). Students need to present an argumentative essay stemming from a topic discussed in class.

Stage 1 (Week 1): Exploring the Topic

During the first week, the class discusses the organizational and structural issues of the argumentative essay, and students participate in a class discussion about the topic of the writing assignment. For this particular argumentative essay, students are asked to research two contrasting positions of a debate about the role of men and women in Spanish-speaking societies. Although the main focus of this class is academic writing, the topics assigned in the course include discussion and comparison of cultural practices in the U.S. and Spanish-speaking countries. Before class, students read several texts such as a fragment of *El eterno femenino* (Castellanos, 1975) and search for additional information on the Web related to women's role in the workforce in Spanish-speaking countries. In class, the students and the instructor compare and discuss the role of women in education, business, and politics in the Spanish-speaking countries and in the U.S to explore similarities and differences among settings. The readings and discussions provide students with content for the writing assignment; however, each pair of students chooses a different subtopic for the argumentative essay, thus providing a variety of arguments and views to enrich the classroom experience.

Stage 2 (Week 1): Working on the First Draft

After the introductory class session, students communicate with each other in pairs via online chats using Blackboard (see below) and are asked to complete the first draft of the assignment in their wikis during the following five days. When working individually, students enter the wiki at different times; they also work collaboratively on their essay when participating in the chats. Each student's work can be viewed in the wiki history, which also allows the instructor to observe what each student has added or changed.

Stage 3 (Week 1): Providing Feedback

The instructor has a day and a half to provide students with feedback regarding content and organization of the text monitored in the wikis. The instructor provides the feedback within the wiki to keep the dialogue in the same medium. This also enables students to more easily review those areas highlighted by the instructor. Although students can see the posted comments in the wikis, they are not allowed to make any further changes until after the ensuing class discussion.

Stage 4 (Week 2): Learning to Revise

In this stage, the students and the instructor work together in class on revising content, structure, organization, and form of several students' writing assignments, which are presented anonymously.

This in-class session is helpful because it guides students towards efficient revision methods and thus towards more successful learning outcomes.

Stage 5 (Week 2): Completing the Assignment

After the in-class discussion, students review and finish their assignment in one week using the same wiki format and chats. Students are not required to communicate a specific number of times or to address specific topics, but are encouraged to discuss content, organization, and form based on the type of revision needed. By this stage, they are required to conduct the communication in Spanish. In general, students revise the essay and communicate with each other several times before handing in their final draft to the instructor.

Table 1: Schedule and Activities

Schedule	Activities
Week 1, Day 1	In-class discussion about topic, organization and structure.
Week 1, Days 2–5	Students work collaboratively on their writing assignments using wikis and chats.
Week 1, Day 5	Students turn in their first draft using wikis.
Week 1, Days 6–7	The instructor provides comments in the wikis (within two days).
Week 2, Day 1	In class, students and the instructor comment on a few of the students' essays, reading for content, structure, and accuracy.
Week 2, Days 2–7	Students continue working collaboratively on their writing assignments using both wikis and chats.
Week 3, Day 1	Students complete the writing assignment in their wikis.

III. Implementation

The activity described was implemented in an advanced Spanish writing course at a mid-size U.S. East coast university in the Fall semester of 2007. Recognizing the linguistic and social benefits of collaborative writing, the instructor of a 3-credit intensive writing course at the university level introduced the use of wikis and chats to enhance students' writing. The main goal of the class was for students to achieve academic writing skills in Spanish by working on a series of writing activities that included the development of argumentative and expository texts. In the class, which meets once a week for two and a half hours, writing had been traditionally taught as an individual experience. Students worked individually on their writing assignments, with the exception of the prewriting activities, which were conducted with the entire class. The instructor expected that, by adding a collaborative writing component, students would demonstrate an improved ability to state a clear thesis, develop their ideas, provide a clear organizational structure to the essay, and focus on grammatical accuracy.

Tools

After an analysis of various wikis, the instructor created a wiki page specifically designed for the course using PBworks (http:// pbworks.com). This type of wiki was selected mainly its for ease of use and because it allowed students to clearly compare corrections from one draft to the next. The instructor created a main wiki page in which she posted information: (a) regarding the course, (b) the assignments to be completed during the semester, and (c) links to the pages of the students' assignments. Similarly to a traditional Word document, wikis enable students to create, transform, and erase their work. The working document, however, is stored on the Web rather than residing in each student's computer or flash drive. Thus, learners do not have to wait until their partners send them the latest version of their writing by email, but can constantly access their latest drafts by checking their wiki. An additional benefit of wikis is their tracking system, which allows teachers and students to track who, what, and when changes are made.

To foster students' exchange of information, the instructor selected the voice and written tools available in Blackboard (Version 7.1), the university's course management system. These oral and written chats are web-based communication tools that enable students to communicate in real time about the argumentative essay from the comfort of their homes. The instructor created chat rooms in both written and voice modes for each pair of students, and gave them the choice of the chat mode most convenient for them. Regardless of what synchronous mode of communication students chose, they were required to archive their conversations. To ensure that students were acquainted with the features of wikis and chats, the instructor took them to the language lab at the beginning of the semester for training in the use of the online communication tools. Two additional visits to the language lab were made to ensure that further questions and concerns were addressed; these could include how to write an argumentative essay and how to revise it on the wikis, or the mechanics of how to log in to the wikis correctly so that the instructor could establish each student's degree of authorship of a jointly produced work.

Originally, because the instructor did not know the students, she paired them in alphabetical order. She was careful to pair Spanish-native speakers with Spanish-native speakers and foreign language learners with foreign language learners to avoid situations where Spanish-native speakers would dominate the writing exercise. After the first month, the instructor re-arranged the student pairs to better suit the students' needs in terms of schedules, language level, or personality.

During the two weeks in which the writing activity took place, students alternated the use of wikis and chats depending on their needs. Although each pair of students employed the wikis and chats in different ways, some general trends emerged (see Oskoz and Elola, 2010). First, using the chats, students worked together to present a clear thesis, to obtain adequate supporting evidence and to organize the essay in accordance with a pre-established genre (i.e. argumentation). Second, students worked individually to research the content and to write their assigned part (e.g. introduction or conclusion), often adding paragraphs without much connection between them; they also addressed grammatical issues. Third, via chats, students reconsidered their ideas and manipulated them in the wikis until the required two opposing positions of the argumentative essay started to take shape. It was at this stage of deliberation and revision that students began to bring coherence to their essay and also started to pay more attention to the grammatical aspects. Fourth, students revised their work, often individually, in the wikis.

IV.   Reflections and Recommendations

To understand the potential benefits of collaborative writing and the integration of wikis and chats in a writing class, we examined students' essays for content, organization, and grammatical accuracy. At the end of the semester, we also asked them for feedback regarding the writing process.

Regarding content, organization, and accuracy, we found that students first addressed global aspects of the writing process, i.e. content and organization, followed by accuracy. Content and organization were the major components in students' online conversations, as directly reflected in their wiki writing. While working collaboratively, students placed great emphasis on the statement of the thesis, the supporting and opposing arguments, and the essay structure. Linguistic accuracy, however, was much less frequently addressed in student interactions. Although highly attentive to the precision of their written language, students seemed to consider language accuracy to be more of a personal endeavor and hardly discussed it in their chat interactions.

Students' reflections on the writing experience mirrored the processes they followed in constructing the essays and the online interactions. Working together using online tools, students had the opportunity to receive and share ideas, and to be challenged by their writing partners. Working with another person forced students to be prepared and organized before each collaboration. Yet the results and reflections of students showed that, while they perceived that these online tools helped them with the content and organization of the essay, they also felt that the tools did not improve their language accuracy. Despite various other challenges, such as difficulty in scheduling meeting times, uncertainty about grading, technical problems with the voice chat, unresponsive partners, and the inability of the wiki to highlight spelling errors, students tended to agree that working with a partner within the wiki and chat environments did help them with the writing process.

Implementing collaborative writing using wikis and chats, while beneficial, is not free from challenges, as issues of group dynamics, schedules, working styles, and technical problems can hinder any collaborative endeavor. Several students were reluctant to work with another person for a graded assignment, did not understand the professional implications of collaborative work, or regarded the use of wikis and chats as inappropriate for academic purposes. Therefore, in order to maximize the potential that online tools bring to the collaborative experience, there is a need for careful planning to ensure students' acceptance and understanding of the collaborative writing process and its implementation with these online tools. Our recommendations, pertaining to the understanding of the collaborative endeavor and the implementation of wikis and chats in the writing process, can be adopted for writing in foreign-language, second-language, and first-language contexts. They are as follows:

1. Help students understand the value of collaborative writing in a context that goes beyond the classroom. Students need to recognize that collaborative writing prepares them "for the increasingly complex and interconnected global society in which they live and work" (Moore, Fowler, and Watson, 2007: 46), and for which they are required to be professionally prepared.
2. Convey to students the value of wikis and chats in an educational context. Help them make the transition from using

such applications for strictly social purposes to using them as fully-fledged learning tools embedded in a collaborative, social context.

3. Provide students with ample practice in the use of the on-line tools (even those students who are technologically advanced). Offer students clear, detailed handouts that include step-by-step illustrations of the different features of the tools employed (e.g. how to look at the history in the wikis, or how to archive and retrieve their own conversations in the voice chats). Hold class in a computer writing lab or language lab at least twice early in the semester so that students can practice working with the tools under teacher guidance. During the first visit, introduce students to these tools in an academic context. During the second visit, answer questions and address concerns regarding their use.

4. Let students practice collaborative writing with online tools by introducing several non-graded activities. These activities will allow students to familiarize themselves with the features of wikis and chats, and will help them adjust to working with their partners (e.g. learning the steps involved in accessing voice chats, finding their pages in the wiki, and developing a working relationship with their classmate) before they embark on their graded assignments.

5. Suggest to students how to use the wiki-chat combination to develop their writing. First, students can start with the chats to work on thesis, organization, structure, and task planning. Second, students can work on their individual parts (or however they have divided the work) in the wikis. Third, students can use chats to discuss their work and the instructor's feedback. Fourth, students can fine-tune their writing in the wikis.

6. Remind students that using wikis and chats allows them to work at their own pace, from the comfort of their homes. It takes time for some students to comprehend that working via wikis and chats frees them from physically meeting

with their partners to work at the library or in a writing or language lab.

7. Observe student dynamics of the working partnerships. Not all pairs of students will work alike. While some pairs of students will immediately develop a productive working relationship, other students will not work well together. After the first non-graded assignments, change partners as appropriate. Identify those pairs whose proficiency levels are too unequal and change partners, in order to avoid situations in which the most proficient partner dominates the writing task. Similarly, identify those students who benefit from their partner's work without contributing. When grouping students, allow them to pair up with a classmate with whom they have already developed a successful working relationship in previous classes.

8. Provide clear assessment guidelines. Students' anxiety levels easily rise when they realize that their grade depends on the process and product of collaboration with another classmate. Clearly establish the assessment procedure to be followed, including: analysis of who, how often, and what changes are implemented in the wiki drafts; listening to or reading the online conversations to assess collaboration; and looking for quality of content, organization, and accuracy in the final drafts. Use at least one of the non-graded activities as an example of how the grading will be conducted, in order to help students understand the assessment process in a non-threatening context.

9. Alternate individual and collaborative writing tasks. While collaborative writing teaches students to perform in a social context, individual writing prepares them to become independent thinkers and autonomous workers; both types of skills are necessary in the professional world.

Working collaboratively in this new approach to writing, students can reflect on the subject matter of their compositions, and more importantly, on the writing processes involved in academic writing. Allowing students to compare their individual work with that of their partner also expands their knowledge of the subject matter. Given that the learning occurs in a social environment, there is the opportunity for students to grow as writers, hypothesize about their language style and writing performance, and readjust their previous notions regarding academic writing in a positive way.

References

Brown, John S. and Adler, Richard P. (2008) Minds on fire. Open education, the long trail, and learning 2.0. *Educause Review* 43: 17–32.

Castellanos, Rosario (2000) *El eterno femenino* (13th edition). México Distrito Federal: Fondo de cultura económica.

DiCamilla, Frederick J. and Antón, Marta (1997) Repetition in the collaborative discourse of L2 learners: A Vygotskian perspective. *The Canadian Modern Language Review* 53: 609–633.

Ede, Lisa and Lunsford, Andrea (1990) *Singular Texts/Plural Authors*. Carbondale: Southern Illinois University Press.

Hirvela, Alan (1999) Collaborative writing: instruction and communities of readers and writers. *TESOL Journal* 8: 7–12.

Moore, Anne H., Fowler, Shelli B. and Watson, C. Edward (2007) Active learning and technology: designing change for faculty, students and institutions. *Educause Review* 42: 43–60.

Oskoz, Ana and Elola, Idoia (2010) Meeting at the wiki: The new arena for foreign language collaborative writing. In Mark J. W. Lee and Catherine McLoughlin (eds.) *Web 2.0-Based E-Learning: Applying Social Informatics for Tertiary Teaching* 209–227. Hershey: IGI Global.

Storch, Neomy (2002) Collaborative writing: Product, process, and students' reflections. *Journal of Second Language Writing* 14: 153–173.

Swain, Merrill and Lapkin, Sharon (1998) Interaction and second language learning: Two adolescent French immersion students working together. *The Modern Language Journal* 82: 320–337.

Subject Index

Author Index

CPSIA information can be obtained at www.ICGtesting.com
Printed in the USA
270238BV00003B/1/P

9 781845 534530